Parenthood the Swedish Way

Dr Cecilia Chrapkowska is a board-certified specialist in paediatrics. She works at Astrid Lindgren's Children's Hospital at Karolinska University Hospital, Stockholm, and regularly appears as a child-health expert in national Swedish magazines and newspapers, and on radio and television.

Dr Agnes Wold, PhD, is a professor and senior consultant in bacteriology at the Sahlgrenska University Hospital in Gothenburg. She first became internationally renowned for her seminal paper published in *Nature* in 1997 on nepotism and sexism in peer-review practices, and has been a columnist for Sweden's largest newspaper and for the political magazine *Fokus*.

Parenthood the Swedish Way

a science-based guide to pregnancy, birth, and infancy

Dr Cecilia Chrapkowska and Dr Agnes Wold

Translated by Stuart Tudball and Chris Wayment

SCRIBE

Melbourne • London

Scribe Publications
2 John St, Clerkenwell, London, WC1N 2ES, United Kingdom
18–20 Edward St, Brunswick, Victoria 3056, Australia
3754 Pleasant Ave, Suite 100, Minneapolis, Minnesota 55409, USA

First published in Swedish by Wahlstrom & Widstrand as *Praktika for Blivande Foraldrar* in 2017
First published in English by Scribe 2020
Published by agreement with Ahlander Agency

The advice provided in this book has been carefully considered and checked
by the authors. It should not, however, be regarded as a substitute for
individual medical advice. Neither the authors or their representatives nor
the publisher shall bear any liability whatsoever for personal injury, property
damage, and financial losses.

Typeset in Portrait 12/17pt by the publishers
Printed and bound in the UK by CPI Group (UK) Ltd, Croydon CR0 4YY

Scribe Publications is committed to the sustainable use of natural resources
and the use of paper products made responsibly from those resources.

9781911617938 (UK edition)
9781947534834 (US edition)
9781925713916 (Australian edition)
9781925693621 (ebook)

Catalogue records for this book are available from the National Library of
Australia and the British Library.

scribepublications.co.uk
scribepublications.com
scribepublications.com.au

To all parents who do their best to raise the next generation
of humanity.

Contents

Preface

It was Agnes's daughter Sigrid who prompted us to write this book. She'd had her first baby, and of course she had all sorts of questions, some easy to answer and others more complex. 'What would I do if I didn't have a mother who was a doctor?' she asked, with some indignation. 'Most people don't have that luxury. It's really unfair.' Well, yes. It is unfair. And, if you choose to be a bit provocative, you could also say that it's a problem about democracy. We'd like to believe that our society, which is often referred to as an 'information society', gives reliable information to all those who need it. But that's not always the case.

As expectant and new parents, you will be overwhelmed with advice about pregnancy and parenting, whether you ask for it or not. Friends, bloggers, authorities, grandparents-to-be, and self-appointed experts will want to help you be the right kind of parent. And you'll listen, because when you are a new parent, or are about to become one, there is nothing you want more than to do the right thing. And, of course, the man-ufacturers of all the baby paraphernalia know this, too, and they'll be sending a sea of advertisements your way once the search engines have detected that you've looked up 'groin pain + pregnancy signs?' or 'best cures for morning sickness'.

And it won't be long before you realise that it's difficult to make use of the information, because a lot of the advice is contradictory. One day, you'll read how vital it is to carry your baby in an anatomically correct baby carrier, and the next you'll be told that the same carrier can damage your baby's spine and that you should use a soft sling instead. One day, you'll be told breastfeeding is the only way to go and never to use a dummy. Then one friend will tell you how bottle-feeding saved his relationship, and another will recount how a dummy got her baby to sleep for at least a few hours a night. You'll read that your baby must have a totally salt-free diet, and then hear that babies need a certain amount of salt. If you don't have friends or relatives who are experts on the human body and child development, you can soon feel way out of your depth.

Between us, we have eight children and four grandchildren, so we understand how alone and afraid you can feel when faced with the responsibility for a newborn baby. But we are also medical doctors and researchers. Cecilia is a board-certified specialist in paediatric medicine and is studying for a PhD in vaccination research, while Agnes is a specialist in clinical bacteriology and immunology and a professor of clinical bacteriology. As doctors, we are trained to understand how the body works, and as researchers we are trained to read, summarise, and sometimes challenge scientific articles. Over many years, both singly and together, we have focused on picking apart advice on pregnancy and parenting and we have debunked a number of myths — such as the idea that drinking wine during breastfeeding will harm your baby, or that cleaning your home will help prevent allergies.

The aim of this book is to pass on this knowledge to you. Over the course of writing *Parenthood the Swedish Way*, we have read several hundred additional scientific papers and discovered many fresh myths that we tackle head on. We are women of science, so we put facts first. Where there is solid research in a field, we present the results of that work. If there is a lack of reliable research (which happens more often than you might think), we say so. The sources for each chapter are listed at the end of the book.

Importantly, as feminists we advocate for parents to equally share both the responsibility for and the practical care of their child. We believe that this sharing gives both parents the chance to establish a healthy, lifelong relationship with their child and to preserve their own relationship in the face of the inevitable stresses of parenthood. As well, a fair division of parenting gives each parent the chance to achieve financial independence and a liveable income into the future.

For the most part, there will be two parents expecting a baby, so we address both parents in describing what we think you need to work out together before your baby is born. If you're expecting a baby on your own, feel free to skip over the sections of the next chapter that don't apply to you and go straight to the section on 'The life jigsaw puzzle: from many pieces to two'. If, as may be the case, there are more than two of you planning a child together, it's perhaps even more important to reach early agreement on how you'll work together to look after the baby. In this instance, change our use of 'both' and 'half' to fit your situation.

In chapter 1, we look at the important things to consider together before your baby is born — especially decisions about how work and childcare will be divided between you. The way we see it, today's unequal distribution of parenting creates major social problems, and we are convinced that shared parenting is a good way of dealing with these problems. In chapter 2, we examine the fundamentals of pregnancy and prenatal care, and discuss common complications you need to be aware of. We also discuss prenatal screening and diagnoses, and some infections that can affect a foetus during pregnancy. In chapter 3, we present our scientific review of the advice most commonly given to pregnant women. Let us say from the outset that while some advice is undoubtedly important, not all of it stands up to close scrutiny. Chapter 4 focuses on the actual birth and the stages of labour. Chapter 5 looks at the feeding of a newborn baby and considers both breastfeeding and bottle-feeding options. We discuss how you choose which feeding method to use, and what you need to do to get the feeding to work. And we discredit many myths about breastfeeding and bottle-feeding. In chapter 6, we explain how to wean your baby, when it is appropriate to begin solids, and with what foods. Chapter 7 looks at babies' sleep, with a review of various sleeping methods currently advocated. Chapter 8 provides a guide to baby poo, vomiting, crying, and colic — information about what's normal and what's not— as well as a science-based approach to colic treatments.

Chapter 9 deals with infections and immune defences; chapter 10, with vaccinations; and chapter 11, allergies — all important subjects you need to understand to avoid getting sucked in by the myths and untruths that do the rounds. In chapter 12, we examine what is truly dangerous to infants and what the actual causes of infant death are today, as opposed to what are scare stories. And finally, in chapter 13, we outline where the research on children's personality development currently stands. We discuss what is important for infants, what factors you can and can't influence as a parent, and what you can afford to be more relaxed about.

Having a baby is extremely hard work, and perhaps at this time, more than any other in life, it's important for parents to be able to concentrate on the absolute necessities. We hope this book will help you to do just that.

CHAPTER ONE
Looking ahead

When you're expecting a baby you become the target for a barrage of messages. The internet is awash with pregnancy and mummy blogs, and websites which lead you to believe that the most important things are preparing the perfect nursery, buying a new car with the best safety rating, and making sure that whoever of you is not carrying the baby works hard to provide for the family. But all these things are not so important. What is really vital to establish is that you can provide for yourself now and in the future, and that as prospective parents you have laid the groundwork for a fair and solid partnership. This chapter aims to give you the tools to do just that, and to suggest other worthwhile preparations for your baby's arrival.

PARENTAL RESPONSIBILITY AND CARE

When you don't have children, you can live as carefree a life as you want. As long as you earn enough money for food and rent, it feels as if your life is your own. Things may not be entirely equal, but when there is enough time and money to satisfy each partner's needs, there is often no reason to overanalyse your general life situation. Some relationships work less well from the beginning, and yet they produce children. If you are in such a relationship, it's even more important that you try to make shared plans; otherwise, there is a risk that your relationship will fall apart under the stresses of parenthood. If you already have a relationship that is high in conflict, try to do the early planning with the help of a family counsellor.

Having a baby will take away most of your free time at a stroke, and land you with the responsibility for looking after a new person and providing for them for the next 18 years. This is not a voluntary relationship; it's your obligation under the law. The responsibility for providing for your child ceases when the child comes of legal age, but the parent–child relationship — whether good or bad — continues for the rest of your life.

The biggest change for new parents is the sheer amount of work and responsibility involved in taking care of a child. The time spent on housework rises dramatically, while the time for paid work and your own interests shrinks. These changes in work and responsibilities need to be divided between parents in some way. In our view, the way this division of labour is planned for and achieved will have a major impact on your future life.

There is a biological imbalance built into most relationships between expectant parents: one of the parents will carry the baby in her womb and the other won't. For some reason it's common for that skewed division of labour to continue once the baby is born. 'Out of habit', the person who carried the baby and did all the pregnancy work usually carries on doing the majority of the work involved in caring for the newborn baby, and has her freedom and finances curtailed far more than the non-child-bearing parent.

Don't use the 'out of habit' method to plan for the future after you give birth. Instead, read on and use the tools you need to plan for a family life that is fair and nurturing. Good partnerships give both parents the opportunity to help care for a child and to receive the love in return that is such a reward. Equitable shared parenting gives a child the sense that their parents are pleased to have them around. No child should feel like a difficult problem for their parents to deal with.

FAIRNESS: A VACCINE AGAINST RESENTMENT

Resentment occurs when one party in a relationship feels that they are not getting their fair share of something — often freedom, time, or money. The emotion of resentment can be a healthy and natural defence mechanism. Resentment should be taken seriously as a warning sign that one person in a relationship may be being exploited. In the best case, resentment can prompt the person in a lesser position to work towards establishing an equal and fair situation. But if the exploited party feels unable to redress the balance, the unfairness and resentment can grow. An imbalance can poison the relationship between parents if it tips over into bitterness and perhaps, over time, into loathing.

Fortunately, there is an excellent way to protect against the toxic effects of resentment: undertake to share your parental responsibilities, housework, and work entitlements fairly. And we mean sharing the parenting down to the most minute level. There will come a time when you have not a had a full night's sleep for longer than you can remember, when the laundry basket never seems to empty, and the mountain of dishes and pans in the sink risks setting off an avalanche. At this point, 'more or less fair' is not going to cut it — the millimetres, or seconds, count.

Striving for absolute fairness is often seen as a little childish and petty. If you truly love each other, you're above all that, aren't you? Don't fall into this trap of thinking. You won't have any regrets if you share everything equally. But if you share things unequally, there is a major risk that at least one of you will regret it. In the worst case, both of you could end up feeling cheated by the other. It's like when you're giving sweets to two siblings: you might get away with giving three lollipops to one and one to the other, but you're much more likely to avoid discord if the children each get two lollipops — and preferably of the same colour!

LEGAL ASPECTS OF PARENTING

If absolute fairness sounds dull and unromantic, what about the legal aspects of parenting? Considering your legal rights and responsibilities as parents-to-be might not be the most memorable task of your relationship, but it is certainly one of the most important.

In all countries, there is legislation covering the rights and duties of parents. Some aspects of these laws are quite similar all over the world, such as the idea that parents have a shared responsibility for giving their children a safe and nurturing environment, for sending them to school, and for making decisions on their behalf during their childhood, but the details differ between countries.

It is important to understand the difference between the legal term 'parental responsibility' (in New Zealand, this is called guardianship) and the living arrangements for, or day-to-daycare, of the child. Parental responsibility refers to all the rights, duties, powers, responsibilities, and authority which by law a parent has in relation to a child and its property. So if you are expecting a baby together, it's important to realise that as parents you will hold parental responsibility together for the next 18 years. For all major decisions regarding the child, legal parents will have to agree. It doesn't matter whether in the future you don't want to be together in the same room; you're still going to have to work together. It's best to understand the implications of your legal position from the beginning. There is nothing like a custody battle to bring out the worst in people, and it's certainly not in the best interests of a child to have parents fighting over them.

In Australia and the UK, a woman who gives birth to a child automatically obtains parental responsibility. If she is married, her husband or wife will automatically share parental responsibility. For unmarried male partners, registration on the birth certificate guarantees legal parenthood. For unmarried female partners, legal parenthood can be granted if the fertility treatment has been done in a licensed clinic and if a consent form is signed by both mothers-to-be before the date of conception.

If a child comes into a family through adoption, the legal responsibilities transfer to the parents who adopt the child. For male same-sex couples who are planning children via surrogacy, the legal situation surrounding legal parenthood is complex. In this case, and for situations where more than two parents are planning children, we recommend that you seek specific legal advice.

When a child's legal parents are living together, the practical parenting and care of their children is carried out jointly. You will need to agree on how the work will be divided between you, and whether other adults, such as step-parents, grandparents, or other relatives and friends, will be involved in the practical parenting. The existence of lasting relationships with several adults is a major asset for children, both in the short and long term. Bear in mind, however, that if a child develops a close parent–child relationship with a person who then disappears from their life entirely, it can cause major distress. Try to avoid this scenario, if at all possible.

PARENTAL LEAVE: THE SWEDISH EXPERIENCE

Sweden has generous parental benefits in a system that has developed since the 1930s, when the first maternity benefits were introduced. In 1974, the maternity benefit consisted of six months paid maternal leave. Recently, as a result of the work of the Swedish feminist movement and a progressive political majority, the maternity benefits were changed

PARENTHOOD THE SWEDISH WAY

into parental benefits, giving parents six months of paid parental leave to divide as they wished. The Swedish state encouraged fathers to take their share of the parental leave, via information campaigns and also television advertisements featuring well-known Swedish personalities advocating for fathers to follow their example and take parental leave.

Since then, the system has evolved, and today Sweden still has among the most generous parental-benefit provisions in the world. The state covers parents or guardians for 240 days of paid parental leave each. For 180 of these days, parents are entitled to 77.6 per cent of their regular salary (and often more from their employer if a collective agreement applies). One parent can transfer days to the other parent, or to their partner if they are married or have other children together. A single parent receives 480 days of parental benefit. In addition to these paid days, a parent of a child under 12 months is entitled to take unpaid parental leave, and they may choose to do so when the other parent is at home on parental benefit.

This relatively long history of parental benefits has created an opportunity to study the effects on the family of different choices regarding the share of parental leave. A study published in 2007 examined the experience of men who took parental leave when they were given the option in the 1970s, and compared their experience to those men who turned down the option. The study showed that men who took parental leave had a lower risk of premature death than those who turned it down.[1] Even after the researchers controlled the results for education, financial status, and country of birth, the increased life expectancy of fathers who had taken parental leave remained. We can speculate on the reasons for this finding. Maybe the fathers who were closely involved in the care of their children also became better at looking after themselves and their own health. Maybe they created closer relationships with children and grandchildren that gave them a greater sense of meaning and increased their ability to hold onto their lust for life into the autumn of their years.

12

LEARNING TO BE A PARENT

There is only one way to learn to be a parent in practice, and that is to take full responsibility for childcare, without the other parent being on hand to help, correct, and comment. Only then can you get to know your baby and develop confidence in your caring skills. This has a biological basis, as experiments on rats have shown.

In the 1960s, researcher Jay Seth Rosenblatt sought to find out which hormones govern the way rat mothers take care of their offspring.[2] A mother rat shows several behaviours aimed at protecting and feeding her young. She licks them, builds a nest for them, and lays down on her side so they can suckle. Rosenblatt's plan was to give certain hormones to female rats that had not yet produced young in order to test their effect on these maternal behaviours. The female rats were given baby rats to look after. Since the females were not producing milk, the young were replaced regularly so they wouldn't starve. After a few days, Rosenblatt was surprised to see the female rats behaving like 'mothers' even though they hadn't given birth themselves. They placed themselves in the sucking position, built a nest, and licked the young. A group of female rats that had not given birth and not been given any hormones displayed the same behaviour even though their own sex-hormone-producing organs had been removed prior to the experiment.

Then Rosenblatt introduced the ultimate control: male rats. Baby rats were placed in a cage with the male rats and, much to the researcher's surprise, after a few days the male rats placed themselves in the sucking position, licked the young, and built nests. The caring behaviour in the males was not affected by the removal of their testicles. His conclusion was that rats of both sexes have neural circuits in the brain that control 'maternal behaviour' and that are activated by contact with their helpless young. No sex hormones are required to trigger these neural circuits. However, if the neural circuits are not activated through use, they remain dormant. And like anything else that is controlled by the brain, parental behaviour becomes considerably better

13

with practice. Rat 'fathers' usually don't behave like rat 'mothers', simply because in nature they never get to take care of their young.

Humans are just as much mammals as rats are. As Rosenblatt's experiments demonstrated, parental brains are programmed to take care of helpless babies. But the neural pathways have to be activated, and the more we use them, the better they work. We have to practise being a parent, just as we have to practise riding a bike.

This biological research sheds some light on the well-known fact that a stunning inequality in parenting skills can quickly develop if one parent stays at home full-time and the other goes off to work. The person at home practises their care regime hour after hour. The newborn baby also has circuits in their brain that make them a specialist in getting older children and adults to feel tenderness and want to take care of them. It's not long before the baby learns exactly which signals work best on the person in front of them. And nature ensures that the infant focuses most on charming and demanding care from the one who is present nine times out of ten. Since two individuals — baby and care-giver — are adapting their newly activated neural circuits to each other, this natural mutual adjustment leads to the development of a strong preference for the person who is at hand. This happens with devastating efficiency.

The partner who is at home for just a few hours in the evening has limited opportunity to train the neural caring circuits and interpret their baby's signals. The baby doesn't get to practise the particular play of emotions and facial expressions that this human would fall head over heels for. And there's no need for the baby to try too hard, as there is almost always another parent nearby who has had much more training and whom the infant has got to know extremely well. For whole days, the baby and the parent in the carer role have been developing their relationship and seem to understand each other well, while the non-carer parent becomes something of an outsider. After just a few weeks of absence, the relationship with the parent who is away during the day seriously falls behind.

It is, of course, possible to catch up and to develop a good, deep relationship, even if you begin in earnest when your child is several years old. However, at this later stage there is a risk that the child will remain politely uninterested in a parent who was not there from the start. If you leave it too long, a pattern is likely to be reinforced whereby one parent understands and responds to the child's signals and the other parent just looks on, not knowing what to do. We've talked about the toxic nature of resentment; it is no fun at all dealing with a howling, writhing baby who wants to get away from you and who immediately becomes happy and calm in the presence of the other parent. You should therefore plan so that each parent is at home just as much as the other, developing their parental skills and getting to know the baby equally well. Consider this time as an investment in the future. If you want to make sure you count as a fully-fledged parent, it's much, much safer to begin your training when the baby is newborn.

How many times have you heard radio interviews with ageing fathers who express regret at not having spent more time with their children when they were little? A Swedish female MP has recounted how, in her experience, shared parenting from the outset led to a different quality in her relationships. She was at home from birth for three of her four children, because at that time only mothers were allowed to take parental leave. By the time her fourth child was born, Swedish law had changed, and fathers were also able to stay at home, enabling both parents to share the parental leave equally. Today, when, as adults, the MP's children phone home, only the youngest is just as happy talking to whichever parent happens to answer, but the three oldest will always ask to speak to their mother, even if their father answers the phone.

Of course, it may often feel scary when you're faced with a crying newborn and you have no idea what to do. Just remember that everyone is equally awkward and bewildered to begin with, and only practice will make you better equipped and more confident. We know that throughout human history people have been successfully taking care of their own children, and other people's children as well.

There are plenty of public commentators who declare that it's better for a mother to take the lead 'at least in the beginning', and that infants need to bond to one person at a time, but there is no research to support these assertions. Much of this thinking harks back to psychoanalytical theory from the 1950s. After World War II, in the USA and other Western countries, women who had gone out to work in manufacturing were encouraged to return home and not compete with men in the labour market. The ideal of the housewife took centre stage, and psychologists adapted their theories to explain that this way of living — with the mother as the active parent, and the father as a guest in the home — was best for children. However, this model of the nuclear family, with one parent at home, is a relatively recent phenomenon. Throughout the development of human societies and across cultures, young children have been looked after by mothers, aunts, siblings, and various other caregivers.[3]

PLANNING FOR PARENTAL LEAVE

During pregnancy, you will need to plan who should take care of your child during their first year of life, and how you should adapt to your new financial situation. It's important to investigate what parental benefits you are entitled to and to find out the rules for parental leave in your country.

In Australia, employees are entitled to 12 months' unpaid parental leave when they or their partner gives birth to a child, and up to 18 weeks' paid parental leave when they are the primary carer. In New Zealand, depending on employment status and history, the primary carer is entitled to between zero and 12 months' parental leave, some of which might be transferred to the other parent. In the UK, mothers may take up to 52 weeks' maternity leave after giving birth, some of which is paid. Since 2015, they have been able to share 50 weeks of their maternity leave with their partner if they wish.

Unpaid parental leave, shared parental leave, maternity leave, and related entitlements vary in each country, and can be complicated. We suggest you seek advice from your own workplace, the government leave provider, if that's possible, or your union. Your maternal child health nurse will also have information to assist you.

In Australia and the UK, there is a father/partner benefit of two weeks' paid leave intended to be used directly after the birth of the child. These two weeks are very special. The baby has no daily rhythm, the birth mother's body needs to recover from the process of labour and delivery, and both parents are generally quite dazed by the whole experience. The chaos tends to be punctuated by moments of wonder, joy, and gratitude for the newborn. The only thing that needs to be planned for during these early days is that you will both be at home, and that the parent who did not give birth will do as much as possible of the housework and tending to the baby — perhaps with the help of relatives or friends, if you have such people to help out. If you, or your family and friends, have spare time and energy before the birth, it's great to stock up the freezer with home-cooked or ready-made meals. These preparations will prove very helpful, because it can feel almost impossible to prepare a meal in those first few weeks after the birth, and a breastfeeding mother can be hit by hunger pangs many times a day!

In our experience, it is a good idea to have both parents at home together even after the first two weeks. Reaching the 14-day mark with the birth mother fully fit, the feeding well-established, and the baby sleeping for extended periods is the exception rather than the rule. For someone who is exhausted, sleeping poorly, and feeling confused about how their newborn baby works, it can feel like a nightmare when the other parent slips off to work and re-enters the 'adult world', leaving you alone to try to tame the chaos.

If it is at all possible for you, taking into account your financial and employment situation, we strongly recommend that you consider extending the shared leave a bit, if possible even six to eight weeks after the baby is born. We have never heard anyone express regret about taking one or two months together in the early days. Towards the end of the first month, life tends to become a little more predictable, and you can find more time to enjoy the experience with your baby. Everything is better, and easier, when shared, and it could be your smartest investment ever to spend some of your days on joint leave at the beginning.

Swedish parental leave is extremely flexible and can be taken in smaller portions, so you can work half days, every other day, or every other week. Those who have tried it often highly recommend this model. Both parents are able to maintain contact with their job or studies — with their adult life — and with some of the individual routines that so many find vital their own wellbeing. At the same time, both parents are able to learn about parenting together. You both experience the developmental stages, joys, and challenges at the same time. It is much easier to handle problems when you can discuss and work through them together. If you alternate professional and home life, both parents become involved in developing their own parenting style, and both also get to spend a few hours of adult life outside the home every day. The power of this model for keeping your spirits up should not be underestimated.

If one parent takes many months of leave initially, and the other quickly returns to paid work, there is a risk that they will have very different opinions about their respective roles. The parent who is at home can become irritated with the working person when they fail to enthusiastically take over the housework and parenting duties as soon as they come home. The working parent can easily feel that the parent at home has had a nice, relaxing time while they need a rest from dealing with the demands and conflicts at work or contending with an unpleasant commute.

ADVANTAGES OF AN EARLY RETURN TO WORK

Before you have a child, it is almost impossible to imagine how you will be robbed of so many things you took for granted. It is a radical lifestyle change to no longer have the ability to sleep through the night, or to go to the toilet in peace, or to shower when you want, or to keep your clothes clean for longer than three minutes. Maintaining contact with your regular social life and working life does most people the power of good. Going back to work part-time makes life with a child and the related housework much more enjoyable for the vast majority of parents. Your previously mundane workplace can even take on a tinge of glamour.

It is also worth remembering that maintaining contact with your work has other benefits. Of course, fine words are spoken about how a person on parental leave should not be overlooked in the yearly adjustments of salary, but in practice it is quite understandable for managers to invest more in those who are actually at work than in those they haven't seen for the past year.

For some reason, many people are of the opinion that splitting parental leave across alternate weeks, working part-time, or adopting some similar schedule, is difficult for employers, who prefer that a parent takes the full year off. This may be true in some workplaces, but there are certainly at least as many employers who would prefer you to maintain contact with your work during parental leave. Think about what you and your partner want, and then ask your managers how your ideal timetable could be made to work. Your employers may not have given much thought to the subject, so try to have these discussions early.

PROVIDING FOR YOURSELF

In purely financial terms, parenthood is a loss-making deal. The first major loss is the reduction in take-home pay. In Sweden, during the year that at least one parent needs to be on parental leave, that person receives between 77.6 per cent and 90 per cent of their salary, depending on the rules of their collective agreement.

If there is more than one parent in the household, it's extremely important to shoulder this loss in work income equally. Even if you can combine your incomes for as long as you live together, your future livelihood is likely to depend on how much each of you has earned over the course of your working life. It seems strange to have to think about old age when your pregnancy test has just come up positive, but it is important. Consider what kind of grandparent you hope to be to your children's children in 30 or 40 years: a poor pensioner who can barely afford to cover their daily expenses, or a comfortably off pensioner who can take their grandchildren to the café, and take their grown-up children out to dinner and perhaps on holiday?

The most common argument for the Swedish 80–20 model, whereby the birth mother takes most of the parental leave, is that it makes financial sense for the man to take very few days of leave and for the woman to take a lot. However, this is a false argument. It has been shown that fathers with low incomes take less parental leave than fathers with high incomes. And even if the mother is a high earner, this does not stop her taking parental leave. Even in households where the woman earns a higher salary, she is usually the one who spends more time at home.

One of your most important duties as a parent will be to make sure you can provide for yourself and your offspring throughout your life. Why are we talking about financial matters in a book about bringing up children? Precisely because everyone who works professionally with children — paediatricians, teachers, social workers, and psychologists — knows there is a much greater risk that a child will have problems of various kinds if their parents experience significant financial hardship. A lack of money reduces options with regard to jobs, education, and housing. These social outcomes affect you and your child, so it is your duty to do what you can to provide for yourselves.

Usually, for men, the need to provide for themselves has been drilled into them since childhood. Most men are comfortable seeing themselves as both a loving partner and a careful financial provider. Many women, on the other hand, have learned through films, books, magazines, social media, and other people that dwelling too much on money and career is a little vulgar. It is not vulgar. Boring, perhaps. But no more boring than sorting laundry and ferrying children to activities. Financial security is a necessary foundation for a good life.

Providing for yourself means ensuring you have a job that can maintain a reasonable standard of living for yourself, and your children, for your entire lifespan. This doesn't mean that you shouldn't share your finances with the person you live with. On the contrary, it can be practical to merge your incomes and share all the expenses to come, particularly if you have children together. It can also be good to help your partner through periods of low income, such as during illness or study. Whether you are in a married or de facto relationship, you have a legal obligation to support each other financially as the need arises.

Providing for yourself means not neglecting your working life, and especially not your own professional development, in favour of your partner's career, in the mistaken belief that this will be good for both of you. A relationship in which one partner has a good income and the other a significantly lesser income is often the breeding ground for resentment. If your relationship later breaks down, as about a third of relationships involving children do, the person without the means to earn a living is left in a very difficult situation. You may not be able to afford a suitable home for you and your children. You may never be able to afford a holiday. You may be wholly dependent on a minimal pension for the last 30 years of your life. And, most dangerous of all, you may not be able to leave a relationship that has come to be filled with hate, loathing, and even violence, simply because you lack the financial means to be independent. For your sake and for the sake of your children, we firmly believe that you should nurture your working life, and make sure you are capable of providing for yourself — at every stage of your life.

UNEQUAL PARENTING — IT EVEN HAPPENS IN SWEDEN

Even in a country with very generous parental leave provisions, equal shared parenting is by no means a foregone conclusion. On average, Swedish men give away hundreds of paid days of parental leave to their female partners. Sweden is often held up as a land of equality, but in fact women take around 80 per cent of the parental leave for children under

21

the age of two. Four lollipops to the one parent and one to the other. Regardless of whether you see your child or your job as the lollipop, this is not a good strategy if you want to share the parenting and have a good career.

We often hear about the fantastic advances we've made in Sweden with fathers getting involved in the care of their children, but are the claims true? Certainly, men took less parental leave 50 years ago than they do now, but what is often overlooked is the fact that women also took significantly less parental leave then than they do today. In the 1970s, total parental leave under Swedish law amounted to six months; up until the mid-1980s, it was nine months. A woman who in the 1980s took 100 per cent of her parental leave was away from her job for nine months, which is half as long as many of today's mothers, who take leave for at least 18 months. Paradoxically, by allowing parents to negotiate an unequal use of their parental leave entitlements, Sweden's extremely generous parental leave scheme, which was designed for equality, may have reduced Swedish women's contact with the workforce.

Unequal participation in working life can cause devastating discrepancies in lifetime pay and retirement savings. A study by Ylva Moberg at Uppsala University showed how Swedish parents' incomes change after the birth of their first child.[4] She compared parents in heterosexual couples with mothers in lesbian couples. In the same-sex female couples, the women tend to share the parental leave more equally. Another Swedish study of two-mother families showed that the majority divided their parental leave 50–50. There appeared to be a correlation between equal parental leave and a strong desire for equal parenting.[5]

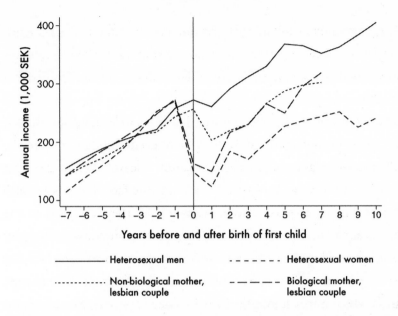

Development of annual income from work (at 2008 rates) for parents in heterosexual and lesbian couples. Source: Moberg, Y., *Är lesbiska föräldrar mer jämställda? (Are lesbian parents more equal?)*, IFAU Report, 2016.

In this diagram, we can see that the heterosexual women earned just as much as their husbands in the year before the birth of their first child. Following the birth, the income of these women fell dramatically, while the men's incomes fell slightly in the first year and then continued upwards. The income gap between the mother and the father remained intact throughout the ten years that the study lasted (and probably thereafter as well). In the lesbian relationships studied, the pattern was entirely different. Immediately after the birth of the child, the incomes of the mothers who gave birth fell almost as far as for their heterosexual sisters. But after two years, they had caught up with their wives, and the income disparity between the lesbian mothers had disappeared. Instead, they followed an income trend that tracked somewhere in between that of the heterosexual women and the heterosexual men.

Moberg's study is an important illustration of how the 'normal' division of parenting in heterosexual relationships (or what we've previously referred to as the 'out of habit' method) can give rise to substantial financial differences between women and men. Pay rates over time feed into retirement incomes. Sweden's disproportionate rates of female pensioner poverty is probably due not only to poorer pay for women, but also to unequal sharing of day-to-day parenting. Don't make the mistake of believing that this has been relegated to the past — as we've discussed above, today's Swedish women are taking more parental leave than ever, yet still the disparity remains.

Are men's jobs more important?

It seems as if many people perceive men's jobs to be more important, exciting, and rewarding than women's jobs, thus rationalising the fact that women take the lead in the home. Let's examine this argument. The six most common jobs for Swedish men (in descending order) are salesman, warehouse worker, lorry driver, programmer, carpenter, and metalworker. The six most common jobs for women are nurse, teacher, childcare worker, preschool teacher, care worker, and office worker. We can see that women and men have very different jobs, and that women's jobs focus mainly on care and education, usually in the public sector. Many jobs are important, but it's hard to understand how, in general, men's jobs can be considered more important to society than women's jobs.

The Swedish 80–20 model not only deprives fathers of their parenthood, but also makes it hard for women to focus on their careers. How interesting or boring you find your job may to some extent depend on how much you commit to it. If you're away for a long time, things change, and you may feel out of place when you return to work. New employees may have carved up all the more enjoyable tasks for themselves, leaving the duller ones for you.

Studies by the Karolinska Institute have examined what characterises women on long-term sick leave, as compared to women actively participating in the workforce.[6] The women on long-term sick leave report that when they were at work they felt unhappy and inadequate, and that at home they always took the main responsibility for the children. A higher proportion of the women on long-term sick leave were part-time workers than their sisters in full-time work. The most common causes for long-term sick leave among Swedish women are mental-health problems such as depressive and anxiety disorders, or diagnoses related to muscular pain such as lower-back pain and fibromyalgia.

Studies like this can never give us any clear understanding of causality, but we believe these factors are related: a person who always prioritises family and housework risks falling behind in their job and not keeping up with changes in work practices. That increases the likelihood of them disliking their job, and fuels feelings of inadequacy and stress, which are known risk factors for depressive and anxiety disorders. It's just like with parenting and housework: if you don't practise, you lose your skills.

Swedish women are, on average, better educated than Swedish men, as has been the case since the 1980s. This ought to counter any expectations that women should put their career on the back burner in favour of their partner's career, but clearly it hasn't worked out that way. Even when both partners have jobs that to an outsider look basically the same, the man's 'incredibly important' job often comes first. In one family we know, it was taken for granted that the mother would be the primary caregiver, as she was a computer teacher, which, according to the father, was ideal for combining with parental leave. And what was his job, which was so poorly suited to parental leave? He was an IT coach.

Any claim that men's jobs can't be combined with parental leave is obviously outdated nonsense — even leaders of political parties take parental leave these days. In 2018, one of them, New Zealand's prime minister, Jacinda Ardern, gave birth to her first child while in office. She took six weeks off duty with her newborn child, and thereafter her partner, Clarke Gayford, stepped in as the child's primary caregiver, travelling with the family to the United Nations general assembly meeting when their baby was three-and-a-half months old.

Breastfeeding as an argument for unequal parental responsibility

The second major justification for the unequal split of parental leave concerns the issues surrounding breastfeeding. We have dedicated chapter 5 to an in-depth exploration of feeding a newborn, but we want to explode the myth here and now that breastfeeding prevents equal parenting.

Swedish breastfeeding parents are legally entitled to breastfeeding breaks at work, so even those who want to breastfeed can return to work early on. This is also the case in New Zealand, but unfortunately not in the UK or Australia. If you want to breastfeed your baby at work, talk to your employer, even in the UK and Australia, as no law allows the employer to deny you this opportunity. It's also possible to take a breast pump to work. A breastfeeding mother can then pump milk once or twice during the day, so the other parent can bottle-feed the baby when the breastfeeding parent is at work. It's also perfectly possible to combine breastfeeding and baby formula. (See chapter 5).

But, above all, the breastfeeding argument only applies to the very early part of parenting. After six months of age, an infant shouldn't be relying on breast milk to meet all their nutritional needs. (See chapter 6.) While many women prefer to continue breastfeeding after six months, in practice this tends to mean offering the infant breast milk for the morning and evening feed. After six months (a third of the parental-leave allocation in Sweden), there is thus absolutely nothing stopping a breastfeeding mother from working full-time.

Interestingly, we have learned that the same argument about breastfeeding is also used by same-sex couples who don't want to share things equally. A small number of the families in a study of Swedish lesbian parents with small children applied the same 80–20 model as the average Swedish family. Such couples reasoned along similar lines to heterosexual couples where the mother takes most of the parental leave; they claimed that pregnancy or breastfeeding kept the birth mother at home, while the paid job was the reason for the non-birth mother to spend most time out of the home. A degree of conflict about jobs and parental leave arose among the non-equal lesbian couples. However, the majority of lesbian families shared things more equally. In most cases, their babies were breastfed, but they didn't consider that breastfeeding was an argument against equal sharing.

THE PARTNERSHIP CONTRACT

When a baby is born, there will always be a certain amount of chaos, so you will need to plan in advance to avoid falling into the 80–20 model or the default model of your society, whether it's 80–20, 70–30 or 99–1, 'out of habit'. We suggest you draw up a partnership contract before the baby arrives. It should contain a plan for the split of parental leave and care in the first year. A partnership contract lays the foundation for active and equal involvement by both parents. Shared parenting is important for children throughout their lives, whether you stay together for a long time or go your separate ways. If the child has developed a close relationship with both parents from birth, those ties are likely to last forever.

If you think that talking about going your separate ways at this stage is a little depressing, it might make you feel better to learn that research shows the risk of divorce is lower if the parents have shared the parental leave with their first child.[7] It's hard to be sure of the reasons for this, but, as we explain above, sharing both the burdens and the joys equally is likely to be good for your relationship, as is having a reasonably similar view of what is and isn't important. You have a better chance of discussing your way to a consensus if you develop your parenting side by side, instead of one parent increasingly taking the lead and the other barely keeping up with their child's development. The same research has shown that parents who shared the parental leave with their first child are more likely to go on to have a second child.[8]

Don't listen to those who think it's unromantic, cold, and calculating to talk about how you organise the care of your child and your individual working lives before the baby arrives. There is certainly nothing romantic about stumbling into unequal parenting simply because you didn't want or dare to make a plan ahead of time. You'll never regret making reasonable plans, and just because you've made plans doesn't mean you can't change them to account for unforeseen circumstances. You plan your holidays and house purchases, so why on earth wouldn't you plan some of the most important aspects of your life: future parenthood and the sharing of parental responsibility?

THE LIFE JIGSAW PUZZLE —
FROM MANY PIECES TO TWO

In Sweden, people use the phrase 'the life jigsaw puzzle' as a way of illustrating how tricky it can be to make the myriad pieces of 21st-century life fit together, with or without children. But we maintain that when you are a new parent, there is no complicated life jigsaw puzzle. There are only two things you will absolutely have to manage: taking care of your child, and providing for yourself and your child. Everything else — exercise, travel, book club, Twitter, home-baked bread, family parties, kitchen renovations, volunteering — can be scaled back for a while and picked up again later. You don't need to live in a spotless home or eat artfully composed meals. These are details you can opt for when you have time, later on.

How can we so confidently say there is no life jigsaw puzzle? Why are there interior-design blogs, Instagram accounts, and countless magazines about home furnishings if they are not important? Why is every magazine full of advice about how vital exercise is for your health, if it's okay not to do it? We can really only speculate. Financial interests may, of course, play a role. The home-furnishings industry turns over enormous sums each year in Sweden and around the world. If we lived now the way we once did — renovating and furnishing the home when you move in, at the age of 30, and then keeping the furniture for the rest of your life — many people would lose their jobs and livelihoods.

It's not quite as obvious whose financial interests lie behind the marketing of 'needs' such as baking cupcakes, wrapping 24 mini-presents for a homemade Advent calendar each year, or constant cleaning. These activities are expected to be carried out by a mother with no payment involved. In her classic 1991 book *Backlash: the undeclared war against American women*,[9] American author Susan Faludi describes how every advance in society made by women has been followed by a step backwards, whereby it is insinuated that women should retire back to the home. (This occurred after World War II, as we noted earlier.) One such typical backlash to the successes of the women's movement in the 1970s and 1980s was the 1990s trend for 'cocooning', which promoted the importance of withdrawing to the cosiness of your own little world. Yes, it can be nice to curl up on the sofa now and then, but you don't have to invest lots of time and money in that. All you need is a blanket.

Physical exercise is good for you. But exercising is much more important for teenagers who would otherwise be sitting in front of their computers, and for middle-aged people who drive everywhere and sit still at work. A parent of a young child gets so much incidental physical activity — many children demand to be carried around as extra weight when you're cooking, picking up Lego, or shopping — that the risk of unhealthy inactivity is minimal. And while providing for and caring for children can't be postponed until later, physical exercise can be put on hold for a few years. Forgivingly enough, exercise has the same positive effect whenever you do it.

There is no reason to feel bad about not jogging or going to the gym while your child is young. If, on the other hand, fitness is one of your major interests and part of your lifestyle, it can be one of those things you do if and when you get a little time to yourself, just as others would prioritise reading the newspaper or going to a concert now and then. It's best to realise that such needs have to be pretty much shelved during the first year. There'll be plenty of time for other interests later on.

All the talk about the 'life jigsaw puzzle' or a 'work-life balance' can sound harmless, but it's a sly way of equating the two most important things in your life — your relationship with your child and your liveli-hood — with significantly less important things. This formulation can lead you to make the wrong decisions, even decisions that will affect your whole career and future life. Trying to solve the 'life jigsaw puzzle' may lead you to believe that getting to go to aerobics once a week is as urgent as going to your workplace one day a week. Nothing could be further from the truth. The former can be fun, but the effect will be gone after a year; the latter is a vital investment in your career and lifetime earnings. Think for a moment about why the 'life jigsaw puzzle' metaphor is so common in magazines aimed at women, and so uncommon in men's conversations. Could it be because of an inclination to see women's work and careers as something quite trivial, with about the same significance as a trip to the cinema? Never, ever fall into the trap of thinking that way.

Isn't your relationship a vital piece of the puzzle?

You will often be advised, whether by family and friends, professional family therapists, or self-appointed experts with popular blogs, about the importance of 'keeping the romance alive' in your relationship during your child's early years. By all means, do this if you wish, but we believe that, as new parents, the most important quality to develop in your relationship as new parents is good companionship. Initially, there won't be much time for your individual needs, or for maintaining a relationship, but that time will come once you've begun to get the hang of caring for your baby and getting enough sleep.

Research shows that a couple who share parental leave and work equally divorce less often than those who split it unequally. We believe that shared responsibility, solidarity, and companionship serve as a kind of glue that will hold the relationship together. We are, however, not aware of any research showing that maintaining romance by eating out at restaurants, going away together, or cultivating shared interests reduces the risk of divorce. Such activities won't do any harm. But equal parenting is still a more important investment, because it will remain an asset whether you live together for the rest of your lives or decide to go your separate ways after a few years. Being on the same page and sharing responsibilities as parents lays a firm foundation for working together, either in a loving relationship or in a parental relationship after a split.

If you are able to do things together that you did before you had children, that's great. Some parents manage to get adult time alone, particularly if they have grandparents or other free child-minders nearby, or can afford to pay a babysitter. But if you only have time to take care of your children and your career during those early years, don't think you've done anything wrong, or that this will necessarily damage your relationship. On the contrary, you've prioritised the two most important aspects of life.

As you will have gathered, we believe that, ideally, parenting should be shared equally. Even so, the current norm in Sweden is 80–20, which appears to be considered equal enough. In Australia, 5 per cent of fathers took primary parental leave as their child's primary caregiver, and in the UK just 1 per cent of couples took up the option of shared leave after the initial two weeks' maternity and paternity leave after the birth. Unfortunately, those who try to share 50–50 will sometimes have to put up with critical comments from colleagues and relatives, and not least from those who split the parenting 80–20, 90–10, or 99–1. You're naturally more sensitive to such comments when you're exhausted and busy taking care of a baby. But if you've agreed on the 50–50 model, you will need to support each other. Remember that those who get most worked up when they see equal parenting are basing their views on prejudice rather than facts, often seeing it as an indirect criticism of their own arrangements.

LIFE AFTER PARENTAL LEAVE

Once your parental leave ends, it will be time to re-engage with your working life. In Sweden, publicly subsidised high-quality daycare has been widely established in the last few decades. In the 1970s, there were few daycare centres, and working women struggled to find an acceptable life–work balance. Consequently, high-quality affordable daycare for all became one of the most important political goals for the feminist movement of that time, and it succeeded. Today, all children in Sweden above one year of age are guaranteed a place at a daycare centre within three months of their parents applying for one.

We cannot put enough emphasis on the importance of daycare to give women the ability to keep working or continuing their careers while their children are still young. And, as we've already mentioned, keeping on working is of the highest importance both for yourself and your children. If you have access to affordable daycare of an acceptable quality, use it. If not, try to find other solutions. Maybe you could organise something with other parents in your neighbourhood — a kind of daycare cooperative, where you share the care of each other's children. If you live close to your parents, they might be able to provide invaluable help.

How much time you as parents can or should devote to work during the first years of your children's lives will vary. It is not always possible or preferable for both parents to work full time, especially not if you have to add commuting time to a heavy full-time schedule. We suggest you discuss this matter while you are expecting your child. If some of you commute, maybe this is the time to change your place of work to somewhere you can easily reach by bike. If you have two cars, selling one of them could make your financial situation much easier to handle.

When you are clear about how much time you both will be able to devote to work, we suggest you split this time equally. It is probable that both of you will have to change your working situation to some extent, which is of course not surprising, taking into account that you are entering a completely new phase of life. Traditionally, in Sweden as well as in all other high-income countries that we know of, working part-time has been the responsibility of the mother.

An unequal sharing of the time available for paid work risks reinforcing a vicious cycle — for the part-time worker, work may become increasingly uninteresting, while the demands at home never ease off. The full-time worker continues to evolve his or her career, and has less and less time for and involvement in parenting and home maintenance. This has long-time consequences. More than one-third of women in Sweden work part-time, not just during their children's early years (when the figure is even higher), but even after the youngest has started school.

Study combines well with having young children. You can take advantage of flexible hours and the ability to study when the child is asleep. In Sweden, we also have the great luxury of taxpayer-funded higher education with no tuition fees, and free childcare for students. If you have a dull job you'd rather not go back to, or a job where you can't work full-time, sign up for a course of study instead. You can begin once your baby is six months old — by then, breastfeeding is usually down to one feed in the morning and one in the evening, and so the other parent can look after the baby during the day. It's usually less tiring to study full-time than to work full-time. In addition, further education offers the benefits of better pay over your lifetime and greater retirement savings.

STUFF YOU (DON'T) NEED FOR YOUR CHILD

We've already said that having a baby is a loss-maker financially, and there isn't much you can do about that at a household level. You do, however, have control over how much you spend on baby accessories. You don't need much at all to start with. A newborn needs a few clothes, a lot of nappies, something to be carried around or pushed in, and a car seat (if you have or use a car). If you choose to feed your baby on formula, you will need to spend money on the formula and bottles; if you choose to breastfeed, the mother will eat more, and so groceries will be a little more expensive. A changing table can be handy, but it isn't an absolute must. A bed sounds important, but in fact homes are full of cots that babies have never slept in (see chapter 7), so hold off on buying a cot — there are other alternatives that may be more suitable to start with.

There are masses of companies that want to sell you baby accessories. They thrive on expectant parents who want to be fully prepared and who don't know yet how few things a newborn really needs. These companies fund parenting magazines and parenting sites through advertisements and product placement. It pays to be smart as a consumer. Don't be taken in by special offers, and don't buy anything unless you're absolutely sure you'll need it — and, even then, don't purchase until you feel the need. In particular, be sceptical about any type of product that is said to monitor or improve your baby's health and safety. Purchasing unnecessary products is just throwing money away, and many monitors create more anxiety than peace of mind.

Don't buy new baby clothes if you will be offered hand-me-downs from friends or relatives. Seek out second-hand items; babies grow out of their clothes in the blink of an eye, and since they are used for such a short time, they don't get worn out, so there is enormous turnover. Baby clothes are a popular present from friends and family, so you may receive quite a lot that way when the baby is born. If you enjoy buying cute baby clothing, go right ahead, but remember that this shopping is being done for your own amusement, rather than the child's actual needs.

Also, buy second-hand goods, while bearing in mind that there are some items that may pose a safety risk. Information on the safety risks of items such as prams and strollers, cots, and car seats is readily available on the internet.

After a few years, you might need larger accommodation, and if you have more children, you might end up needing a bigger car. One financial tip, however, is to look for a small-size car seat that will fit into the old car. Another option if you are mostly travelling short distances is to swap the car for an electric cargo bike.

The older the children get, the more they cost. The best way to anticipate these costs is to draw up a financial plan. Set a realistic monthly budget based on the income you will have during your parental leave. Tailor your consumption to this level during the pregnancy. Save the rest, as the extra funds will be much needed later. Make sure the savings amount is transferred automatically from your account as soon as your regular pay comes in. If you wait till the end of the month, there will rarely be any money left to save.

IN BRIEF

It's important to get a grip on your personal finances, to become self-sufficient if you aren't already, and to plan parental leave and parental responsibilities fairly, right from the time of conception. Prepare for the baby by getting nappies, a pram or a carrier, a few clothes, and formula and bottles if you don't intend to breastfeed all the time. Buy second-hand where you can, and don't buy anything unless you absolutely know you're going to need it. Don't believe in the myth of the life jigsaw puzzle — and only decorate a cute nursery if it honestly makes you happy, and you have time for it.

CHAPTER TWO
Pregnancy facts

Expecting a baby is not just about making mental preparations and planning parenting roles and expectations. In most expectant families, one of the parents-to-be is pregnant and will carry the baby in her womb for nine months. How women experience their pregnancies varies widely: some find it relatively easy and others find it difficult. In this chapter, we write about what happens during the different stages of pregnancy, some common problems and less common complications, and the health checks that we recommend to ensure a safe pregnancy. These are things that we believe every pregnant woman and their partner should know. The chapter concludes with a comprehensive guide to prenatal screening, and diagnostics. We also describe some infections that can harm the foetus. We've included this information because we know many people have questions about this area, but if you would prefer not to read about these problems, feel free to skip them, and go on to the next chapter.

In the previous chapter, we encouraged the idea of sharing parenting absolutely equally. Unlike parenting, the hard work of pregnancy can't be shared. In families where both parents can bear a child, the inequality can be redressed with the next pregnancy, but in the majority of families only one parent has a womb and will need to bear all the family's children.

Whatever your situation, it's important to value the job of pregnancy as the grand contribution to humanity that it is. During pregnancy, a woman's body is redirected to satisfy the needs of her womb and foetus, often to the detriment of her own needs. This includes major hormonal changes aimed at ensuring that the pregnancy progresses well. These same hormones also tend to cause mood swings, tiredness, morning sickness, a frequent need to urinate, constipation, and pelvic pain. The side effects of pregnancy can't be shared fairly, but it's important to make sure the pregnant parent gets extra care and attention, and that the non-pregnant partner is supported to provide both empathy and practical support. Having the non-pregnant parent take on more of the housework during pregnancy is another way to create a little fairness.

From a global and historical perspective, childbearing has been not only hard work but also truly life-threatening. Thankfully, this is no longer the case for most women in high-income nations, but we still have a way to go globally to ensure a safe pregnancy and delivery for all women. Even in high-income countries such as Sweden, Australia, New Zealand, and the United Kingdom, there are unequal risks accompanying pregnancy for different groups of women. In general, poor immigrant women and indigenous women experience higher rates of negative health outcomes during pregnancy and childbirth, which we know is as a result of their lower access to and thus use of healthcare services. These inequalities are important to tackle politically to reach the best possible maternal and child health for all in the future.

In the meantime, if you belong to a group that has a statistically increased risk of poor health outcomes, bear in mind that this does not mean you are doomed to a risky pregnancy. Even though inequalities in health on a societal level are most efficiently tackled through political action, your body will work exactly like the bodies of women who happened to be born in more privileged groups.

NINE MONTHS/40 WEEKS

Most pregnancies last for around 40 weeks, which is just over nine months. When calculated from the moment of fertilisation, a full-term pregnancy is 38 weeks, but traditionally the start date is calculated from the first day of the last menstrual period before conception. This convention accounts for the extra two weeks.

If your period is very regular and you take a pregnancy test on the first day that you're late, you are considered to be at week 4 by the time you receive a positive test result, despite the pregnancy only having been underway for two weeks. Fertilisation by the sperm takes place in the fallopian tube, and the fertilised ovum (egg) begins to divide as it makes its way down towards the uterus (womb). A week or so after fertilisation, the fertilised egg attaches to the lining of the uterus, and the placenta begins to form. By around week 4, the growing placenta has produced enough of the human chorionic gonadotropin (hCG) hormone that it can be measured in the urine using a regular home pregnancy test. There are (more expensive) tests that measure even lower levels of hCG and can detect a pregnancy a week or so before an overdue period.

If your menstrual cycle is irregular, or you don't really keep track of it, you won't know what week you are at when you discover that you're pregnant; in this situation, it's common to have an ultrasound scan that measures the size of the foetus to work out how far into the pregnancy you are. The more expensive home tests are a waste of money. As hCG levels in urine vary so much between different women, this method of pregnancy dating is way too inaccurate to pay extra for.

CHOICE OF PRENATAL CARE

As you will see in this chapter, even though most pregnancies are uncomplicated, pregnancy complications are not uncommon. Some of them, such as pre-eclampsia, may be asymptomatic for several weeks or months before a sudden deterioration leads to life-threatening disease. By attending prenatal check-ups, most complications will be discovered in time, and treatment will be given before any danger has occurred. As we said earlier, going for your pregnancy check-ups is the most important step you can take for yourself and for your baby.

In Sweden, the choice of prenatal care is easy, based on a single system: tax-funded midwife-led maternity centres that all deliver the same care, from which parents-to-be choose one — often the closest to their home or workplace.

In the UK, the National Health Service offers free prenatal care by midwives. You can get in touch with them either directly or through your GP. If you already know where you want to give birth, there may be prenatal services connected to your chosen birth place, and you can enrol in their program directly. Some midwifery services offer continuous care by the same team of midwifes during pregnancy and childbirth, which many women find gives them a sense of security. In some studies, that kind of care has also been associated with lower levels of complicated deliveries. All midwifery services follow the same NHS program for prenatal check-ups, and are thus safe alternatives.

Especially in London, there are private wings of public hospitals that, in addition to good-quality maternity care and delivery, offer hotel-standard accommodation during delivery and after childbirth, a very welcoming and luxurious environment for prenatal care visits, and all the extra services you may ask for. This might be the most comfortable choice for those who have private insurance or can afford it themselves. Given the high level of care at the NHS maternity centres and hospitals, remember that your chances of getting a healthy pregnancy and child are the same in publicly funded care.

In Australia, you have to make a choice between midwife-led and obstetrician-led maternity care. Both could be provided by a public hospital, funded by your private health insurers, or provided by a private hospital. If you choose a service that is part of a hospital, it is natural to plan for a birth at the same hospital. If you choose a private practitioner, there is often a choice of birthing place coupled to your choice of prenatal care provider. In chapter 4, we write more about your choice of birthing place. In Australia, as in the UK and Sweden, maternity care follows a standard program set by national authorities based on scientific evidence regarding what is safe for mother and child.

Remember that it is important to have confidence in your doctor and midwives, and if you don't feel comfortable you should always ask for an alternative practitioner, or go elsewhere, if that's possible.

The nine-month pregnancy is divided into thirds, known as trimesters. The following sections give an overview of what happens to the foetus and the pregnant mother during the three trimesters.

FIRST TRIMESTER (WEEKS 1–12)

Over the course of the first trimester, the fertilised ovum develops into a foetus, and the body's organs are formed. By the end of the first trimester, the foetus is around 6 centimetres long and weighs about 60 grams. Most pregnant women experience a number of symptoms, mainly tiredness and morning sickness, over this period. However, the 'baby bump' is not very visible at this stage, and, since there is a considerable risk of miscarriage during the first trimester, many women choose to keep the pregnancy private.

Morning sickness

Half of all pregnant women feel nauseous and vomit, and another quarter feel nauseous without vomiting.[1] It is commonly thought that the sickness is worst in the morning (hence the name 'morning sickness'), and while this is true for some women, it is just as likely to come and go throughout the day. Around one-third of women suffer so much that it affects their ability to work and their close relationships.

The most severe form of pregnancy-related nausea and vomiting is called hyperemesis gravidarum, which affects 0.3–1 per cent of pregnant women. Women with this condition vomit frequently, lose weight, and become dehydrated. Considering the prevalence of nausea and vomiting during pregnancy, and how much suffering it causes, you might think that tireless research would have identified what causes it, and would have found effective treatments by now. However, research on the condition is scarce, so we still don't know much about why it happens. If the vomiting is so bad that you can't keep down any fluids, you need to seek medical assistance, and you may need to be hospitalised on a drip. There are prescription drugs that can help combat moderate pregnancy-related sickness, although they are unfortunately not always effective against hyperemesis gravidarum.

The nausea and vomiting is most likely related to the placenta rather than the foetus. In the very uncommon disorder called molar pregnancy, or hydatidiform mole, an abnormal placenta develops from a fertilised egg, but no foetus forms. Molar pregnancies are usually characterised by severe nausea and vomiting — obviously related to the placenta, as there is no foetus. On average, smokers and older pregnant women have a smaller placenta than non-smoking young mothers, and they also tend to feel less nauseous. There is also a very strong link between hCG levels in the blood over different weeks of the pregnancy and the proportion of pregnant women with nausea and vomiting at this time. While hCG is formed in the placenta, it may not just be the hCG but something else from the placenta that causes the nausea and vomiting.

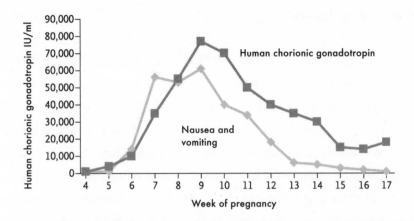

The proportion of women who feel sick at some point during their pregnancy and the level of human chorionic gonadotropin (hCG) in their blood at that time. Source: *New England Journal of Medicine.* 14 Oct 2010. 363(16): 1544–50.

So is there any point to morning sickness? Perhaps. The nausea during pregnancy is thought to be linked to the sense of smell, which becomes hypersensitive — many pregnant women hate all overpowering smells, which can give them a feeling of nausea. There are people who are born without a sense of smell, a condition called anosmia. In a small-scale study, a researcher noted that women with no sense of smell rarely felt nauseous during pregnancy. A pregnant woman's hypersensitivity to smells and her strong tendency to feel sick may thus be connected.[2] It could be an instinct that has evolved as a way to avoid rotten food and other hazards.

The brain controls nausea and vomiting. There is plenty of research into medicines that can stop the nausea and vomiting which accompanies chemotherapy and when waking up after an operation — but little research specifically relating to pregnant women. The problem is that many medicines that have been shown to treat nausea and vomiting have not been tested for their safety or efficacy during pregnancy.

Studies into the effect of different treatments on pregnancy-related sickness provide no clear guidance, and they are few and far between.[3]

Ginger seems to have some effect in certain studies, but the required dosage is unclear. A daily 10 milligram dose of vitamin B6 (pyridoxine) has been shown to work quite well in some studies.

Unfortunately, there are no reliable studies into whether you can influence your sickness by eating or drinking specific items, or by organising your meals in a particular way. In fact, we could only find one small experimental study of how different kinds of food affect pregnancy-related sickness.[4] The researchers studied 14 women who were given different types of meals, and found that protein-rich food led to less sickness than carbohydrate- or fat-rich food with the same overall calorific value. They also found that liquid food caused fewer problems than solid food.

This lack of knowledge means that if you are affected by nausea and vomiting during your pregnancy, you'll have to test different things for yourself, and ask your friends what worked for them. Some people find relief by consuming something small before they get up, so you could try keeping a few biscuits and maybe a flask of a favourite drink next to your bed. Another suggestion is to eat more often and in smaller portions. We have heard anecdotally that sparkling water and raw carrots work for some women — it's a matter of finding what works for you. Make sure you steer clear of frying smells, and cigarette smoke, and whatever smells cause you to feel sick. And for everyone else, it's about respecting the pregnant woman's aversion to odours.

Carry on working, if possible. The vomiting can be more depressing, and the pregnancy can feel even more endless and hopeless, if you're lying at home feeling ill. You may find that by concentrating on work you can settle the brain and manage the sickness with an occasional vomit in the privacy of a bathroom. It can be a good idea to carry a plastic bag with you, just in case! It may be a slight comfort to know that pregnancies accompanied by sickness and vomiting are less likely to end in a miscarriage than pregnancies with no sickness. Don't let this worry you, however, if you're one of those who aren't sick; you may well be one of the lucky quarter who never feel ill and who enjoy a happy pregnancy.

Bleeding

Around one in four pregnant women will bleed at some point during the first part of their pregnancy. A small amount of bleeding is usually not significant, but a larger bleed or repeated bleeding may be a sign that there is something wrong. Below, we go through the different conditions that may lead to bleeding and what you should do in each case.

Major bleeding without abdominal pain

If you experience heavy bleeding with no abdominal pain, so that you bleed through several sanitary pads in a few hours, it is important to seek immediate medical assistance. Such bleeding is often caused by a miscarriage. If you otherwise feel normal and don't have a stomach ache, you don't need to call an ambulance; getting a lift or a taxi to the emergency department is fine. If you feel dizzy, faint, or have cold sweats, your body is signalling that you have lost too much blood, and you should urgently get an ambulance to hospital.

Minor bleeding without abdominal pain

Minor bleeding not accompanied by abdominal pain does not require emergency medical care. While it could be a sign of miscarriage, it's more likely to be a normal phenomenon in a completely normal pregnancy. Minor bleeding of this kind needs to be checked by a gynaecologist, and your prenatal healthcare provider will be able to inform you about where to go for this check-up.

There are two good reasons to avoid an emergency unit for light bleeding if you have no abdominal pain. The first is that you may be made to wait for a long time, because women with greater, more dangerous bleeding or other acute problems will always come a long way ahead of you in the queue. Emergency rooms are not a pleasant environment.

45

They are designed to deal rapidly with life-threatening conditions, so when it is finally your turn to be examined at 3:30 am, there is a risk that you'll be seen by an exhausted night-shift gynaecologist who does not have the capacity to give you the sympathetic treatment you need. A long time in the emergency waiting room is not good for a person who is worried about a miscarriage. In this situation, it is less stressful to sip a hot chocolate and watch television at home on the sofa while you wait for a planned appointment the next day.

The second reason to avoid the emergency waiting room is that the doctor you will meet in the evening and at night is more likely to be a tired doctor a long way into his or her night shift. You have a greater chance of obtaining an accurate assessment of your baby's condition at a planned daytime appointment.

Ectopic pregnancy

In one in a hundred pregnancies, the fertilised egg doesn't implant in the lining of the uterus, but elsewhere. Most commonly, it attaches to the fallopian tubes before it reaches the uterus. This is called an extrauterine, or ectopic, pregnancy. An ectopic pregnancy is not viable because the embryo can't grow to term outside the uterus.

Initially, an ectopic pregnancy may seem like a normal pregnancy; the pregnancy test will be positive as a small placenta forms and releases the hormone hCG, which is what the pregnancy test measures. In nine out of ten cases, the ectopic pregnancy is discovered due to pain in the lower part of the abdomen. If you experience considerable pain when newly pregnant, you should see a doctor for an ultrasound. If you have already registered with the obstetric unit of a hospital, that's where you should go; otherwise, ask your midwife or GP for a referral.

If you generally feel fine, you can do this as a daytime appointment. If you have severe stomach pains while also feeling increasingly dizzy, with cold sweats and sickness, you should call an ambulance to get you to the nearest hospital as quickly as possible, no matter what the time

46

of day. You may be suffering major internal bleeding, which can quickly become life-threatening. Often, but not always, there will be some vaginal bleeding. You may also have a bleed in the abdominal cavity that is not revealed through vaginal bleeding. This is a serious situation that requires an emergency operation and blood transfusions.

Miscarriage

Miscarriages are common: approximately 15–25 per cent of all identified pregnancies end in a miscarriage, and 80 per cent of these occur before week 12 of the pregnancy.[5] There are also a large number of miscarriages that happen early, before a woman knows she's pregnant. This has been shown in studies where women trying to get pregnant were asked to send urine samples to a research lab several times a week so a pregnancy test could be performed. Once the heartbeat of a foetus has been detected in an ultrasound scan, the risk of miscarriage reduces to a few per cent.

Many miscarriages happen because an embryo that has formed does not have the attributes needed to develop into a foetus. This applies in particular to early miscarriages, where between 50 per cent and 80 per cent are thought to be due to chromosomal abnormalities in the foetus.[6] The majority of miscarriages are nature's way of dealing with mistakes that occur in the complex processes that lead to the formation of eggs and sperm, fertilisation, and the development of an embryo. You must not blame yourself for a miscarriage; it is almost always due to the intervention of nature. A healthy foetus and placenta have an enormous capacity to remain in place in your womb and are not easily dislodged.

Most women who experience a miscarriage do so only once, with the next pregnancy leading to the birth of a child. Only around one in a hundred pregnant women have three miscarriages in a row. If you are in this group, it is important to see a gynaecologist who can check for underlying problems and see whether there is any treatment you can be given to reduce the risk of miscarriage during future pregnancies.

Factors that increase or decrease the risk of miscarriage

The factor most strongly associated with the risk of miscarriage is the age of the pregnant woman: the older she is, the greater the risk of miscarriage.[7] A rule of thumb is that around 10 per cent of 20-year-olds' pregnancies and as many as 40 per cent of 40-year-olds' pregnancies end in miscarriage. This is explained in part by the fact that the risk of chromosomal abnormalities, which cause many miscarriages, increases with the age of the mother.

The pregnant woman being underweight or overweight is also associated with a higher risk of miscarriage, but the increase is only modest. Other factors associated with an increased risk are alcohol and caffeine consumption.[8] However, there have been no randomised controlled trials (as described later in the book) to study whether the risk of miscarriage can be reduced if pregnant women drink less coffee or alcohol.[9] We therefore don't know whether it's coffee or alcohol themselves that are the villains of the piece.

Vitamin supplements have been tested, but their ability to prevent miscarriages has not been proven.[10] Progesterone treatment has been investigated and found not to protect against miscarriage.[11]

SECOND TRIMESTER (WEEKS 13–27)

The second trimester begins in week 13 of the pregnancy. From this time, the tiredness and sickness tend to disappear, and the belly grows but does not usually feel very heavy, which means that many women find this period the most pleasant of the pregnancy. All the organs are fully formed, but the whole foetus and all the organs have yet to grow and develop. The brain, in particular, undergoes enormous development during the second trimester. Your baby will soon begin to kick and increasingly make its presence felt.

During the second trimester, you will have regular visits with your doctor or midwife, when you will be weighed and measured, and have your urine and blood pressure checked. Towards the end of this trimester, they will also listen to your baby's heartbeat. An ultrasound scan of the foetus will usually be conducted around week 18–19 of the pregnancy.

The prenatal clinic can also provide help with things that can be hard to manage on your own such as quitting smoking, controlling your weight, and getting an addiction under control. Don't hesitate to ask for help if you have such problems.

This will also be the time to attend prenatal classes that provide useful information about birth and parenting. Ask your midwife if she can recommend any classes, or if she runs some herself. These classes are a way to meet other expectant parents in your local area. Having a friend nearby who is also on parental leave can be invaluable to a new parent.

High blood pressure and pre-eclampsia

The most common potentially serious complication of pregnancy is pre-eclampsia, which affects 1–2 per cent of all pregnant women in its severe form, and another 5 per cent in milder forms. It develops during the second half of pregnancy. The first symptoms are elevated blood pressure and leakage of protein into your urine, neither of which you feel. That's why it's so important to go to your scheduled pregnancy check-ups, even if you feel perfectly well. If your blood pressure is elevated, you will be referred to a specialist who will check both yourself and your baby. Anti-hypertensive treatments will sometimes suffice to treat mild hypertension of pregnancy.

If pre-eclampsia develops, aggravation can come quickly. The kidneys lose their ability to keep the blood proteins inside the bloodstream, and you will lose massive amounts of protein in the urine. The low blood-protein levels will lead to swelling of your entire body, and you may gain several kilograms of weight per day, caused by water building up in your tissues. If you feel abnormally swollen, go to your pregnancy clinic to have your blood pressure and urinary protein checked.

In its most dangerous stage, pre-eclampsia affects your brain and may also affect other vital organs such as your liver and blood cells, which is known as HELLP syndrome. Symptoms may appear quickly in the form of severe headaches, cloudy vision, or a sharp pain in the upper abdomen. If you experience these symptoms, you must immediately contact your hospital, and if necessary call an ambulance. If severe pre-eclampsia or HELLP syndrome is confirmed, treatment of the mother and the baby will be carried out in a hospital, and the responsible obstetricians will decide how long it is safe to continue the pregnancy — taking both the mother's and baby's health into account. Severe pre-eclampsia is one of the most common reasons for a baby to be delivered early.

We don't know exactly why pre-eclampsia happens. It is clear that the placenta, the vascular systems, and the kidneys are involved, and it's more common in the first pregnancy than in the second or third, provided that the sperm involved in the different pregnancies come from the same man. It is more common with egg donation, suggesting that immune-system recognition of non-self-molecules is involved. Several studies have shown shared risk factors between pre-eclampsia and cardiovascular disease in later life. For women at high risk for developing pre-eclampsia, low-dose aspirin treatment from the 12th week of pregnancy may be considered.

Premature birth

Currently, it is not possible to save the life of a baby born before the 22nd week of pregnancy. With today's high standards of neonatal care, a baby can be kept alive from week 22, and some babies have even survived being born at the very end of week 21. A large-scale Swedish study of the children born extremely prematurely during the period 2004–2007 shows that 10 per cent of those born in week 22 week survived, compared with 85 per cent of those born in week 26.[12] Neonatal care has since improved, so the chances of survival are now greater.

Babies who are born extremely prematurely run a greater risk of developing both physical and intellectual problems later in life compared with those who go to full term, although many still do perfectly well, attending regular school, providing for themselves as adults, and becoming parents themselves.

If you find yourself in labour in weeks 21–23 of your pregnancy, at the limits of your baby's viability, your obstetrician and neonatal doctor will give you detailed information about what to expect in your particular case. Protocols vary from country to country, but in Australia, for example, it is very uncommon to resuscitate babies before 22 weeks. At 23 weeks, decisions are made on a case-by-case basis. From 24 weeks, a baby will be resuscitated and neonatal intensive care will be started, as its chances of survival are considered high.

If you travel abroad during this stage of your pregnancy, check what neonatal care is available in that country, and what your insurance covers when it comes to healthcare and repatriation if you suddenly go into labour. Many travel-insurance policies don't cover repatriation by air ambulance for premature birth, which can end up being very expensive, as can neonatal intensive care in another country, when your baby can't be transferred home for a time and the hospital costs aren't covered.

THIRD TRIMESTER (WEEKS 28–40)

In the third trimester, the baby begins to reach full size, and the pregnancy can often start to feel very long. Your body expands, and the discreet little baby bump takes on more bizarre forms. The pregnancy hormones loosen the pelvis, which is an advantage for birthing a baby, but can impair your ability to walk painlessly or for long distances. Your breasts will often have grown considerably, and some will produce a little milk. Constipation is more the rule than the exception, because the smooth musculature (the type of muscles that are not controlled by force of will, as found in the intestines and uterus) is kept in a relaxed state by the pregnancy hormones. The combination of constipation with a heavy baby pressing on the genitals and rectum greatly increases the risk of developing haemorrhoids. Thoughts about the birth often become charged with a sense of impending freedom the longer the time goes on. You can read much more about what to expect during the birth in chapter 4.

Go to the maternity hospital if the baby stops moving

For a baby to stay happy and healthy in the womb and to keep growing, it needs constant access to fresh, oxygen-rich blood from its mother via the placenta. Sadly, for reasons not very well understood, in some pregnancies the placenta stops working without any previous signs of distress. When a foetus cannot get enough oxygen, and this is not recognised, it may die in the womb (referred to as stillbirth). In Australia, six babies are stillborn every day, while in the UK the number is around nine per day. Stillbirth happens among all groups, but the risk is higher among indigenous people and among disadvantaged groups.

Besides attending your pregnancy check-ups, you need to be aware of your baby's movements and to promptly go to the maternity hospital for a check-up if the baby becomes much less active than usual.

You'll usually start to feel the movements of the foetus around weeks 18–20. After that, as the foetus grows, you'll feel them more frequently and more strongly. Once the baby has reached a size where you can usually feel it moving, you mustn't ignore a lack of movement. A baby in the womb has periods of sleep that commonly last between 20 and 40 minutes, sometimes up to 90 minutes, and these are times when the baby can be almost entirely motionless. If a period of sleep starts to feel too long, lie down on your left side; because of how the internal organs and main arteries are arranged, this position encourages the blood circulation to the womb. Take note of the time, and how long since you felt movement, and carefully check for movement. If after two hours the baby hasn't moved, or has only moved occasionally, you should go to the maternity hospital for monitoring. In most cases, the baby will wake up and begin moving again. If, on the other hand, the baby is unwell, and the placenta has stopped working, it can be critical to get to the maternity hospital as quickly as possible so the baby can be delivered early.

When Swedish researchers asked 600 mothers who had lost their baby in the latter part of their pregnancy whether they had any idea that there was a problem, 64 per cent answered that they had noticed reduced foetal movement.[13] Many did not know that they needed to seek medical assistance, and some had tried but had received incorrect reassurance on the phone. They therefore didn't seek medical assistance until it was too late, and the baby was stillborn.

VACCINATIONS AND PREGNANCY

The general rule is that you should only get vaccinated during pregnancy if there is a good reason to do so. That means that it's better to wait until after your pregnancy to have vaccinations against viruses or bacteria that you have a very low risk of encountering. On the other hand, vaccination against seasonal influenza virus is specifically recommended during pregnancy, as is a booster vaccination against whooping cough.

The influenza (flu) vaccination is a special case. New flu epidemics arrive every year, usually caused by a new strain against which we lack immunity. To ensure good protection against the current strain, you therefore need a new flu shot every year. For most people, the flu is nothing more than a particularly heavy cold with a high temperature, but in some it can be extremely serious, causing lung inflammation that can require intensive care and even the need of a ventilator. Being pregnant increases the risk of contracting a severe form of flu, which is why pregnant women are advised to get vaccinated.[14] The increased risk is most pronounced during late pregnancy, due to decreased lung capacity when a large womb prevents deep breathing. The increased risk may also be caused by the weakening of the immune system during pregnancy, which prevents the pregnant mother's immune system from attacking the foetus.

Many large observational studies have been carried out to uncover any side effects from vaccinating pregnant women against flu, and so far none have been found.[15] It's quite the opposite. Some studies have shown small associations between having a flu shot and better pregnancy outcomes. It is hard to tell whether this is a vaccine effect (rather an effect of not getting influenza), or if it is due to some other factor that differs between the women who were vaccinated during pregnancy and those who were not, but the recommendation to take the flu shot during pregnancy has good evidence behind it.

Pregnant women are recommended to be vaccinated against whooping cough (pertussis), optimally between weeks 20 and 32. This infection is very dangerous for newborn babies, and they can't be vaccinated until they are two to three months old.

Whooping cough had been quite well controlled by vaccination in both Australia and the UK, but in 2009, incidence figures began to increase. Prior to 2012, four infants died every year from whooping cough in the UK; but in the first nine months of 2012, 14 infants died from the disease. This was declared a national emergency, and vaccination of pregnant mothers against whooping cough was introduced in 2012. Infant whooping-cough mortality has decreased for every year since 2012, and in 2017 and 2018 no infant died from whooping cough in the UK. In 2015, Australia decided to recommend maternal pertussis vaccination based on experiences in the UK.

Upon vaccination, a pregnant woman produces antibodies against *Bordetella pertussis*, the bacteria that cause whooping cough. Those antibodies, which are found in her blood, are transferred to the foetus during pregnancy. (More about how this works can be found in chapter 9.) When the mother is protected from the disease, she can't infect the baby when it is born.

In chapter 10, you will read more about vaccines and how they work, but we will mention here that there are two types of vaccines: live-attenuated vaccines and inactivated (non-living) vaccines. The live-attenuated vaccines contain live virus or bacteria that will not cause infection in an immunocompetent person, but they may cause infection in situations where the immune system is weakened — as it is during pregnancy. Therefore, live vaccines are generally unsuitable during pregnancy.

However, quite a number of pregnant women have had live-attenuated vaccines (for example, when they didn't know they were pregnant) without any harmful effects. This is even true of the vaccine against rubella (German measles), despite the fact that the rubella virus itself is well known for the risk it carries of causing foetal abnormalities.[16] If you're considering getting a vaccination against yellow fever or Japanese encephalitis while pregnant, you should probably give a little extra thought as to whether it's a good idea to travel to a region where there is a high risk of these diseases occurring. If you must travel to such an area when pregnant, seek medical advice to discuss the risks.

Our next section is about screening tests for foetal abnormalities, which is followed by information about harmful infections during pregnancy. If these topics feel too heavy-going for you, feel free to skip to the next chapter.

SCREENING AND DIAGNOSTIC TESTS

The aim of screening and diagnostic tests is to check whether the developing foetus is healthy or not. Screening tests are offered to all pregnant women, and provide a risk assessment for certain foetal diseases. If the risk is high enough, further diagnostic testing is recommended to confirm or exclude disease. In this section, we explain the different types of foetal testing available, and also offer some thoughts about making decisions whether to undergo screening tests or not.

Screening for haemoglobinopathies

In the UK, pregnant women are offered a blood test to determine if they are carriers of any gene that can cause inherited disorders of haemoglobin — an oxygen-carrying protein in red blood cells. We all have two copies of each gene in our DNA. To be affected by these disorders (thalassaemia, and sickle cell disease), a person has to carry two disease-carrying genes. Those with only one disease-carrying gene and one normal gene will not be affected. If two people with one disease-carrying gene each conceive a child together, there are three possible outcomes. Their child could inherit two normal genes, and be healthy; it could inherit one normal and one disease-carrying gene, and be healthy; or it could inherit two disease-carrying genes, and develop the disease.

Thalassaemia major and sickle cell disease are both chronic conditions. Without modern treatment, few people with these diseases will reach adulthood. Today, these diseases can be cured with a blood stem-cell transplantation, which is a high-risk intervention that requires top-level care and a suitable donor. If stem-cell transplantation is not an option, life-long treatment with blood transfusions and treatment to reduce its side effects is required for thalassaemia major. For sickle cell disease, blood transfusions are usually required; but without stem-cell transplantation, a person is likely to suffer from progressive disabilities and painful medical crises.

If a screening test for the carrying of such genes returns a positive result, the mother will be advised to continue with genetic testing of the foetus to investigate whether it will be healthy. In Sweden, as in Australia, these genes are less common than in the UK, and genetic testing is only offered to women with either a family history of those diseases or to those who demonstrate abnormal haemoglobin levels during pregnancy.

Ultrasound scan

In Sweden, Australia, and the UK, you will be offered an ultrasound scan in weeks 17–20. During the routine ultrasound scan, the foetus is measured to determine the stage of the pregnancy, and the practitioner establishes whether there are one or more foetuses, and checks the position of the placenta. The foetus's organs are examined for any sign of abnormalities. If the practitioner suspects serious abnormalities, you will quickly be offered more ultrasound scans conducted by a specialist doctor, perhaps an MRI (magnetic resonance imaging) scan of the foetus, and possibly amniocentesis to check for genetic abnormalities.

If you would like to know the sex of your foetus, you should ask the practitioner — it can usually be seen at this ultrasound. You'll usually also get a picture or two of the baby to take home with you.

Combined ultrasound and biochemical (CUB) test

The combined ultrasound and biochemical (CUB) test is a first-trimester screening for foetal chromosomal anomalies. The ultrasound scan measures the translucency of the fluid-filled area at the back of the baby's neck, and the blood test measures the levels of two substances (beta-hCG and PAPP-A) in the blood. The results of these two tests, combined with the mother's age, are used to calculate the risk of Down syndrome (trisomy 21), as well as trisomy 13 and 18. Trisomy 13 and 18 are genetic disorders that cause abnormalities in the brain and other vital organs; most babies born with these disorders die either in the foetal stage or during their first months of life. People with Down syndrome have moderate to severe intellectual disabilities, and many also have congenital abnormalities of their heart and other internal organs.

Amniocentesis and chorionic villus sampling (CVS)

If the CUB test produces a risk figure above a certain value, further testing will be offered using amniocentesis (sampling of the fluid that surrounds the foetus in the womb) or chorionic villus sampling (CVS)

— where a piece of the placenta is sampled. CVS can be done from week 11, and the earliest that amniocentesis can be performed is week 15. Both tests collect cells with foetal DNA for gene testing.

In both cases, a long needle is inserted into the abdomen, using ultrasound to ensure that the needle does not damage the baby. The samples that are collected are sent to a laboratory, where foetal cells are cultivated until there are enough for the genetic analysis, which can take a few weeks. For the most common genetic abnormalities, quick tests are available that give you an answer within a week. It is important to note that there is some degree of risk to the foetus in performing amniocentesis and CVS. In up to one in 100 cases for CVS, and one in 200 cases for amniocentesis, the sampling leads to a miscarriage, usually within two weeks of the test.

Non-invasive prenatal testing (NIPT)

A relatively new kind of test called NIPT (non-invasive prenatal testing) works on the basis that a small quantity of foetal cells passes over into the mother's blood during pregnancy. A sample of the mother's blood is extracted and used for genetic testing for Down syndrome, trisomy 13 and 18, and other conditions. The test is, in many cases, more accurate than the CUB test, and performing it after the CUB test has identified a high risk avoids the need for amniocentesis in many cases. NIPT is therefore offered in certain situations if the CUB test has shown a risk of chromosomal abnormalities. In contrast to the CUB test, NIPT test gives a yes/no answer, not a risk figure, which is easier to interpret. It is usually accurate; but to confirm a genetic abnormality found in a NIPT test, the health service will always offer amniocentesis as a means of confirmation.

A blood test is much easier to do than amniocentesis, and doesn't carry the risk of miscarriage. NIPT can be performed from week 10 of the pregnancy, and is available in private diagnostic clinics (many of which offer it without a preceding CUB test), but access to it varies in public-health systems. You have to pay for this test yourself. For a higher fee, you can opt to expand the test to check whether your baby has certain genetic syndromes that increase the risk of multiple abnormalities, intellectual disabilities, and health problems.

Early genetic testing

If you know or suspect that you have an inherited risk of passing on a serious genetic condition, you can ask your doctor to refer you to a genetic counsellor or a clinical geneticist for a genetic test before your pregnancy.

If the screening shows that there is a major risk of fatal congenital conditions, you can ask to have early prenatal screening such as CVS in week 10. There is also the option of *in vitro* fertilisation, where each embryo is tested to be sure that it is free from the heritable condition before it is implanted in the uterus. This method is called pre-implantation genetic diagnosis. Another option is egg or sperm donation, where the parent carrying the condition doesn't contribute genes to the baby.

Genetic screening is also recommended if two people who are genetically related plan to have a child together. People who are related share a large number of genes, and run a greater risk than an unrelated couple of passing on the genes that cause genetic disorders. Many heritable conditions require two faulty genes in order to occur, and so a child with one faulty and one complete gene will not become ill, but if two parents transfer a faulty gene each to their child, the condition will present in the child.

What do you want to do with the results of the screening?

If you arrange genetic testing and discover that there are risks associated with the foetus, you will have to make some difficult decisions. It's worth thinking about this before the testing. (If you are the non-pregnant partner, you can also give these matters careful thought, but the legal right to make all decisions lies with the pregnant woman. It is her choice to decide who else she discusses the matter with.)

You may choose to terminate the pregnancy if testing reveals abnormalities and you don't want to give birth to a baby with a particular disorder. Or you may choose to keep the baby, having had time to prepare for the birth and postnatal care in the safest way, and to anticipate life as a parent of a child with additional needs.

If you don't want to know or be put in a position of having to make a choice, you can decline the screening. We recommend a routine ultrasound scan to check where the placenta is positioned, whether you're having twins, and so on. But you can tell your midwife or doctor at this stage that you don't want further testing.

Even though you may have planned in advance what you would do if faced with a worrying diagnosis, you may change your mind once you're fully informed about its implications. It can be difficult making a decision about what to do with a pregnancy following the news of a foetal abnormality. A late termination — usually from week 18 up to the cut-off point where the foetus can be considered viable outside the womb — is generally approved in the case of severe, fatal abnormalities and disorders, and of seriously ill mothers. There are no statistics on what percentage of pregnant women who find out that their baby has a particular disorder decide to terminate or keep their baby.

Sometimes the choice to terminate is not a difficult one. Most pregnant women who find out that their foetus is suffering from anencephaly, for example — where the brain has not developed and there is no chance of survival outside the womb — choose to terminate. Nevertheless, it is a painful experience when the joyful anticipation of a healthy newborn is replaced with grief, and perhaps anger, over what has happened. A late termination will often be a traumatic and tragic experience in itself.

In other cases, with abnormalities that are survivable but that require major medical interventions, or syndromes that most people survive into adulthood but without the ability to lead a fully independent life, the decision is not nearly as clear cut for many parents-to-be, and that is as it should be. Precisely because it can be so difficult, we believe the only right and fair thing to do is to leave the decision to the pregnant woman and allow her to draw on the advice and support of whoever she sees fit.

If you live in a family or a cultural circle where termination is seen as unacceptable, remember that the laws apply to you as much as to anyone else: you have the right to decide which pregnancies you want to carry to term. If you believe that termination is wrong, and you want to continue the pregnancy even if the foetus is not viable, you should naturally do so. If you want a termination, you have every right to keep the termination and, as far as possible, the pregnancy secret. Many people in this situation find it helpful to talk in confidence to a counsellor at a women's health service. If you are religious, talking to someone from your own faith may be important for you.

INFECTIONS THAT CAN CAUSE BIRTH DEFECTS

In cases where birth defects occur during pregnancy, viral infections are the most common cause. Rubella (German measles) used to be a common cause of birth defects, but fortunately vaccination programs have done their job, and German measles no longer poses any real threat to pregnant women in high-income countries. In this section, we discuss some of the other viral infections that can lead to birth defects.

Cytomegalovirus

Cytomegalovirus (CMV) is a very widespread infection that is spread through bodily fluids. Often, the symptoms are so mild that you don't notice the infection, but doctors can tell that a person has had it by the presence of antibodies to CMV in the blood. The infection is harmless to people with a normal immune system. One-third of one-year-olds in Sweden have had CMV, and approximately seven out of 10 pregnant women have antibodies against CMV from a past infection. The figures for Australia are similar, or somewhat lower. In the initial period following infection, the virus is present in the blood, but it then lies dormant inside cells in the body.

If a woman contracts CMV during pregnancy, the virus will enter her bloodstream, and in around 30–40 per cent of cases the infection will be transmitted to the foetus. CMV infection in a pregnant woman is usually asymptomatic, but can include a prolonged fever, throat pain, and swollen lymph nodes. When the virus is in the body's cells, it is not infectious, either to the foetus or to anyone else. However, the dormant virus may become active during a pregnancy, at which point it re-enters the bloodstream and may infect the foetus. The risk of this occurring is about 1–3 per cent.

Each year in Sweden, around 230 babies (approximately one in 500 pregnancies) are born with CMV that they have contracted during the pregnancy. In the majority of cases, these babies have no symptoms at birth, although some show signs such as small bleeds under the skin, effects on liver function, or impaired growth. Of those who are born with CMV but have no symptoms at birth, a further 10–20 per cent will develop abnormalities as they grow up. Damage to hearing and sight and to the brain is possible, with CMV a relatively common cause of congenital hearing impairment.

In Australia, CMV seems to be underdiagnosed and infrequently treated. A survey conducted during a ten-year period (1999–2009) found around 200 cases, 90 per cent of whom had symptoms, mostly hearing loss. Most probably, the great majority were asymptomatic and went unnoticed.

There is currently no treatment for pregnant women with CMV that has been proven to help protect the foetus. Antiviral medication after birth has shown promise in reducing the incidence of hearing impairment in children born with CMV. Let us hope for a future vaccine.

Parvovirus B19

Parvovirus B19 causes the childhood disease *Erythema infectiosum*, more commonly known as fifth disease or slapped cheek. It produces cold-like symptoms together with a distinctive red rash on the cheeks, which then spreads like lace over the shoulders, neck, torso, and upper arms. Around 70 per cent of pregnant women will have already had fifth disease, and will have developed immunity to the virus for the rest of their lives.

The unprotected third of pregnant women remain at risk of contracting parvovirus B19, and, of this group, one in three risks transmitting the infection to the foetus. In at least 90 per cent of cases, infection will not lead to any harm to the foetus. Where the foetus is affected, the biggest problem tends to be the disruption of red-blood–cell development. This problem can lead to prolonged and severe anaemia, which affects the foetus's heart and liver, as well as to an increased risk of miscarriage and stillbirth. A pregnant woman who has contracted the virus will require extra screening to check the foetus for signs of anaemia. Anaemia can be treated in utero with blood transfusions through the umbilical cord.

Unfortunately, there is no vaccine against parvovirus B19, and mothers who are not already immune may become infected, often by children at home, or at work if they work with children. If a child in the family develops the classic rash, and the infection is diagnosed, the mother will most likely already be infected. Preventing infection within the family is practically impossible, but when pregnant you may want to limit your exposure to children outside your own family that have fifth disease. Parvovirus B19 is being spread all the time, but intensive epidemics tend to peak every few years. If you are working at a preschool or children's hospital during an epidemic, and you're not already immune to the disease, you could discuss being reassigned to duties in areas where you won't have contact with infectious children.

Zika virus

The most recent virus to become widely known for causing birth defects is the mosquito-borne Zika virus. The virus was identified a long time ago but hadn't previously attracted much attention or stimulated research, as it causes only mild illness, more or less like a moderate flu. In 2014–2015, however, the Zika virus spread to Brazil, where it hadn't been seen before. Since no one was immune, the entire population was vulnerable, and a Zika epidemic broke out. Following the outbreak, there was a steep rise in the number of babies born with severe brain damage, the cause of which was traced back to the fact that their mothers had been infected with the Zika virus during pregnancy. The virus is found primarily in the southern hemisphere, and has long been present on the African continent and in South-East Asia. From Brazil, the Zika virus has continued to spread across South and Central America. Despite the presence of the Zika virus in the Pacific region, and the fact that travellers returning to Australia have been found to carry the virus, no local transmission has yet been reported.

The virus can remain in the body for months, although exactly how long is unknown. It has been found in a man's seminal fluid more than 180 days after he returned from a Zika-affected area, and it can be transmitted sexually from both men and women to their partners. Intensive research into Zika vaccines and medicines is currently underway. Until a vaccine has been found, the only real protection is to avoid travel to affected areas if you or your partner are already or planning to become pregnant.

IN BRIEF

Pregnancy is a condition in which the body is taken over by the placenta, for better (for the foetus) and for worse (for the pregnant woman). There is little you can do to control the unpleasant effects of pregnancy. But it's important that you make sure to attend your prenatal check-ups, go to the maternity hospital if the foetus seems to be moving less, and go to the emergency department if you experience heavy bleeding or severe abdominal pain. You can read all about smoking, alcohol, diet, and weight in the next chapter. When it comes to certain infections, there is not a lot you can do, except to be aware of the symptoms of potentially harmful infections, take appropriate precautions, and avoid travelling to countries where you might contract the Zika virus.

Remember that once you are pregnant, your chance of a successful pregnancy and birth is nine out of ten, and the further the pregnancy progresses, the less common it is to have complications that endanger your baby.

CHAPTER THREE

Do's and don'ts
during pregnancy

If you've become accustomed to being an independent individual who makes her own decisions about how she chooses to live her life, you may be in for a surprise when you become pregnant. All sorts of people — ranging from friends and acquaintances to health professionals and authorities — will suddenly have a lot to say about you and your life. It may not be easy to discern how much of this is based on actual knowledge and how much boils down to myths, moralising, and general meddling. In this chapter, we aim to help you decipher what is and isn't important advice about how to look after your own health and the health of your developing baby. We explain how research serves as a source of knowledge, and how to look at research with a critical eye. And we look more closely at some of the advice that the authorities give out, and question how much of it is it rooted in solid scientific evidence.

Lifestyle advice was being handed out to pregnant women as far back as the Old Testament. The Book of Judges, chapter 13:2–3, reads:

And the angel of the Lord appeared to the woman and said to her, 'Behold now, thou art barren, and bearest not, but thou shalt conceive and bear a son. Now therefore beware, I pray thee, and drink not wine nor strong drink, and eat not any unclean thing.

The Book of Judges depicts a walled patriarchal society. It's mostly about tribal warfare, but sometimes women make an appearance. Jephthah sacrifices his daughter, for example, as a burnt offering to God as thanks for helping him defeat the Ammonites. And the Levite gives up his concubine to a mob so they will rape her and leave him alone. In Exodus, it is made clear that an unborn baby belongs to the man of the family and that he determines its worth:

When men strive together and hit a pregnant woman, so that her child comes out, but there is no harm, the one who hit her shall surely be fined, as the woman's husband shall impose on him.

Much has changed since Old Testament times. Married Swedish women were granted legal majority almost a century ago — in 1921 — at the same time as they were given the vote. Pregnant women also have legal majority, and the right to determine what happens to their own body. But taboos against their drinking wine or strong drink, and eating anything unclean, persist to this day.

Many pregnant women describe feeling that their rights over their body are not always respected. Their round belly is suddenly seen as a piece of public property that strangers and vague acquaintances feel entitled to pat or comment on. Such behaviour towards a person who isn't pregnant is unthinkable.

Within health services and public-health organisations, pregnancy is seen as providing a window of opportunity to introduce lifestyle changes that are considered good for the population as a whole. Pregnant women are seen as being more receptive than the general population to health advice because they are understandably anxious not to cause harm to their unborn baby.

Pregnancy is a very particular condition. We believe that, to the best of their ability, anyone who is pregnant has a moral duty to avoid behaviours that could damage their unborn baby. But we also feel that the organisations publicly dispensing advice have a duty to critically assess their advice before announcing potential harms, especially because women are very sensitive to such advice during pregnancy. Advice about what is and isn't safe for you during pregnancy should be given only to protect you and/or your baby. Pregnant women should not have to bear responsibility for helping to solve public-health problems. They certainly have the right to choose for themselves whether they want to change their lifestyle during pregnancy.

In this chapter, we go through the current advice on unclean food and strong drinks: what the research actually says; which advice is important for protecting the unborn baby; and which advice has more to do with improving public health. We also include relevant information about medication, vitamin pills, and smoking.

But we begin by explaining how researchers determine what is true or false.

SCIENTIFIC TRUTHS AND HALF-TRUTHS

Scientific methodology has developed in the Western world since the 17th century, when researchers began to conduct experiments instead of speculating about how everything worked, especially about how the phenomena they considered were expressions of God's great plan. We have since learned that experiments are the safest source of knowledge, as long as they are performed correctly. In the perfect medical experiment, participants are randomly selected to receive either the active treatment or an inactive placebo, with the latter serving as the control group. Participants do not know which group they are in, and nor do those carrying out the study. A study such as this is called a randomised controlled double-blind trial, and it offers the most valuable evidence in medical research.

Observational studies

However, many of the questions we want answers to cannot be studied using randomised controlled trials.[1] For example, if we want to know how much alcohol you can drink during pregnancy without harming the foetus, an experimental study can't be done. No research ethics committee would approve a study in which pregnant women were to be randomly given different amounts of wine, or none, during their pregnancy to investigate how much alcohol causes birth defects.

When experiments are not possible, we have to make do with observational studies. Researchers can observe a group of pregnant women, for example, and can study those who drink a lot, a little, or none at all, and see what happens with their pregnancies or babies. Observational studies give us a great deal of knowledge, but they have their limits and pitfalls. Here, let us consider what is required to determine the risk to the foetus of drinking alcohol during pregnancy.

First of all, researchers need a selection of study subjects who are as similar as possible to the group they want to later advise. If they want to draw conclusions that are relevant to Swedish women, for example, they need to study well-nourished women from high-income countries. Studies of women in deprived areas in a country where substance abuse and undernourishment are more common would not provide a suitable basis for reaching conclusions on the effect that alcohol has on Swedish women's pregnancies.

Second, the level of alcohol consumption needs to be measured in as reliable a way as possible. There are no blood tests that can show with any accuracy how much alcohol a person has drunk, so researchers have to ask pregnant women to tell them. To obtain answers that are as honest as possible, it is desirable to conduct the study in an environment where it is acceptable to at least drink a little while pregnant; otherwise, not everyone will dare tell the truth. It is also important to ask these questions during rather than after the pregnancy. If a long time has passed since giving birth, mothers would be unable to recall all the details of their alcohol consumption, and there is a considerable risk that mothers with problematic children would feel guilty and over-estimate their alcohol consumption during their pregnancy. Conversely, mothers who have well-behaved children are much more likely to forget and downgrade at least parts of their alcohol consumption.

Third, the researcher must take account of the phenomenon known as confounding. A confounding factor is something that, in this case, both affects the likelihood of having a baby with abnormalities and is more common among people who drink alcohol than among those who do not. A good example is smoking. Smoking causes low birth weight. Smoking and alcohol are also correlated: women who drink alcohol also smoke more often than those who do not drink. If drinking mothers give birth to particularly small babies, this may be due to the smoking or the alcohol (or both). If the researcher's analysis fails to take into account the effect of the smoking, it will be easy to believe that the alcohol is the cause of the low birth weight.

There are statistical methods for eliminating the effect of confounding factors, but they can only be applied to those that are known and included in the analysis. In this example, we can examine women who smoke but do not drink, and mothers who drink but do not smoke, and measure the birth weight of their children. But many confounding factors are either unknown to researchers or are unmeasurable, and so cannot be screened out in the analysis. This inherent problem makes it very difficult to prove causal links through observational studies.

Researchers often disagree about how to interpret the results of observational studies and animal experiments. On the other hand, as scientists, they are trained to change their stance if new research proves an existing theory to be wrong. A single randomised controlled intervention trial on humans is able to overturn thousands of old observational studies at a stroke, proving the opposite of what was previously held to be true. An example of this is how researchers and doctors believed it was good for women to take oestrogen pills during menopause until a randomised controlled trial showed hormone therapy to be harmful due to the increased risk of blood clots and breast cancer.[2]

Smoking

There are some areas where the research leads to clear and unambiguous conclusions about behaviours that a pregnant woman should absolutely try to avoid. Smoking is one of these. Smoking during pregnancy increases the risk of the foetus dying in the womb. Smoking is also associated with babies, on average, being born earlier and smaller.[3]

The good news is that the number of women smoking is falling year on year. If you haven't already given up smoking, pregnancy is the time to quit, or at least to cut down the number of cigarettes you smoke to the very minimum. Ask for help from your GP or prenatal-care provider if you don't think you can give up on your own.

Nicotine replacements such as gums or pills are good alternatives to cigarettes when you are not pregnant, but unfortunately not when you are pregnant. Nicotine constricts the blood vessels, including those supplying the placenta and thus the baby. In Sweden, nicotine use in the form of snus, which is a non-smokeable tobacco product, is common. According to a reputable 2016 Swedish study, the risk of premature birth is just as high for snus-taking as it is for smoking.[4] There is also a greater risk of a newborn baby having breathing difficulties if it has been exposed to snus during pregnancy than if it has been exposed to smoking.[5] The advantage of snus over smoking is that it's less harmful to the mother's own health, as it doesn't damage the lungs, but taking snus is bad for the foetus. This is probably also valid for all other forms of nicotine use. Whether vaping (or e-cigarette use) is more or less harmful for the user than cigarettes is not known, regardless of what the vaping industry tries to tell us. For a foetus, nicotine is nicotine, and vaping is not recommended.

Alcohol

The angel's advice in the Book of Judges implies that even in pre-Christian times, children born to alcoholic mothers tended to be born small or to not develop normally. In modern times, the condition now known as foetal alcohol syndrome (FAS) was presented in the scientific journal *The Lancet* in 1973,[6] and in 1979 Gothenburg doctor Ragnar Olegård described the harsh consequences for children whose mothers abused alcohol during pregnancy.[7]

FAS affects a large proportion of children born to mothers who actively abuse alcohol during pregnancy,[8] and manifests as poor growth, brain damage, and a particular facial appearance with a flattened-out philtrum (the groove between the nose and upper lip), a thin upper lip, and narrow eyes. Children with FAS often have severe behavioural problems and intellectual disabilities. Heart problems are also more common in this group than in the wider population.

More recently, the FAS diagnosis is often made together with foetal alcohol spectrum disorder (FASD), which is a diagnosis that does not require the typical facial appearance of FAS sufferers. To receive a FASD diagnosis, a child needs to have had documented foetal alcohol exposure, and to exhibit some intellectual, behavioural, or developmental problems. The FASD diagnosis is somewhat problematic, as the condition can be caused by factors other than prenatal alcohol exposure.

The prevalence of FAS varies greatly between different populations. In Sweden, after the introduction of free abortion services in 1975, the number of children with FAS rapidly decreased, and now, more than 30 years later, only nine new cases of FAS are diagnosed among children born in Sweden each year, out of 120,000 births — a rate of less than one in 10,000 live births. On the other hand, among children adopted to Swedish families from eastern European countries, the prevalence of FAS in a recent study was almost 30 per cent. In Australia, several studies show that rates of FAS are higher in indigenous communities where alcohol abuse is more common and where it is harder to access healthcare, including abortion care.

Regularly drinking large quantities of alcohol during pregnancy is very harmful to the developing foetus. If you have an alcohol problem, it's necessary to treat it — preferably in advance, but at least as soon as you discover that you're pregnant. At the same time, it's vital that maternity clinics, addiction clinics, and social services have good resources for treating women who have an active addiction problem and want to continue their pregnancy. For women with an active addiction who don't want to have a baby, good access to contraceptives and terminations is critical — the success of these policies in Sweden today is probably the key reason why the condition is very uncommon.

Are small amounts of alcohol harmful?

Swedish authorities issue strict advice that, for the sake of safety, pregnant woman should not drink alcohol under any circumstances. Similarly, in most Western countries, including the UK, Australia, and New Zealand, the authorities now advise pregnant women not to drink alcohol at all. This advice is a fairly recent change; for example, the official advice in the UK until 2016 was to have no more than one or two drinks a week.[9] The introduction of the stricter guidelines is usually justified by the inability of the relevant health authorities to determine a safe lower limit for drinking, or by the authorities reasoning that it is most prudent to tell women that no alcohol is the only safe level, as designating any low level as safe would encourage over-consumption by women who struggle to control their drinking.

Abstaining from alcohol when pregnant is a perfectly good choice to make. But we believe that the current total-abstention policies are not factually based, and cause unnecessary anxiety and guilt in women.

Since we published the Swedish edition of this book, we've had many expressions of appreciation from mothers who, finally, could stop thinking about whether that drink they had the day before their positive pregnancy test caused their son's ADHD, or whether the glass of wine they had in early pregnancy might have caused the leukaemia their daughter developed.

At the same time, we want to emphasise again the need for effective and available care for expecting parents who have an alcohol addiction. Not only is alcohol toxic to the developing foetus, but being addicted carries a high risk of the mother not being able to take sufficiently good care of her child. For those who are, or have been, addicted to alcohol or drugs, it is important to exercise great caution and avoid the risk of relapsing. A key approach in overcoming an alcohol addiction is to abstain from alcohol completely. An addict who wants to see whether it's possible to drink a little alcohol without relapsing should really do so at a responsible remove from their pregnancy. But it's a bit of a leap in thinking to suggest, for example, that a woman trying to get pregnant who opts out of a champagne toast at her sister's wedding has any effect on women with a serious alcohol addiction.

Support for the current 'no safe limit' guidelines is based on the claim that research indicates there is no safe lower limit of alcohol consumption in pregnancy. But this claim is not quite true. Our review of the literature in this field shows that a great deal of good observational research has been conducted in this area, and we've chosen to present it here. It's a lengthy presentation, so skip over it and go straight to the next section on food during pregnancy if this issue doesn't concern you.

The review indicates that, with the exception of a slightly higher risk of miscarriage early in the pregnancy, there is no statistically significant association between foetal abnormalities and the consumption of up to five to six standard glasses of wine a week, as long as you drink fewer than three standard glasses at a time. Due to random variation (chance), there will always be the odd study showing either positive or negative effects of drinking small quantities of alcohol. For this reason, researchers never rely on individual studies, and instead compile numerous studies, judging the quality of these studies along the way. In meta-analyses, the researchers compile the results from different studies mathematically, while review articles list the results of a number of articles, often with a general assessment of their findings.

There are many studies, using various methods, that have investigated the effects of low-to-moderate consumption of alcohol during pregnancy. It's a difficult field of research.[10] The ways of measuring alcohol consumption vary across studies, but to make a general assessment, we've converted all measurements to the standard unit of a Swedish standard glass of alcohol (where one glass equals 12 grama of alcohol, which is equivalent to a large glass of wine [150 millilitres], a strong beer [330 millilitres], or a shot [40 millilitres] of strong spirits).

As mentioned above, there is no statistical proof that drinking up to five to six standard glasses a week will adversely affect the foetus, so long as fewer than three standard glasses are consumed at a time (with the exception, mentioned above, of a slightly higher risk of miscarriage early in the pregnancy). A meta-analysis from 2011, which includes 36 studies on the subject, found no evidence of negative effects on birth weight, or premature birth, from the consumption of fewer than 5.8 standard glasses a week.[11] A systematic review from 2007 also shows no evidence of negative effects such as miscarriage, intrauterine foetal death (stillbirth), growth restriction, premature birth, low birth weight, or growth abnormalities, including foetal alcohol syndrome, accompanying the consumption of fewer than seven standard glasses a week.[12] In a meta-analysis of more than 130,000 pregnancies, researchers found no difference in the number of babies born with abnormalities when they compared babies whose mothers had drunk two to fourteen glasses a week in the first trimester of the pregnancy with those whose mothers had not drunk any alcohol at all.[13] A 2014 meta-analysis of 34 studies found no correlation between alcohol consumption of up to 6.8 standard glasses per week and a number of neuropsychological outcomes in the child (attention, behaviour, intelligence, sight, motor development, and language skills).[14] Researchers who conducted a systematic review of 39 scientific papers in 2010 found no difference in motor development between children whose mothers had abstained from alcohol and those whose mothers had drunk up to seven standard glasses per week during pregnancy. The studies looked at children aged between four months and four years.[15]

On the other hand, several studies do show an increased risk of damage to the baby when alcohol consumption exceeds one standard glass per day. The aforementioned meta-analysis from 2011 shows that the risk of low birth weight starts to increase at the equivalent of 5.8 standard glasses per week, and the risk of premature birth increases at 8.7 standard glasses per week.[16] The meta-analysis from 2014 shows a correlation between lower intelligence in the child and what is known as 'binge drinking' (occasionally drinking more than four-and-a-half standard glasses of alcohol in a short period of time).[17] The systematic review from 2010 shows a correlation with poorer motor development in children whose mothers drank more than 10 standard glasses a week.[18]

Most of the studies into the effects of alcohol have looked at women at or beyond the end of their first trimester, when the greatest risk of early miscarriage has already passed. They have, therefore, not been able to study the effects of alcohol specifically on early miscarriage. A Danish study of more than 90,000 women shows an association between drinking as little as half a glass of alcohol per week and a slightly higher risk of miscarriage before week 16 of the pregnancy, but not after that point in time.[19] It is not possible for such a study to show whether there is any causal link, but anyone who wants to avoid an early miscarriage would be well advised not to drink any alcohol during the first trimester.

If you've consumed small amounts of alcohol while pregnant and not had an early miscarriage, it might be comforting to know that nothing in the research suggests you've damaged your baby.

FOOD DURING PREGNANCY

The second piece of advice in the Book of Judges — not to eat unclean food — is also highly relevant to pregnant women today. Most countries give advice to women about what they should eat and what should be avoided during pregnancy. Much of the advice about what you should eat during pregnancy is the same as what you should be eating when you're not pregnant: plenty of fruit and vegetables; half a litre of low-fat dairy products daily; fish two to three times a week; meat, poultry, lentils, or beans every day; as well as pasta, rice, potatoes, or some other carbohydrate (preferably wholegrain) each day. And then throw unsaturated fat into the mix.

If you follow this basic advice, you'll get all the nutrition you need. You don't have to be too particular, as not all the advice is strictly evidence-based for pregnant women. If you usually eat full-fat dairy products and prefer non-wholegrain pasta, you're free to continue with that during pregnancy without any risk to your own health or that of your baby. There is no scientific evidence to indicate that pregnant women should drink skimmed milk; it's just that the health authorities consider pregnancy as the ideal time to establish 'good eating habits'.

Your baby is very good at sourcing the nutrients it needs from you and your reserves. If you're careless about your diet, you are the one who will become undernourished, with the baby only becoming affected in starvation situations. Conversely, you can't optimise your child's chances by eating a particular diet, since the placenta takes care of everything itself by drawing either on the foods you put into your body or from your body's stores. If, prior to pregnancy, you're following a specific diet or avoiding many foods, think about whether you can compromise on your principles while you're pregnant. A strict diet that excludes many foods will increase the risk that you may suffer nutritional deficiencies. If you have a restricted diet (due to an illness or allergy), or if you really want to continue with your diet, visit a dietician for tailored nutritional advice before and during your pregnancy.

There is also well-founded advice on what you should specifically avoid while pregnant, or what is considered 'unclean food' for pregnant women today. The basic advice is to avoid eating fish loaded with high doses of environmental toxins, and to avoid contracting the bacterial infection listeria and the parasitic infection toxoplasmosis.

Fish

Pregnant women are warned against eating certain types of white fish, because it contains mercury. For example, the British NHS recommends that they not eat any shark/flake, marlin, or broadbill/swordfish, and no more than two tuna steaks or four medium-sized cans of tuna a week.

The Swedish National Food Agency recommends that pregnant women not eat white fish such as perch, pike, pike-perch, and burbot, as well as large predators such as fresh tuna, swordfish, large halibut, shark, and skate more than two or three times a year.

Food researchers are currently debating the recommendations regarding mercury. Although someone who eats extremely large amounts of fish may consume more mercury than is recommended, it's also known that fish in itself is good for the foetus, and this probably balances out any effects from the environmental toxins. No negative effects have been seen in children born in places where people eat a lot of fish and have relatively high exposure to mercury.[20] On the contrary, the children of fish-eating mothers are generally better developed.

In this context, it is perhaps worth mentioning that middle-aged and older women in a large Swedish study had lower mortality rates, particularly from cardiovascular disease, the more mercury they had in their blood.[21] Naturally, this is not because mercury is good in itself, but because the mercury came partly from fish the women had eaten and partly from their amalgam fillings. Those who retain many of their own teeth generally also have more fillings left, and so have more mercury in their blood. In summary, most of the evidence indicates that fish is a healthy food and that it's foolish to avoid it for fear of the toxins in fish — the benefits win out.

If you want to be absolutely on the safe side, choose fish that isn't on your country's warning list. But remember, having some servings of fish on the warning lists will most probably not hurt your child.

Shellfish

Shellfish such as mussels, clams, and oysters have high nutritional value. However, they may contain bacteria and viruses from waters where they were grown. Some of those can cause gastroenteritis; in the US, vibriosis, a bacterial infection that can be severe, has been coupled to the consumption of raw shellfish. We therefore recommend that you only eat cooked shellfish while pregnant. And it is preferable to buy your shellfish, as commercial fishing areas are controlled for harmful toxins and bugs. If you collect shellfish yourself, make sure the area you use is safe.

Listeria

Listeria bacteria are just about everywhere, but they are not particularly dangerous unless you are pregnant, old, or have a weak immune system. In rare cases, the bacteria can cause septicaemia (blood poisoning) in these groups of people. If you contract septicaemia from listeria while pregnant, there is a high risk of stillbirth. However, listeria infection in pregnant women is extremely uncommon. For example, Australia reports approximately seven cases per 300,000 births; the figures for Sweden are similar, with one to three cases annually per 115,000 births.

The listeria bacteria differ from other bacteria that require heat to flourish — listeria grows well even at fridge temperature. This is why you can often find listeria bacteria on cold meats, smoked salmon, and other food that has been in the fridge for a while. In the majority of cases of listeria infection, authorities are unable to trace the source of the bacteria. Sometimes there are cases of concentrated outbreaks that are traced back to cold meats, rockmelon (cantaloupe melon), unpasteurised milk, and certain soft cheeses.

If you want to be on the safe side, avoid processed, ready-to-eat deli meats, chicken, and poultry, soft cheeses, seed sprouts, pre-cut fruits (especially melon), and other foods that have been prepared and packed. Cooking, frying, or baking foods in the oven will kill any listeria bacteria.

Toxoplasmosis

The parasite *Toxoplasma gondii* commonly occurs in the intestines of cats, such as our domestic cats and the wild lynx. It doesn't make the cats ill, but the parasite's eggs that are excreted in cat faeces can infect humans, rats, and other mammals. Around 20–40 per cent of people in Australia have been infected by the parasite without having noticed; these people have antibodies against toxoplasma, produced by their immune system. But if a pregnant woman is newly infected, the foetus can become infected in the womb. Around one to two in 1,000 Australian mothers become infected, and in one-fifth of these cases, the infection also affects the foetus. An infection during foetal life may result in serious damage to the developing brain, eyes, and hearing, but in many cases, no harm is evident. Some 40–50 Australian infants can be expected to be born with a toxoplasmosis infection each year, based on the calculated risk (1.5 per 10,000 live births) from a study performed in Perth in West Australia. A woman who was infected by toxoplasma before her current pregnancy, and has antibodies to the parasite, cannot transmit the infection to the foetus in her womb.

The toxoplasmosis parasite can be found in meat (particularly game, lamb, and pork), and toxoplasma eggs may be found in lettuce and berries. The health advice is to make sure meat is well cooked, to carefully rinse lettuce and fruits, and to wash your hands after contact with soil, raw meat, vegetables, and fruits. Direct contact with cats is rarely a source of transmission.

Toxoplasma is rarely found in beef, and it is mostly beef that people are served rare. The rule about well-done meat is therefore perhaps a little overstated, since the risk of contracting toxoplasmosis from beef is small. If you want to be absolutely sure you won't be infected with toxoplasmosis, you can either cook the meat to at least 67°C, or freeze it for three days before you cook it, after which it doesn't need to be well done, because any parasites will have been killed by freezing.

The risk of contracting toxoplasmosis is why pregnant women are advised against emptying cat-litter trays. However, if you live with a cat and its litter tray (and the cat is a carrier of toxoplasma), you've probably already been infected and will have developed antibodies, so you are highly unlikely to become newly infected. We do, however, believe it's reasonable for you to be released from litter-emptying duties and other cleaning tasks when pregnant if you live with another adult. If you live alone, you will need to empty the litter tray; just don't lick your paws clean afterwards — wash them instead.

Common symptoms of toxoplasmosis in a pregnant woman are swollen lymph nodes and extreme tiredness, but muscle pain, headaches, and other flu-like symptoms also occur. If the infection is discovered during pregnancy, it can be treated with antibiotics to reduce the risk of serious complications for the baby. If you're pregnant and have these symptoms, go to your doctor and ask for a blood test for toxoplasmosis.

DIETARY SUPPLEMENTS AND VITAMINS

It's hardly surprising that manufacturers of multivitamins and dietary supplements heavily target their marketing to pregnant women. There is a large market for dietary supplements across many parts of the rich, developed world, and many of them are marketed specifically for use during pregnancy. However, the evidence is inconclusive as to whether they have any positive effects on well-nourished women in high-income countries.

A 2015 scientific review of studies into multivitamin supplements during pregnancy showed that they do by far the most good in low- and middle-income countries.[22] Only two studies had investigated the effect of multivitamin supplements (which contain several vitamins and minerals, plus iron and folic acid) during pregnancy in rich countries, and both came from the UK. The more relevant study, which was conducted in 2010, involved 410 women who were given multivitamins or sugar pills. The study showed no difference in the outcome of the pregnancy between the two groups, which suggests that vitamin pills provide no benefit for pregnant women or their babies. The second study was published in 1937, when the UK is certain to have enjoyed a much lower level of nutrition than today, and should be seen as less relevant to us. By contrast, in poor countries where large swathes of the population are undernourished, multivitamin tablets have been proven to reduce the risk of giving birth to a baby with a dangerously low birth weight.

Some vitamins and minerals — such as vitamin D, iron, and folic acid — have been ascribed greater importance than others. We go through each of them below in more detail. Supplements are recommended in certain countries and situations. If you take a pregnancy multivitamin pill, it will most likely contain the recommended amounts of these vitamins and minerals (with the exception of iron for certain women, as you will see below), and you do not have to take the separate pills. Ask your prenatal practitioner if you have any questions.

Vitamin D

Vitamin D is formed by the skin when exposed to sunlight. The vitamin is important for the absorption of calcium, which in turn is important for strong bones, but it also has many other more-or-less clear functions in the body. The Australian Bureau of Statistics found that one in four Australian adults suffer from a vitamin D deficiency, although in most cases at a mild to moderate level. (Similar results have been reported throughout the Western world.) Severe deficiency leads to soft bones — rickets — but we don't see this disease any more. The significance of milder deficiencies, including vitamin D deficiency during pregnancy, is less clear.[23] However, it may be worth asking for a vitamin D test at the clinic to see whether you need to treat a vitamin D deficiency by taking a preventive vitamin D supplement.

Iron

The body needs iron to form haemoglobin, which is the protein in the red blood cells that transports oxygen from the lungs to all the cells in the body, and myoglobin, which is the red substance in muscles that absorbs oxygen from the haemoglobin. It is important to include iron-rich foods such as meat, chicken, seafood, dried beans, and lentils, and green leafy vegetables, in your diet.

Iron-deficiency anaemia is very common among women who menstruate, particularly if they also follow a vegetarian diet. (Red meat is undoubtedly the best source of iron.) Anaemia has a negative impact on a pregnancy, and results in a heightened risk of premature birth and low birth weight. Your pregnancy-care practitioner should test your iron levels with a blood test at the start of your pregnancy and recommend an iron medication if your levels are low. Take this medication if it is recommended to you, but don't worry too much if you still have a slightly low red-blood–cell count (haemoglobin level). If one iron medication gives you side effects (usually constipation or diarrhoea), ask if there is another option. (All iron supplements give you black stools, so that's unavoidable, unfortunately!) The amount of iron in multivitamin pregnancy supplements is not enough to treat anaemia and iron deficiency, which is why you have to take a separate medication if your blood-test results show you need it.

Folic acid

It is generally recommended that all women who are planning to get pregnant should take a folic acid supplement to reduce the risk of their foetus developing spina bifida. After some randomised controlled trials showed that an extra folic acid intake had a positive effect, Australia,

North and South America, and several countries in Africa and the Middle East introduced policies in the first decade of this century for the fortification of grains and cereals. After this fortification, a reduction in the number of babies born with spina bifida was seen. At the same time, however, ultrasound screening for spina bifida during pregnancy, and/or legalised abortion, also became more widespread. No country in Europe has adopted fortification, but the incidence of spina bifida still decreased in Sweden from 0.55 per 1,000 births in 1973 to 0.29 per 1,000 births in 2003. By comparison, the incidence in Australia is considerably higher, at 1 per 1,000. Genetic influences, ethnicity, and other factors contribute to the risk of spina bifida.

It is probably sensible to follow the recommendation and take the supplement. The dose you receive is around ten times higher than what you get from food, so you can't obtain an equivalent amount simply by changing your diet. It is recommended that you take the supplement from the moment you begin trying to become pregnant. But if you have an unplanned pregnancy, you don't need to be overly concerned about putting the baby in danger by not having taken the folic acid supplement.

Iodine

Iodine is an important mineral needed for the production of thyroid hormones, which are important for growth and development. Inadequate iodine intake during pregnancy increases the risk of severe mental impairment and a restriction of growth in newborns.

Foods that are good sources of iodine include seafood and seaweed (including nori and kelp), eggs, meat, and dairy products. Because it can be hard to get enough iodine from food sources, many countries have introduced policies for the iodisation of salt. Consequently, using iodised salt in cooking and as table salt is recommended. You don't have to oversalt your food to get enough iodine — just let your taste guide you to the right amount.

Due to the re-emergence of iodine deficiency in Australia during a period when iodised salt was not the standard, iodised salt is now added to all commercially sold bread in Australia and New Zealand, with the exception of organic and unleavened bread.

Pregnant and breastfeeding women have increased iodine requirements. In Australia and New Zealand, iodine supplementation of 150 micrograms per day is recommended for women planning a pregnancy, throughout pregnancy, and while breastfeeding. In the UK and Sweden, supplements are not generally recommended.

Vitamin A

Although vitamin A requirements do increase during pregnancy, vitamin A supplements are not recommended for pregnant women in high-income countries where vitamin A deficiencies are uncommon. This is because an excessive intake of vitamin A may cause birth deformities.

The best way to make sure that you are getting enough vitamin A is through food sources such as milk, fish, eggs, and butter. Multivitamin supplements for pregnant women contain either no level or low levels of vitamin A, while those not specifically for pregnant women may contain higher amounts. Therefore, if you use a multivitamin supplement, use one specifically formulated for pregnant women.

HOW MUCH SHOULD YOU EAT? AND IS BEING OVERWEIGHT HARMFUL?

During pregnancy, you will need a little more food than usual, and for most people the increased demands are well regulated by elevated hunger once the sickness of the first trimester has passed. The amount of weight that a pregnant woman gains varies a great deal; around 12 kilograms is typical.

If you are considerably overweight even before your pregnancy (with a body mass index, BMI, over 30), there is a greater risk of you incurring complications (gestational diabetes, pre-eclampsia) and of you needing a caesarean section.[24] It is also more common for babies of overweight mothers to exceed their expected size for the gestational dates, and even for a stillbirth to occur.[25] The more overweight a pregnant woman is, the greater the risk of brain damage such as cerebral palsy in their baby, which is largely due to oxygen-deficiency problems during the birth.[26] If you're already pregnant, it is not a good idea to begin the kind of regular dieting program that is aimed at non-pregnant adults, as a restricted regime will provide far too little nourishment for you and your growing baby. You can, however, improve the conditions for you and your baby by adopting a special diet and physical-activity program suitable for pregnant women.

There are numerous studies of programs for overweight pregnant women that are based on recommendations and support for changes in diet, and for increased physical activity. While the effects are far from dramatic, these programs generally result in a certain reduction in weight gain and a modest reduction in the risk of high blood pressure and perhaps gestational diabetes.[27] There may also be a slightly reduced risk of giving birth to an overly large baby.[28] Although the effects are slight, there is certainly no suggestion of any danger in following such a program. If you have the drive and motivation, ask your GP or midwife whether there is any group you can join to try and get your weight under control during pregnancy.

Remember that no one has the right to demand that you take part in such a program. It is part of the job of the doctor or midwife to raise the subject, but it is not the place of your neighbours, relatives, or friends to discuss your weight if you haven't chosen to do so with them. If you don't have the energy or opportunity to try to control your weight during pregnancy, you are fully entitled to leave it alone. The vast majority of midwives will understand and respect this if you tell them, and if you find your doctor or midwife to be less than supportive, you should consider switching to someone else.

If you have an eating disorder, or have had one in the past, there is a major risk that the disorder will become more active during pregnancy as your body changes and you gain weight. Doctors and psychiatrists are very familiar with this situation, so just make sure you tell your midwife, obstetrician, or GP if you've had such problems, and if you still have one, contact your eating-disorder clinic. Also tell your partner, and ask them to look out for signs of a relapse and, if necessary, help you to seek medical care. It will be easier to treat the problem early on, but it can be very difficult to ask for help yourself — that's the nature of an eating disorder.

If you feel unwell, have a craving for specific items, or are completely turned off by something in particular, try to find food you can eat. The dislike of certain foods can be extremely strong during pregnancy, so try to work around it if possible. If you can't face half a litre of skimmed milk a day, try ricotta in your pasta sauce instead. If you're off green salad, try a fruit smoothie. And don't forget that these feelings will pass.

MEDICINES

All medicines known to cause serious foetal abnormalities are only available on prescription. If you take any ongoing prescription medication, ask your GP in advance what you should do about your medicines when you become pregnant. If you're already pregnant, contact your doctor for specific advice. When prescribing to fertile women, doctors have a duty to explain about medication that is known to have both mild and severe effects on foetuses, so you should be well informed about whether you're taking such medicines.

However, there are some over-the-counter medicines that are also best avoided during pregnancy. One example is the common pain tablets that contain non-steroidal anti-inflammatory drugs (NSAIDs), such as ibuprofen, diclofenac, and naproxen. These medicines are suspected of potentially increasing the risk of miscarriage in early pregnancy, and of potentially causing foetal heart and kidney side effects if taken in late pregnancy. Pain tablets that contain paracetamol, at the appropriate dose, are a safer choice in pregnancy.

Natural remedies and medicines ordered online

Natural remedies may sound harmless, but first impressions can be deceptive. When the authorities conduct checks of such medicines, they find that many of these 'natural preparations' contain high doses of common pharmaceuticals, often of the prescription kind, that are not declared on the pack. The fact that something comes from the plant kingdom is no guarantee of absence of harm; there are plenty of cases where so-called natural remedies have had serious side effects. The same is true of unlicensed online pharmacies, which may sell pills that contain substances other than the ones claimed. Buying them can therefore be something of a risk lottery, and we recommend you give them a miss.

DEPRESSION

Those who work with pregnant women and new parents recognise that depression is a common problem among this population.

Between one-fifth and one-tenth of pregnant women appear to suffer from some degree of depression during pregnancy or in the early stages of parenthood following birth. But it is as yet unclear whether these rates of depression are any higher than for women who are not pregnant or are recent mothers. In any case, depression is common, particularly in women, whether they're pregnant or not. Since the symptoms of depression are quite similar to some of the normal symptoms of pregnancy — lethargy, body pain, constipation, nausea, insomnia, and poor appetite — it can be quite tough to diagnose depression at this time, particularly if the symptoms are not terribly prominent.

If you feel devoid of happiness; if you can't see any point to your pregnancy, or to life in general; and if you feel that no one understands your situation, don't hesitate to seek help. First talk to your GP or midwife, and they will be able to refer you on. If the situation is really serious — if you are having intense suicidal thoughts, can't sleep at all, or suffer constant anxiety — and you need urgent help, call a public helpline or go to the emergency department of your local hospital.

A typical symptom of depression is that everything feels hopeless and pointless. This perception can prevent people from seeking help. In the case of a really deep depression, you might even feel that your life is worthless. Feelings of guilt and shame also accompany deep depression, and form an effective barrier against telling someone how you feel.

But the sense of hopelessness is caused by the brain not working properly. Depression can be treated effectively these days with a range of therapies that usually involve cognitive-behavioural therapy (CBT) alone or in combination with antidepressant medication. The cornerstone of the CBT approach is to help you establish good sleep and food routines, and get more active. When you have depression, it's easy to end up in a vicious cycle of isolating yourself from friends, becoming a night owl or staying in bed, eating less, more, or poorer food, and not leaving the house. All this makes the depression worse. It's usually not possible to break this vicious cycle all by yourself when you suffer from depression. You need help.

Treat your depression, even when pregnant

Many pregnant women with depression or anxiety are terrified that their baby will be damaged by medication or treatment. In fact, it's very important to get treatment for depression during pregnancy — not only to reduce the suffering of the expectant mother, but also to improve her chances of being able to take care of her baby well, and to cope with the major changes that come with being a new parent. For exactly the same reason, the partner of an expectant parent needs to get help with any depression or anxiety problems they have prior to or during their partner's pregnancy. Your GP can offer advice on where to turn. A meta-analysis found an increased risk of both premature birth and having a baby with a low birth weight in women whose depression during pregnancy goes untreated.[29]

The type of antidepressant drugs called selective serotonin reuptake inhibitors (SSRI) have been through meticulous testing and appear to have no long-term effects on a baby's development. If you have depression, or suffer anxiety or obsessive-compulsive disorder and you need medical treatment, your doctor will probably recommend that you continue with the treatment while pregnant, at least if the medication is of the SSRI type, both so that your symptoms are reduced and your ability to cope with caring for your baby is strengthened. Since SSRIs carry a risk that a baby will have certain difficulties switching from life in the womb to life outside, the baby will need to be observed more closely after birth for breathing difficulties or low blood sugar, but these problems will pass. It is important to give birth in hospital if you've been taking SSRI medication during pregnancy, due to these increased risks. If you're on other types of medication, discuss the matter with your psychiatrist.

Electroconvulsive therapy sometimes needs to be deployed during pregnancy, as it is the most effective medication against severe depression, but also against some other severe psychiatric disorders such as mania. This carries certain risks, particularly because you're anaesthetised during the procedure, but it's the fastest, most effective, and sometimes the only treatment for really deep depression. Electroconvulsive therapy should only be performed on pregnant women following consultation between their obstetrician and treating psychiatrist.

IN BRIEF

Never forget that you are still an independent adult with responsibility and power over your own life, even when you are pregnant. Many people will want to offer more or less well-meaning advice about your lifestyle, and you may feel that your personal privacy and right of self-determination are suddenly not nearly as clear-cut as they were before. But your boundaries are as worthy of respect as ever, and your right of self-determination remains intact. There is certain advice about eating and drinking that you can take on board if you want to minimise controllable risks for you and your baby during pregnancy. Your GP or midwife is right to inform you about health risks and support your lifestyle changes if you so wish, but it is up to you to decide what you want, and don't want, to do. We do recommend that you heed the advice to stop smoking, and remember that active substance abuse (including alcohol abuse) and pregnancy don't go together — and nor do substance abuse and parenthood, for that matter.

CHAPTER FOUR
Birth

If you're looking for advice on how you can maximise your chances of a good birth, you won't have to look far. The Internet, books, parenting magazines, and social media all offer an abundance of information about preparing for birth and birthing methods. Hypnobirth, orgasmic birth, water birth, and yoga birth all promise fantastic experiences. In this chapter, we don't discuss these options. Instead you'll be able to read exactly how a birth happens, and will be reassured that you're not alone if you think it's bizarre to liken a birth to an orgasm.

Looking into the vast array of prenatal preparations and birthing 'methods' can teach you quite a lot about how a normal birth works. As well, having something to think about during birth, such as breathing or posture, can give you a sense of control, and nip any feelings of helplessness and chaos in the bud.

There is, however, no scientific evidence that methods of relaxation and dealing with pain make for faster or less painful births. Anyone who promises that they do is guilty of false advertising. They also don't make birth safer; you absolutely don't need to breathe 'correctly' to ensure that the baby gets enough oxygen. Conveniently enough, the body controls all this automatically — willpower has nothing to do with it. So if you don't have the time, money, or desire to enrol in a lengthy private birthing course, you might be relieved to know that things will work out just as well without. In a short prenatal course, you — with your partner or support person, if that's what you want — can learn the basics of how a birth works and what to expect when you are in hospital. Such courses are offered within most public healthcare systems.

LABOUR AND BIRTH

You will find that the birth process is generally described as comprising three stages: stage one is the labour; stage two is the delivery of the baby; and stage three is the delivery of the placenta. The labour itself is divided into three phases: phase one is the latent phase; phase two is the active phase; and phase three is the transition phase.

Labour usually begins with contractions. With a first birth, contractions usually come irregularly for a day or so, maybe more. Early labour, when the contractions are more than three minutes apart, is called the 'latent phase'. If this phase becomes drawn out, it can be very frustrating. Many women head to hospital during this time and have to return home with the bad news that they're not yet in the active phase of labour. The practitioner checks this by measuring how much the cervix has opened (dilated). All that maternity hospitals can do to help women in the latent phase is prescribe strong pain relief based on morphine. If you need it, ask for it.

Sometimes labour begins with the waters breaking. Many women describe hearing a sudden pop and then feeling like they've wet themselves. When the waters break there is generally a lot of fluid rather than the little watery discharges that you may have already experienced. These small discharges might be either normal vaginal discharges, or might indicate that the mucous that has been plugging the cervix during pregnancy is coming away.

If you think your waters have broken, call the maternity hospital for instructions. You'll probably be asked to come in to be assessed.

The colour of the amniotic fluid is checked. A brown or green colour indicates that the baby has pooed in the fluid, in which case, you will need to be monitored to check that the baby is not distressed. If the amniotic fluid is colourless and everything is normal, but the cervix hasn't dilated enough, you may be sent home to wait for contractions. And if the contractions don't start within a day, you'll be called in to have the labour induced.

Eventually, labour will move into what's called the 'active phase', when the contractions usually become regular and occur around three minutes apart. These contractions tend to be more painful than those in the earlier latent phase. You should head to the maternity hospital if you require pain relief. A midwife will check the dilation of your cervix by inserting two fingers into your vagina (many such examinations are generally required during a vaginal delivery); if the cervix has dilated and the labour is in active phase, you may be kept in hospital.

Once on the labour ward, you'll have a few different types of pain relief available to you. The most effective is epidural anaesthesia (EDA), which involves an anaesthetist injecting an anaesthetic into your lower back at the point where the nerves from your uterus and pelvis enter your spine. Many women get good relief from laughing gas (nitrous oxide), although it can cause some to become confused and start to hallucinate. While this can be disturbing, it's not dangerous because nitrous oxide disappears from your body as soon as you stop inhaling it. Transcutaneous electrical nerve stimulation (TENS) helps some women. Sterile water injections under the skin are another option. It is very painful for a few seconds, like being stung by a swarm of wasps: the idea is that this stimulates the body to produce extra pain-killing endorphins, which help by numbing the labour pains.

When the cervix has dilated to 10 centimetres, and the baby's head has descended through the fully expanded vagina to the pelvic floor, labour enters its third 'transitional' phase — which is when you will feel the urge to push. The baby's head has to pass through the pelvic floor muscles and the vaginal opening first, and then the baby's body usually slides out without any problem. Sometimes this stage is less painful than the first stage, and many women report a sense of relief at finally being able to start pushing. However, the pushing phase is very painful for most women. Like 'a blowtorch between the legs' and 'pooing out a melon' are just two descriptions of what it feels like. After anything from a quarter of an hour to a few hours of pushing, the baby usually comes out on its own, cries, and is placed on the mother's belly or chest.

The feeling of seeing your tiny baby for the first time can seem unreal. Most mothers experience very strong emotions after giving birth, and some don't want to let go of their newborn for a second. Others are just exhausted and want to be left alone to sleep. In this case, the other parent, or the birth partner, can get to know the baby and let the birth mother rest. There is nothing wrong or strange about being tired, sad, angry, or frightened following a birth.

The third, and final, stage of labour involves pushing out the placenta, which isn't usually too taxing, and then any damage to the genital area needs to be investigated and stitched up. Despite all the pain and sometimes suffering, many women afterwards describe their vaginal delivery as a very positive experience, and find that their body is remarkably quick to forget how much pain was actually involved. Others never forget the fear or the pain, and elect to have a caesarean section for future births.

Complications associated with vaginal delivery

By far the most likely outcome is for both mother and baby to be fit and healthy after the birth, but complications can occur along the way. It is common for a birth to progress slowly, in which case the doctor or midwife may put you on an oxytocin drip — oxytocin is a hormone that stimulates contractions of the uterus. They can also break your waters, which usually induces labour. To do this, the doctor or midwife performs a vaginal examination and inserts a thin device through the vaginal passage. This device looks a bit like a crochet hook, and is used to carefully pop the amniotic sac bulging through the cervix. Inducing labour in these ways makes the contractions more frequent and more painful, but usually moves the labour forward.

Another complication occurs when a baby's blood supply to the brain is restricted by the umbilical cord becoming compressed as the uterus is squeezed during contractions. This problem will show up on the foetal monitor, which records the baby's heartbeat during labour. If this happens when the mother is on an oxytocin drip, the midwife or obstetrician will try to ease the contractions by halting the drip. Sometimes that is sufficient for the blood flow to recover.

If the problem persists, and happens in early labour, the vaginal delivery will be halted and a caesarean section will be performed instead. If it happens later, during the pushing stage, attempts will be made to speed up the process using a vacuum extractor or forceps. The vacuum extractor is a round metal or plastic cup, about 5 centimetres in size, that is inserted into the vaginal opening and attached by suction to the baby's head. When the mother has a contraction, the obstetrician gently pulls the chain that is attached to the cup, to help the baby come out. A forceps is an instrument shaped as a pair of large spoons that the obstetrician places around the baby's head to help guide the baby out through the birth canal. Mothers' experiences of this process vary: some are relieved that the labour is finally over; others find it a hideous feeling. Nevertheless, the vacuum extractor or forceps is useful when the baby needs to come out quickly, and it has saved countless babies from injuries they would otherwise have suffered due to oxygen deficiency.

After the baby's birth, the mother needs to push while the midwife gently pulls the umbilical cord so that the placenta detaches from the uterus lining and comes out. Sometimes this fails, and the placenta has to be removed surgically under anaesthetic. In some cases, the placenta may only partially detach. This can cause severe bleeding and can require urgent surgery.

Once the placenta is out, the uterus needs to contract. The area of the uterus lining where the placenta was attached is like a wound, full of open blood vessels. The bleeding is stopped by the contraction of the muscles in the uterus, but sometimes the uterus fails to contract, and the blood vessels continue to bleed. The problem can usually be fixed with an injection of a uterin- contracting agent and by massaging of the uterus to stimulate uterine contractions. Occasionally, this approach doesn't help, and a new mother can quickly lose several litres of blood. In this situation, a blood transfusion and emergency surgery are required. Although major bleeding is uncommon, it can't be predicted; this is one of the main reasons we suggest giving birth at a hospital that routinely handles a large number of deliveries, which means it will have more staff available and relevant experience to guide it should it have to deal with sudden life-threatening complications. The presence around the clock of obstetric, anaesthetic, and neonatology staff is also a very important safety factor to take into account. If you do not find such a hospital for delivery, having obstetric, anaesthetic and neonatology staff on call from home is the second-safest option.

Quick deliveries and a long distance to the hospital

Some women give birth extremely quickly, or experience so little pain during the latent phase of their labour that they suddenly get second-stage contractions before they reach a hospital. Fortunately, such quick deliveries rarely involve complications for the baby or the mother, although they can naturally be overwhelming and frightening for both the woman and her partner. If you experience the urge to push before you get to the hospital, call the emergency services and ask for an ambulance. While you wait, they will connect you to ambulance personnel to guide you through the process of labour over the phone. If you have a long car journey to get to the hospital, make sure you pack a blanket, as well as towels to clean the baby and the mother, in case the baby ends up being born in the car. But when there is little chance of making it to the hospital in time, it's better to stay at home and call for an ambulance.

If you live a long way from the hospital, it might be a good idea to check into a hotel, or to stay with a friend or relative near the hospital for the week before your baby is due. You might also want to consider having a planned induction of labour. In some Australian hospitals, induction is performed for this reason; in others, not. If you face many hours of driving on bad roads, it could be a safer option for both parents and baby.

Muscle tears

Several muscles run between the coccyx and the front of the pelvis, forming the pelvic floor and below that the perineum, and not all these muscles share the same orientation or function. The muscles of the pelvic floor and the perineum provide support for the lowest internal organs: the uterus, bladder, and rectum. If the pelvic floor were to be removed, they would fall out. A healthy pelvic floor keeps the vagina closed at rest, so no air gets in, and it can create contractions around the vagina during orgasm. The pelvic floor is also important for keeping in urine and, in part, for holding gases and faeces inside the rectum. In the latter case, the anal sphincter muscle, which forms a strong ring around the opening of the rectum, also plays an important role.

Because a baby passes through this intricate system of muscles during birth, there is a considerable risk that some muscles will tear in the process of labour, particularly with first birth. These tears, or lacerations, are divided into four categories: a first-degree laceration involves no muscles, and only the mucous membrane in the vagina; a second-degree laceration involves the perineal muscles, but not the anal sphincter; a third-degree laceration extends partially or completely through the anal sphincter; and a fourth-degree laceration tears the mucosal lining of the rectum.

An injury suffered in a vaginal delivery increases the risk of urinary incontinence in later life, and of weakening the pelvic floor, which can lead to the uterus dropping into the vagina (prolapse). A less common complication is faecal incontinence.[1] Certain sexual problems, such as painful intercourse, or a sense of being fully open and not feeling any-thing during penetration, can occur after a vaginal delivery.

In Sweden, historically, the maternal examinations carried out immediately after birth were not thorough enough. Many women, therefore, did not find out about the tears they'd suffered, even though having such information could have led to the damage being repaired. Many were told by their practitioner, 'You had a little tear, but we've given you a couple of tiny stitches', and they went away happy. In fact, some of these women suffered quite a sizeable muscle tear that would have healed much better with a proper repair procedure. The maternity-care service in Sweden has recently concentrated its resources on improving these examinations and damage-repairs, which is excellent news.

Under-diagnosis has made it difficult to obtain a consensus on the best strategy for preventing tears. Swedish mothers appear to experience a large numbers of tears, with between 3 per cent and 8 per cent of first-time mothers suffering third- or fourth-degree tears, compared with just under 1 per cent in nearby Finland, for example. Some people suggest that the Finnish practice of midwife-led assistance during the pushing stage is the reason for their low tear rate. In this method, the woman lies on her back in stirrups during the pushing stage. Her midwife has full control over the perineum, and holds the baby's head in place until the tissue has stretched enough so the baby can be born without causing any tearing. When it's needed, the midwife usually cuts 4–5 centimetres through the skin and muscle of the perineum to give the baby space to squeeze out. (This is called an episiotomy.).

A major Swedish observational study shows an increased risk of sphincter damage when mothers deliver in a squatting position, or on a birthing stool.[2] Lying on one's side was associated with the least risk of sphincter damage. Several decades ago, when Sweden used the more old-fashioned Finnish method, the reported levels of tearing were also low, but since then generations of midwives have been trained in the use of freer methods for the pushing stage.

When Finnish obstetrician Katarina Laine moved to Norway, she was appalled by the high rate of sphincter damage (4 per cent). She brought Norwegian midwives and obstetricians together to learn the Finnish method, and sphincter ruptures rapidly fell by half.[3]

The message from all this is that amid the exhilaration and drama of giving birth, it's important not to overlook the impact that birth has on a woman's body. And to make sure you ask as many questions as you want to. If you want to follow the Finnish way, ask for a controlled pushing stage with slow delivery, protection for the perineum, and a cut if things look tight. And whatever the method for the pushing stage, demand a proper examination after delivery. If you're not given clear information, ask what degree of tearing you had, and ask for the torn muscles to be repaired and for the midwife to get help from a more experienced colleague or a doctor if she is unsure. There are good grounds to believe that thorough examinations and repairs to tearing lead to fewer long-term complications than simply stitching up what is visible.

If you have lasting problems with urine, gas, or faecal leakage after birth, or if you experience odd sensations during sex, consult a gynaecologist with expertise and an interest in the pelvic floor and perineum. If the gynaecologist doesn't have any clear answers, ask them for a referral to another expert. Help is out there! If you have problems, don't be fobbed off with advice about doing pelvic-floor exercises. If the muscle is torn, tensing the two parts isn't going to help; it's never going to heal by itself, no matter how many exercises you do.

Caesarean section

The alternative to a vaginal delivery is a caesarean section (commonly known as a C-section). During this procedure, the obstetrician makes a 10–15 centimetre-long incision through the abdomen, and expands the hole by pulling the edges of the incision forcefully apart. The intestines are moved to one side to access the bladder, which sits on top of the uterus. The bladder is loosened from the uterus, which is cut with a scalpel. Time is of the essence at this stage, since the cut into the uterus bleeds heavily. The baby is pulled out through the incision, followed by the placenta. The uterus is massaged, sewn up, and repositioned with the other organs in the abdominal cavity. Finally, the abdomen is sewn up. During the operation, you will be under local or general anaesthetic, so, fortunately, you won't feel any pain. You will feel movements, though, which can be a strange sensation, as you are not used to feeling somebody stretching your skin and removing a baby from your pelvis. The pain comes afterwards, with recovery, but there is no reason to hold back on pain relief, which is usually very effective.

A C-section using local anaesthesia (usually a spinal block) is strongly recommended, since putting a very pregnant woman under general anaesthesia carries a relatively high risk of lung complications. Other risks associated with a C-section are damage to the intestines or bladder, and abdominal bleeding, which can require another surgery to open up the abdomen again to repair the leaking blood vessels. Major bleeds from the uterus through the vagina are more common with a C-section than with a vaginal delivery, but are treated the same way. As with all operations, there is a risk of infection resulting from surgery. Delivery via a C-section carries an increased risk of blood clots compared with a vaginal delivery. Symptoms of blood clots include swelling or pain in the legs or groin, shortness of breath, and unexplained headaches. Blood clots are treated with blood-thinning medication.

After the C-section, a scar is formed in the uterus where the surgeon made an incision. Scar tissue is weaker than the uterine muscle, so there is a small risk that the uterus will tear along the scar with future vaginal deliveries. The risk is estimated at around five in 1,000 vaginal deliveries after a C-section. Extra monitoring and readiness for an emergency C-section is therefore required during subsequent vaginal deliveries. The more C-sections a woman has, the greater the risk of the uterus tearing; after two C-sections, Swedish doctors recommend that the next delivery should be caesarean, not vaginal. It's uncommon for a uterus to hold for more than four caesareans, but it does happen.

In a subsequent pregnancy after a C-section, there is a risk that the placenta will attach to the scar in the wall of the uterus. This may result in the placenta becoming difficult to detach after the delivery, leading to a risk of bleeding and, in some extreme cases, the need to remove the uterus.

A C-section also carries slightly increased risks for the baby, compared with a vaginal delivery. There is a greater risk that the baby will need help with starting to breathe, and the risk increases the earlier in the pregnancy the C-section is performed. It's more common for babies delivered by caesarean section to be overweight,[4] and they also have an elevated risk of certain immune regulatory disorders such as type 1 diabetes,[5] asthma, and food allergies.[6] No one knows why a C-section has these effects. One theory is that a vaginal delivery places enormous physical stress on a baby, which may positively affect many bodily functions. Another is that the bacteria transferred from the mother during a vaginal delivery stimulate the baby's immune system in the first few days of life. Babies born by C-section don't receive any vaginal bacteria during the delivery, and instead pick up skin bacteria from the people around them after the delivery.

Caesarean section or vaginal delivery?

In some cases, the choice between a C-section and a vaginal delivery is obvious. If a baby is in the lateral position, or the placenta is completely blocking the opening in the uterus, a vaginal delivery is not possible, and a C-section is the only option. If a baby is lying bottom first (breech), a C-section is often recommended. There is a slightly increased risk of injury to the baby during a vaginal breech birth compared with a caesarean section, but a woman can go ahead with a vaginal delivery if she prefers, as long as the baby is healthy and the labour progresses well. Due to the slightly increased risk to the baby, not all hospitals are willing to assist with breech delivery. If you are convinced that you want to vaginally deliver a baby that is in a breech position, you will do best to find a hospital with experience in these deliveries. Breech delivery outside a hospital is not recommended. For a breech delivery to be reasonably safe, access to foetal monitoring, forceps assistance, and other obstetric interventions are needed.

If none of these situations apply to you, and you still want a C-section, you'll need to explain your reasons to the midwife and to an obstetrician at the hospital. They will ask whether you would consider giving birth vaginally under certain conditions. The reason why they will negotiate with you is that, as we've mentioned above, an uncomplicated vaginal delivery carries the least risk to both mother and baby. If you can't give any particular reason to have the operation beyond the fact that it seems convenient, or that you want to be able to choose the date of birth, you won't be granted a caesarean section in Sweden. In Australia, you can choose a C-section even if you have no medical reasons for doing so.

Fear of giving birth is a common reason for wanting a C-section. Most pregnant women experience fear ahead of a vaginal birth. If the fear is so great that it significantly impacts on your life, you need to seek help from your GP or midwife. It's a common issue, and hospital and maternity clinics should have programs to help with birthing fears. You may be offered extra discussions with the midwife, counselling, psychiatric help, a personal tour of the labour ward, or a promise of a special delivery plan. However, the fear of giving birth is so strong in some women that none of this helps. If you are one of these women, you should insist on not being forced to give birth vaginally.

Could I die during childbirth?

Well, yes, you could, but in affluent and developed countries, maternal deaths are extremely rare. A summary of maternal deaths in Sweden for 1997–2005 shows that around six to seven women per year (out of 120,000 pregnancies) died during pregnancy or in the first six weeks after childbirth, equalling four deaths per 100,000 deliveries. Corresponding figures for Australia, which has approximately three times as many births as Sweden, is 21 maternal deaths per year during 2008–2012, which gives a maternal mortality ratio of seven per 100,000 women who gave birth. The rate is similar in Canada (seven per 100,000) and the UK (nine per 100,000), while the risk in the US is considerably higher, at around 20 per 100,000.

The most common causes of death are blood clotting, bleeding, and infections. Pre-eclampsia is a very rare cause of death — less than one woman per year in Great Britain and one woman every second year in Sweden dies from pre-eclampsia.

To put the figures into perspective: in 2015, 92 Swedish women aged 20–39 died of cancer in Sweden, and 201 died in accidents, of which 94 were certainly suicide. It is thus around 30 times more common for a woman of a fertile age to die in an accident than to die during childbirth.

Another perspective to consider is the global picture. The most common causes of death associated with pregnancy and birth globally are birth-related bleeding, serious infection, pre-eclampsia, labour complications, and unsafe abortions. All of these risks can largely be treated or prevented through good gynaecological care (which includes free and safe abortions) and maternity care. In 2015, it was most dangerous to be pregnant in Sierra Leone, where 1,360 in 100,000 mothers (over 1 per cent) died during or immediately after pregnancy, which is 270 times higher than the risk in Sweden. But even in Sierra Leone, the maternal mortality rate has been halved over the past 15 years. The difference in maternal mortality rates even between countries with good socio-economic standards shows that it is possible to minimise the risk of maternal death during delivery.

WATCHING YOUR PARTNER GIVE BIRTH

When a birthing mother has a partner, the partner in most cases attends the birth. Many find watching their partner give birth quite frightening, but it can also be an overwhelming and incredible experience. For many mothers, the comfort of having their partner with them during the birth is extremely important; they may be the only person they want to talk to in this situation. (With a vaginal birth, you can generally choose to have an additional support person in the room with you.)

It is a good idea to talk through how you think you will each react, before the birth. Think about how you manage stressful and painful situations, and what you each need from the other person. Attending prenatal classes together can help prepare you for this. An important task as a partner can be to advocate for the mother and ensure that she feels comfortable with the midwife. Check this during the labour when the midwife goes out of the room for the first time, and if the partner giving birth doesn't feel comfortable, ask for a different midwife. This is perhaps the most important factor you have control over during birth: getting help from a midwife whom the birth mother trusts.

DOULA

A doula is a woman whose specific task is to support a woman giving birth. Doula services have emerged in Sweden and in other countries in recent years, and are a welcome addition to most labour wards, as far as we know. In Australia, some women choose to engage an independent midwife for their regular prenatal and postnatal check-ups, and to support and advocate for them in hospital during labour and the early days after giving birth. If you can afford it, it can be worthwhile, as the staffing levels at maternity wards are not always high enough to give you the continuous attention of a midwife during the entire delivery; in Sweden, a midwife supports several women in labour at the same time, as a rule. If you can't afford to hire extra help, be reassured that medical safety is extremely high, not only in the Swedish maternity service, but also in that of Australia, New Zealand, Canada, and the UK.

SHOULD I WRITE A BIRTH PLAN?

It's common to write a birth plan that sets out your wishes about how you want the birth to proceed. There's nothing wrong with doing this, but it is worth bearing in mind that it can be difficult to predict what you'll want during the very particular situation of your birth. It can, however, be sensible to note down any specific fears or past incidents or traumas — such as a late termination, a previous traumatic birth, or an experience of sexual violence — that could bring up difficult emotions during your birth. It's also a good idea to report any history of mental illness, as you may need extra care and monitoring. If you don't want to breastfeed, it's worth writing that down, because the midwives will assume that everyone who has not expressly said otherwise will be wanting to start feeding immediately. Show your birth plan to your midwife, who can give you some feedback on your wishes and fears, and maybe offer you some further suggestions.

GIVING BIRTH AT HOME OR AT THE HOSPITAL?

Many normal births would be just as successful in a home environment with the help of trained midwives, and a small proportion of births in Sweden do take place at home. In the Netherlands, around one-fifth of mothers have home births. There are no gold-standard scientific studies in the form of randomised controlled trials that have investigated whether home births are as safe as hospital births. The studies that do exist compare women who chose a planned home birth with those who chose to give birth in hospital. Some of the studies show no major differences; others indicate that home births are better; and still more come out in favour of a hospital birth.[7] The women who choose to give birth at home are, however, so different from those who choose a hospital birth that it's impossible to separate the significance of the birth location from the bigger picture.

The midwives who help women with home births often have good experiences to refer back to, and are keen to promote the benefits of a home birth, such as comfort, a calm environment, and access to continuous experienced support. The vast majority of obstetricians and neonatal doctors, on the other hand, report that they regularly save the lives of mothers and newborn babies who would not have survived if the birth had taken place at home, without access to intensive care, surgery, and a blood bank. It's a matter of different perspectives — life-threatening complications are uncommon, but doctors in labour wards know that if they do occur, they're going to need emergency medical resources. Anecdotally, we can say that we've never met an intensive-care doctor who would consider a home birth for their own or their partner's pregnancy.

AFTER THE DELIVERY: A BABY'S FIRST BREATH

As soon as a baby has been delivered, they need to start breathing independently. Inside the womb, the placenta provided them with oxygen from the mother's blood, but as soon as the umbilical cord stops pumping, a baby needs to use their lungs. This usually happens automatically: the baby comes out, cries, and begins breathing in air.

Once the baby can breathe, the midwife performs a quick initial inspection to check that the baby's palate is intact and the rectum is open. She will usually also weigh and measure the baby. In addition, it is now common practice to give all newborns a vitamin K injection to ensure that the baby's blood can clot. The standard vitamin K injection has practically eradicated the previously much feared disorder *Morbus haemorrhagicus neonatorum* (commonly known as vitamin K deficiency bleeding, or haemorrhagic disease of the newborn), which used to cause brain bleeds in several Swedish infants each year before the introduction of the vitamin K supplement.

Sometimes, particularly if a baby is born prematurely or has endured a long labour, they can't manage to start breathing unaided. In this case, the midwife or doctor will whisk the baby off to a place containing the equipment that helps babies take their first breath. Depending on where you give birth, this may be in the delivery room or a separate room in the delivery ward. Mostly, all it takes is a few breaths with a breathing mask, and a full-term baby can very quickly be returned to its mother. Watching a midwife hurry off with an apparently lifeless baby can be a very frightening experience for parents. Remember that this is not an uncommon scenario, and that the vast majority of babies come back after a few minutes, all pink and healthy.

When babies are very premature, they need to be placed in an incubator, or humidicrib, to maintain warmth and humidity levels, and sometimes they will need continued help with breathing. If the birth has been very complicated and the baby has been deprived of oxygen, if they have breathed in faecally contaminated amniotic fluid, or if they have a congenital heart or lung abnormality, they may require long-term assistance with breathing, and extended intensive care in the neonatal unit.

NEONATAL CARE

Around one in 10 babies require care in a neonatal unit after birth. Premature birth is a common reason for a baby to need to stay in neonatal care. Another common reason is that sometimes a baby will need help in adapting its lungs to life in the open air, outside the womb. When babies are born, their lungs are full of fluid. In most cases, the blood absorbs the fluid in the lungs during the first few hours of life, but in some babies the process takes longer, and they may need the assistance of a ventilator to blow air into the lungs and expel the fluid over the course of a day or two.

Some babies who are born prematurely, or whose mothers have diabetes, are unable to maintain their blood-sugar levels in the first few days, and will need to be given a glucose drip; if not, an oral glucose gel or formula feeding will help keep their blood-sugar levels at an adequate level. Others may have congenital abnormalities or diseases that require investigation, operations, or medical treatment in this early period. Babies who have been starved of oxygen during the birth are also cared for in the neonatal unit. The time spent in special care can vary between a few hours and, in complicated cases, several weeks.

In many hospitals, parents are able and expected to stay with their sick newborn baby and to look after them as much as they can themselves. Other hospitals may have been built a long time ago, and don't have the space for parents. There is nothing you can do about this, as a parent, but you can ask what the situation is at your local hospital.

THE MATERNITY WARD: ROSY GLOW, OR STICKY, BLOODY, AND CONFUSED?

Following the birth, and once your uterus has contracted, or after the epidural or spinal blockade from a caesarean section has worn off and you can move your legs, you'll be taken to the maternity ward. If you're one of the lucky nine out of 10 mothers with a baby who can breathe independently, was not born too prematurely, and doesn't have any apparent abnormalities, you'll take your baby with you.

Skin-to-skin care is now recommended during the initial period on the maternity ward. This involves the baby just wearing a nappy and being placed on the mother's, or father's, naked chest, with a blanket over the top and a little hat to stop heat loss. Skin-to-skin care is an excellent, and also pleasurable, way to keep a newborn baby warm. If the baby is lying on its mother's chest, it may seek out a breast and begin sucking on it within its first hours of life. Even if you want to bottle-feed, skin-to-skin care is still a good idea; just have a bottle ready for when the baby seems ready to latch on.

New mothers used to be put onto open wards with other new mothers, but now most Swedish mothers are able to stay in private rooms with their baby and their partner. In Australia, private hospitals usually offer single rooms, while public hospitals offer shared rooms with up to four mother-infant pairs in each. It's certainly nice not to have to share a room with strangers when you've just given birth and you have stitches down below, and leaking breasts, and you're coming to terms with looking after a brand-new baby. The downside of private rooms is that no one has any idea how everyone else is doing. Many assume that the other rooms are full of joy and happiness, instant love and perfection, and that they're the only ones who are crying, in pain, and still not feeling the overwhelming love and instant baby-bonding that's described in the books. In reality, everyone on the maternity ward is dazed, and many are in pain. Most are exhausted. When we doctors come around to check families before discharge, the mothers exuding happiness are in a clear minority. The happiness levels are much higher by the time of the two-month check-up at the maternal and child-health centre.

THE BODY AFTER CHILDBIRTH

In the first few weeks after birth, the uterus contracts to its non-pregnant size (smaller than your clenched fist). You are likely to feel this process as cramps, known as afterpains, which are never as strong as the birth pains, but can still hurt. Afterpains occur during breastfeeding, in particular, due to the uterus-contracting hormone oxytocin that is released into the bloodstream when the baby sucks on its mother's breasts. But you'll experience afterpains whether you breastfeed or not, and irrespective of whether you had a vaginal or C-section delivery. Ask for pain-relief tablets if they're hard going.

Whatever the means of delivery, you will have a large wound inside your uterus where the placenta was previously attached. That wound will bleed. The bleeding, called lochia, is like a heavy period that can last for several weeks. It might smell a little, but if it starts to smell really unpleasant you should see a doctor, because it could be a sign of uterine infection. If you also have a high temperature, you need to seek emergency treatment at the labour ward, as a uterine infection can quickly lead to blood poisoning if not treated with antibiotics. If you can't make it to the hospital by yourself, call an ambulance.

After a vaginal birth, your genitals will be stretched, swollen, and often a little sore. Urinating will be difficult, and passing your first stool after giving birth could feel totally impossible. It may be easier to urinate in the shower. Don't hesitate to talk to the midwife on the maternity ward if you're having difficulties, as they're very used to these problems and may have some good tips to share with you. If you become constipated, you should get treatment for it, which could mean receiving an enema. Your genitals will return to their usual unswollen state more quickly than you might think. It is a good idea to exercise your pelvic floor. You'll be given information on how to do this on the maternity ward, so try to remember to do the exercises now and then.

If you had a caesarean section, your genitals will be unchanged, but you will have a large wound in your abdomen that will hurt if you don't take pain relief. Make sure you get some if you need it. In the first few days, you'll have a dressing over the wound, but when it's removed, check the wound daily. If it turns red, swollen, or hot, or it starts leaking around the edges, you will need to see a doctor because you may have an infection that requires antibiotics to allow the wound to heal. To avoid the risk of rupturing the wound, it is important that you refrain from lifting anything heavier than your baby in the first few weeks. Make plans to ensure that someone else is there to take care of the housework when you come home.

IN BRIEF

Babies are delivered vaginally or by caesarean section. It's worth researching both experiences, as well as the various labour and birth scenarios described in this chapter. This knowledge will help you prepare strategies for managing your own experiences. Even with pre-planning, your birth is still likely to be an overwhelming experience over which you have little control. Maternity care in high-income countries with free public healthcare is very safe, so you can rest assured that things will usually work out well for parents and baby in the end, one way or another.

CHAPTER FIVE

Feeding a newborn baby

Few topics are as awash with myths as how, when, and what to feed a baby. And few things can frustrate a parent as much as a baby who refuses to feed. In this chapter, we pin down what is true and false, explain how breastfeeding works, and give practical tips on how you can feed your baby, whether you choose to breastfeed or bottle-feed. We've also got some reassuring news: no, breastfeeding is not essential for bonding with your baby or for keeping it healthy.

There are two options for feeding a newborn baby: breast or bottle. It's a good idea to think about what you (and your partner, if you have one) want to do in advance. But you don't need to commit to either one, of course, as you can combine the methods, or change things later on. So even if you do have a view on how you want to feed your baby, be flexible. Some babies find it easy to suckle and some mothers find it easy to provide lots of milk. Other babies are not good at sucking, and some mothers find it impossible to make breastfeeding work. Certain babies only want the breast, while others prefer the bottle. Many families combine breastfeeding with shared parenting perfectly well, whereas others find that bottle-feeding makes it so much easier for both parents to look after their baby. It's basically a question of whatever works best for your family. The ideal goal is for happy parents, and a baby who gets enough food and grows well, so don't become locked into a particular feeding method too early on.

In many countries, parents are bombarded with so-called official information almost at the level of propaganda promoting the importance of breast milk in keeping a baby healthy and well nourished. This may be critical in low-income countries having to deal with masses of infections, dirty water, and practical difficulties in keeping bottles clean. But in high-income countries, children will be healthy whether they're breastfed or bottle-fed.

The reason that this type of skewed information continues to be spread by health services is that most countries signed a World Health Organisation (WHO) declaration in 1981 (also known as the WHO code) that requires authorities and healthcare professionals to tell parents that breastfeeding is always best, no matter what the facts of the matter are. Essentially, a political decision was taken on a medical issue. This is highly inappropriate, and also contravenes the principle that healthcare must be based on scientific evidence and proven experience.

The WHO code was drawn up against a backdrop of terrible experiences in the 1970s, when companies such as Nestlé pushed breast-milk substitutes hard globally, including in low-income or very low-income countries. The promotional marketing showed fat, happy babies who had been fed on formula. Mothers with little understanding of the products were diluting the expensive powder with too much water — water that was often contaminated by pathogenic bacteria. As a direct consequence, millions of babies died of diarrhoea and blood poisoning. Bottle-feeding in low-income countries was deleterious in two ways: first, the babies were ingesting harmful bacteria via the dirty water, and second, breast milk — but not formula — contains IgA antibodies and other substances that protect a baby against infection.

The cynicism of the infant-formula manufacturers triggered a wave of outrage, and many parents worldwide joined the boycott of Nestlé products. It was to prevent this type of marketing that the WHO produced its International Code of Marketing of Breast-milk Substitutes in 1981. Health authorities were required to inform all women that breast milk is better for their child's health than formula. Initially, the WHO recommended four months of breastfeeding, but this was later extended to six months. Finally, it was decided that babies shouldn't be fed on anything other than breast milk, an approach referred to as exclusive breastfeeding. The latter move came about in the late 1980s with the discovery that babies in some countries were being given many different types of bacteria-laden fluids and solids.[1] By restricting foods other than breast milk, a source of infection was evaded.

Breast milk provides excellent nutrition, and protects against infections, particularly bacterial diarrhoeal diseases and blood poisoning. It is therefore extremely important that babies who live in places where the risk of water-borne infection is high are breastfed. Children in countries with reliable clean water and formula supplies do perfectly well on breast-milk substitute. Serious infections in high-income countries are very uncommon in babies, except in premature babies. In Sweden, premature babies are always given breast milk, usually from a milk bank, because many mothers of extremely preterm babies do not have enough breast milk themselves. In the UK and Australia, the use of milk banks was halted at the time of the AIDS epidemic, and they have only recently gained popularity again, so at present most extremely preterm infants in those countries will receive special preterm infant formula.

Despite all the evidence that shows that the risks associated with formula feeding are restricted to low-income countries, the WHO determined that the same rules should apply around the world. They most likely suspected that if women in high-income countries had continued bottle-feeding, it would have been more difficult to argue that women in low-income countries should breastfeed.

Since then, every imaginable benefit has been claimed for breastfeeding, from reducing the risk that children will be overweight to making them smarter and keeping their blood pressure down. When we scrutinise the scientific evidence behind such claims, we see that the differences between breastfed and bottle-fed children in most studies are so small that they are entirely meaningless to the individual. It's impossible to tell whether the minor differences that have been identified depend on the source of infant nutrition. (We've discussed the problems with drawing conclusions from observational studies in chapter 2.) Repeated studies have shown that bottle-feeding mothers, on average, smoke more, have more of a tendency to be overweight, and are less educated than breastfeeding mothers. It's likely that mothers with higher education levels will tend to be more diligent in following the feeding practices, as well as other health advice, promoted by the authorities.

When breastfeeding and bottle-feeding mothers differ in so many respects, there will be many other possible (and often more plausible) explanations for their children developing differently than their choice of infant nutrition. For example, if bottle-feeding mothers, who on average weigh more than breastfeeding mothers, have babies who are also a little heavier, this needn't necessarily occur because of the bottle. Several studies have shown a difference in IQ between breast-fed and formula-fed children; but when the mother's IQ is taken into account by the use of appropriate statistical methods, most of the differences disappear.

Breastfeeding has also incorrectly been ascribed certain magical effects, such as 'strengthening a baby's immune system'. This is simply not true. Breast milk contains antibodies that protect the baby against infections for as long as the breastfeeding continues, but it doesn't make their own immune system any better trained — in fact, quite the reverse. (You can read more about the baby's immune system, and why it needs training, in chapter 9.) The claim that breastfeeding protects against allergies is false, and always has been.

In summary, the health impacts of breastfeeding for full-term babies are minimal and insignificant in circumstances where clean water and high-quality formula supplies are reliable. If you live under these fortunate conditions, choose the feeding method that suits you, your family, and your child. On the other hand, if you can foresee a situation where you won't have access to or can't afford clean water and/or sufficient amounts of high-quality baby formula, it may be a very wise decision to breastfeed. If your child is born extremely preterm, there are also benefits associated with breast milk nutrition, so it would be advisable to try to start breast milk production at the neonatal ward.

A BABY'S HUNGER SIGNALS AND FEEDING REFLEXES

Healthy, full-term babies are able to show that they're hungry from the day they are born. When hungry, a baby will open its mouth and move its head backwards and forwards like a baby bird searching for food; it almost 'pecks' its mother's body with its head. If a baby doesn't get fed, it might place a hand in its mouth and start sucking. And finally, if no one gets the message, it will start bawling! It's well worth getting to know your baby's hunger signals, because it's much easier to give food to a baby who is happy and peckish than to a shrieking ball of anger.

Newborn, full-term babies have three reflexes that help them to drink milk: they open their mouths if you touch the corner of their mouths, they suckle if they feel something pressing against the roof of their mouths, and they swallow when they get liquid in their mouths. A baby that has had enough to eat is happy, calm, and often falls asleep with the breast or the bottle in its mouth. A baby who is hungry may also fall asleep at the breast, but not as happily, and will soon wake again, crying. Ask the maternal and child-health centre for advice if you are having trouble keeping your baby content — your baby might be hungry.

BREASTFEEDING: HOW IT WORKS

Both boys and girls are born with mammary glands. In puberty, girls' mammary glands grow under the influence of the hormone oestrogen, and adipose tissue grows around the glands, creating the shape of the adult female breast. In male puberty, this does not happen, due to low levels of oestrogen, but men or transwomen who are prescribed oestrogen for medical reasons develop breasts of the same type and shape as women's. During pregnancy, the hormone prolactin, formed in the pituitary gland, stimulates the breasts to grow substantially.

Milk is formed by milk-producing cells in the mammary glands. When the baby suckles on the breast, more prolactin is formed as a reflex action; nerve signals go from the breast up to the brain, which controls the hormone secretion from the pituitary gland. Due to this reflex, the more the baby suckles, the more milk is produced.

The baby's sucking on the breast produces a nerve signal that causes the release of the hormone oxytocin, which is also formed in the pituitary gland, but by different cells from those that produce prolactin. The oxytocin causes smooth muscles in the milk ducts to contract (smooth muscles are those that contract and relax without our conscious control), which presses the milk out through tiny holes in the nipple. (Oxytocin is also responsible for contracting the smooth muscles in the uterus when giving birth, and for forcing out a man's semen during ejaculation.)

The milk ejection reflex varies in strength. In some women, the milk comes out like a fountain and the baby just needs to swallow, while others have a weaker reflex. If the reflex doesn't get started, hardly any milk will come out of the breast when the baby suckles. Sometimes it can take several minutes after the baby has started sucking before the reflex kicks in. This delay can be stressful, so if it happens to you, make sure you have peace and calm, and take your time while you wait for the reflex to engage. You'll know when the ejection is working, because the baby will take breaks from sucking on the breast to swallow milk.

Many women report feeling the onset of the ejection reflex in their whole body, and it's reasonable to assume that the release of oxytocin is what they are actually noticing. A significant number also report strong emotions associated with this sensation. Some talk about a wonderful sense of peace and contentment (these women also tend to really enjoy breastfeeding), while others experience strong feelings of anxiety and depression. The latter usually stop breastfeeding quite quickly, which gives them a feeling of liberation.

The condition of experiencing negative emotions associated with the ejection reflex has been given a name: Dysphoric Milk Ejection Reflex (D-MER) — but the scientific literature on this includes only a couple of case reports.[2] Until more research has been conducted into D-MER and any potential treatments, it may be worth acknowledging the symptoms and considering stopping breastfeeding if the unpleasant emotions are intense.

Establishing breastfeeding

If the birth has gone well and mother and baby are both healthy, the midwife will usually place the baby in just a nappy on the mother's bare belly. The newborn baby will often then look up, crawl towards the nipple (which has grown and darkened in colour during pregnancy to make it more visible), and eventually latch on. We're not talking about a little rosebud mouth that gently shapes itself around the nipple — no, the baby clamps on like a piranha! At least, it will if it has a good sucking reflex.

It is important for the baby to take in as large a part of the breast as possible. It should have its mouth full of breast, so the nipple ends up a long way back in the mouth. This causes the baby's sucking reflex to kick in. If the baby has a proper grip, the breast should fill the entire mouth. The mouth should be wide open, and the bottom lip should curl over so you can see its inside. The baby's head should be so close to the breast that the cheek touches, or almost touches, the breast. Don't be afraid that your baby won't get any air when its whole mouth is full of breast; newborn babies breathe through their noses, while at the same time swallowing milk. 'Chin in, nose clear' is a good rule of thumb for getting a baby to latch on correctly.

If your breast doesn't go far enough into your baby's mouth, it will be incredibly painful when your sensitive nipple takes the full force of the sucking. It is the pressure on the breast just behind the nipple that engages the ejection reflex, so nipple sucking will be both painful and inefficient. Some babies open their mouths wide but don't latch onto the breast properly, in which case it can help to squeeze together the front part of the breast and push as much of it as you can into the baby's mouth, and then rub the nipple a little against the roof of the baby's mouth to get the sucking reflex going. If your baby doesn't open its mouth, you can poke your nipple at the corner of the mouth or against the lip; this will cause most babies to open their mouths. When you want to detach your baby from your breast, simply poke a finger into the corner of its mouth. This will let air in and release the grip.

If you intend to breastfeed, make sure you don't leave the maternity ward until you've received help from the midwife with getting the baby to properly latch onto your breast. This is a crucial step in getting the breastfeeding started and feeling comfortable. It often takes a few days of practice, but you'll soon get the hang of making your baby latch onto your breast correctly. When you reach a stage of breastfeeding in positions other than lying on your back in the maternity-ward bed (sitting, lying on your side), remember that the baby should be stomach-to-stomach with you. You might well need cushions or some other support initially, so ask the midwife for help. Some hospitals organise for midwives to visit mothers and babies at home soon after discharge, and private midwives generally provide postnatal care.

Milk

In the first few days, your milk production won't have properly started, and all that is produced is a few drops of straw-coloured, slightly sticky fluid. This is called first milk, or colostrum. It is sometimes claimed that colostrum contains unique substances that are missing from the later mature milk. That's not really the case. Colostrum does contain higher concentrations of antibodies and white blood cells than mature milk. On the other hand, only a couple of teaspoons of colostrum are produced each day, compared with decilitres of milk per day later in the breastfeeding period, so the overall quantity of antibodies that the baby consumes each day is around the same across the whole breastfeeding period. There has been a tradition in some cultures to discard the colostrum, which was thought to look unpleasant. This is quite unnecessary.

Babies are adapted to consume minimal quantities of milk in their first few days, and it's normal for them to lose a little weight after birth. After a couple of days, the milk will begin to flow, and it will feel like your breasts are about to burst. They swell up, not just because of the milk, but also because of the fluid that collects in the tissue under the influence of hormones. Sometimes the breasts can become so hard (and bumpy) that the baby finds it hard to get a grip. In this case, you'll need to squeeze a little of the fluid away to soften up the nipple. Place your fingertips, including your thumb, just behind the nipple. Then press gently but firmly straight in towards the rib cage. You don't want to be pinching the actual nipple. What you're doing is using tiny, tiny movements to push away the surplus fluid from around the nipple. Hold your fingers in place for a minute or so before letting go and giving your baby the breast. You will find pictures and detailed descriptions of this 'Cotterman's hold' or 'flower hold' on specialist breastfeeding websites. Bear in mind that this engorged phase will pass after a few days — this isn't how your 'new breasts' are going to stay.

How often should a baby breastfeed?

The question of how often you should breastfeed has had many different answers over the years. From the 1950s up until the late 1970s, the brochures handed out in maternity wards stated that mothers should try to leave a gap of four hours between each feed. This wasn't exactly easy to achieve, and many mothers felt quite guilty about sneaking in a feed 'between meals'. Things were even worse in the 1940s, when mothers were told that if the baby was picked up from its cot and fed other than at the prescribed times, it would never be punctual and clear-headed.

Today, the pendulum has swung in the other direction, and there is a belief that it is a mother's duty to be in a state of constant readiness, to ensure that the breastfeeding goes well and that the baby gets enough to eat. There is just as little scientific support for this approach as there was for the four-hour rule. In fact, your feeding pattern is something you (and your baby) get to decide. If you're happy for your baby to feed little and often, that's fine. If you want a few hours away from breastfeeding, for example, so you can study, or pop into town without the baby, you can often get your baby used to this later on. Initially, though, you will rarely have more than one or two hours between feeds. Many babies use food to get to sleep, and indeed this is the easiest way to get a young baby to nod off. Babies like sucking, so if you don't want yours to be constantly latched on to your breast, you might want to keep a dummy to hand.

The practical benefit of breastfeeding is that, as long as everything is working properly, it's self-regulating. The breasts produce more milk when they are empty, through the prolactin reflex. If the baby needs more milk for a while, they will suckle more often. After a few days, the milk production will have increased, and you can once again stretch out the interval between feeds.

It is often suggested that all mothers can breastfeed and that no one has too little milk. This is not true. Throughout history, there have always been mothers who have been unable to produce enough milk, and if a baby couldn't be fed by another woman, it would become undernourished or starve to death. In the 1960s and 1970s, babies were weighed regularly, sometimes after each feed, and as soon as they failed to gain weight, the healthcare professionals were quick to recommend the bottle. Nowadays, you might hear the assertion that if the mother simply breastfeeds intensively, as often as she can, more milk will be produced. But this doesn't always work. It is basically true that milk production increases when a baby sucks more, but this may not be enough.

If your baby never gets full and doesn't gain weight, and if intensive breastfeeding for a few days doesn't help, you need to change strategy. Use a bottle as a supplement. Research shows that you can carry on for quite a while with a combination of bottle and breast, and even phase out the bottle later, if milk production increases. A scientific review from 2016 shows that newborns who received breast-milk substitute in their first days on the maternity ward under a feeding plan were slightly more likely to be breastfed at the age of three months than babies who didn't receive formula in the first few days as part of a feeding plan.[3]

There is absolutely no harm in a baby being given a bottle of breast-milk substitute now and then, even if you want to breastfeed. It's also absolutely fine to give the baby a bottle if you want to sleep in one morning or go out in the evening and you don't have any surplus milk to express and store in the freezer. If you want to get back to work quickly, partial bottle-feeding is a possible solution. Another strategy is for the other parent on parental leave to bring the baby to your work at feed time. You can also store a breast pump in a break room at work and pump out a feed there, to maintain a supply of breast milk in a bottle for your baby at home.

If you want to express your breast milk often, an electric pump is a good idea. There are some wonderfully designed models with carry cases — and a cooler section for the milk — that are specifically aimed at working mothers who breastfeed. Another option is to hire a pump from the hospital. They tend to be heavy and unwieldy, but work well.

Women who have masses of milk can pump and sell their milk to a milk bank. Most neonatal units in hospitals have access to a milk bank.

Establishing and maintaining breastfeeding can be hard work, week in and week out, but it shouldn't feel hopeless or totally exhausting. If you feel trapped and deprived of any independence, change your strategy. Taking a couple of hours off from parenting to go out for a coffee, see a film, or do something else you've missed won't harm your baby in the slightest.

If your baby won't breastfeed

If your newborn baby doesn't want to feed as usual, can't manage to suckle at all for five to six hours during the day, or there are much longer gaps than usual between feeds at night, it is important to go to the paediatric emergency department at once. A lack of interest in feeding may, of course, be due to a random bout of tiredness that passes before you get to hospital, but it could also be the first sign of a serious illness, such as blood poisoning or meningitis, that needs to be treated quickly.

The best way to check that your baby is getting enough food is to keep an eye on their nappies. A baby should fill its nappy with urine several times a day. If the nappies start to be dry, the baby has probably drunk too little. In this case, top up with breast or bottle, and if this doesn't help and your baby starts to seem tired, go to the hospital or contact your paediatrician for a check-up. You should also go to the hospital if your baby starts to show signs of really struggling to suckle, is breathing heavily, or is sweating when feeding. The baby may just have a cold, but these are also symptoms of heart failure in babies that are just a few weeks old. Heart failure in newborns is rare, but feeding problems due to a cold are one of the most common reasons for newborns to require medical assistance.

Sore nipples and mastitis

Learning how to breastfeed takes a little time, but once you get the hang of it, breastfeeding is generally practical and simple. It can be quite painful to start with, because the baby really latches on in a way that is difficult to imagine. The pain usually passes after a week or so, once both mother and baby have mastered the technique. Two problems that can plague many breastfeeding mothers are sore nipples and mastitis.

At this point, let us remind you how important it is for the baby to take a large enough mouthful of the breast. If this doesn't occur, the wear and tear on the nipple will create a major risk of soreness and cracking. These sores can be incredibly painful. If you have damaged nipples, show your nurse at the maternal and child-health centre. If your nipple doesn't heal, or it continues to be very painful for longer than a day or so, contact a breastfeeding clinic — there will usually be such a clinic at the hospital where you gave birth. Specialist knowledge and, sometimes, antibiotic treatment may be required. Don't wait too long.

It's a good idea to place something in your bra so a sore nipple doesn't catch in the bra fabric. The last thing you want is for the wound to be reopened when you take your bra off. There are special 'breast shells', also called 'nipple shields', that you can buy at the pharmacy, but regular shells you've found on the beach would probably work just as well as long as they are thoroughly cleaned. Nipple-protection cups made of silver are a more expensive alternative. Whether the silver has any special effects has not been studied. The leaves of a white cabbage are a budget alternative that will also do a good job of protecting your nipples.

Mastitis is an inflammation of the breast caused by a blockage in a milk duct that affects many women at some point during their breastfeeding period. It is painful and often accompanied by fever. The key is to try and get the milk to be discharged from the clogged part of the breast, which can be easier said than done. You need to continue breastfeeding, and, when you breastfeed, stroke the breast firmly, but gently, from the site of the mastitis out towards the nipple to encourage the milk to be expressed. No hard massaging! Take ibuprofen or paracetamol for the pain. Mastitis is an illness, so sign yourself off from all housework and all other work with your baby. Get the person helping you (the other parent, or perhaps your own parent or a friend) to look after the baby and bring it to you to feed. If you find it easy to express milk with a breast pump, that can be a good supplement, but, if you don't find it easy, frustrating hours on the breast pump are not going to help – quite the reverse.

If you're not better in two days, you need to seek medical assistance. Sometimes mastitis develops into an abscess in the breast that has to be emptied surgically. Antibiotics may also be required.

Preventing mastitis

Ask any mother or grandmother how you prevent mastitis, and you're likely to get the same answer: don't sit in drafts, and avoid getting your breasts cold! However, no one has scientifically proven these methods of prevention. Considering how painful and common mastitis is, you might expect there to be plenty of scientific articles examining this condition and how to prevent it, but a review from 2010 found no more than five articles reviewing sound studies in this area.[4] Three studied antibiotics, which did not prove their effectiveness for treating mastitis, because the studies were not good enough; one was about breastfeeding education, which was found not to help; and one related to SPC-Flakes. SPC-Flakes are a type of processed oat flakes that can be eaten like breakfast cereal, with milk or yoghurt. They stimulate the body's own production of anti-secretory factor, a protein that is naturally present in the body and may have anti-inflammatory effects. A published study of 28 women showed a reduction in the risk of mastitis in those who ate SPC-Flakes.[5] This was just a small study, but until a larger one is conducted, you can always seek out SPC-Flakes if you want to avoid mastitis.

What can I eat and drink while breastfeeding?

You can eat and drink whatever you want while breastfeeding, with the exception of certain medicines that can transfer to the breast milk and harm the baby. Note that these medicines may be entirely different from those that pass into the placenta, and can damage a baby during pregnancy.

Many GPs are not entirely well educated about drugs and breastfeeding, which may result in them either recommending risky treatments, or, probably more commonly, being unnecessarily cautious. In the UK, the Breastfeeding Network provides reliable information on drugs and breastfeeding, both on their website and by phone. In Australia, you can call the NPS medicines information line in your state. You can also ask your GP to use the internet resource LactMed, which is a database directed towards professionals with scientific-level information on drugs and breastfeeding.

Alcohol moves freely back and forth between your blood and your breast milk when you're breastfeeding. This is because alcohol is soluble in both water (blood and breast milk) and fat. As the cell membrane that surrounds each cell in the body is made out of fat molecules, alcohol passes freely into and out of cells. When you have alcohol in your blood, you will also have the same concentration of alcohol in the neurons of your brain, your liver cells, kidney cells, and all the other cells in your body. Anyone who has ever been drunk can testify that alcohol also passes from the blood into the brain (and back again), even though our blood–brain barrier keeps most other things out. Alcohol also passes between blood and breast milk, across the cells in the mammary gland. The free movement of alcohol means that breast milk will always contain the same concentration of alcohol as the blood. If you weigh 60 kilograms and quickly drink two glasses of wine, you'll have around 0.05 per cent alcohol in your blood (50 milligrams per 100 millilitres). Your breast milk will then also contain 0.05 per cent alcohol, which is 40 times less than the alcohol concentration in low-alcohol beer (2.1 per cent). Such a minimal alcohol level is not going to harm your baby. In fact, many natural foods — including yoghurt, fruit, juices, and other products containing alcohol-forming yeasts — have such minimal levels of alcohol.

Alcohol can't build up in the milk; when the alcohol level in the blood drops, so does the level in the milk, until no traces are left. It used to be that women were scared into pumping out and discarding their milk if they had drunk alcohol, which is completely unnecessary.

When discussing alcohol and breastfeeding, the question always crops up about where the limit lies for how affected by alcohol you can be and still be able to take proper care of a baby. This has nothing to do with breastfeeding. Anyone who has responsibility for a baby should be in full possession of their faculties and able to anticipate and react to any dangers around the baby, comfort them if they wake, and exercise plenty of patience. It doesn't matter whether that person is breastfeeding or not. If the breastfeeding parent has gone out and got drunk with friends while the other parent or a babysitter has looked after the baby, she can breastfeed when she comes home if she wants to, or express milk and let the sober partner feed the baby with a bottle.

It is, however, important that a drunk parent doesn't sleep in the same bed as a baby. Researchers have identified a sharply increased risk of sudden infant death syndrome (SIDS) when a young infant co-sleeps with an adult who is under the influence of alcohol. (See chapter 7 on sleep.)

For a while, breastfeeding women were advised to avoid food that babies could be allergic to, such as peanuts, or foods that tended to cause rashes, like strawberries. This advice has been proven to be incorrect and is no longer official. According to our current scientific understanding, there are no particular foods that you need to avoid when breastfeeding. However, advice is like space debris: once it is out there, it is impossible to take back; it will always continue circling around somewhere. If you have a baby who cries, you'll be given all sorts of tips on avoiding one thing or another. You'll be told that a baby will react if its mother has eaten anything spicy, or it will get a stomach ache if she has eaten beans or onion. No one has studied the issue scientifically, but we suggest that it is not a particularly good idea to start avoiding certain foods in the vague belief that your food is the reason why your baby cries or seems to have a stomach-ache. Unfortunately, crying is something babies do, even if there's nothing wrong with them. (See chapter 8 on colic.) If you try to maintain different diets while at the same time dealing with a crying baby, you might soon find yourself at the end of your tether.

In most cases, it's hard to tell why babies cry, but sometimes it might be due to a food allergy. If that's what you're concerned about, the best approach is to get a doctor to check your baby for allergies, rather than messing with your own diet. The most common allergy in babies is an allergy to cow's milk, followed by an egg allergy. There are enough dietary proteins in the environment and in breast milk for a baby to develop an allergy even when entirely breastfed. In the case of the above allergies, it may be worth cutting cow's milk protein or egg from your diet as well, but this should be done in consultation with a doctor, and not just something you do yourself. Bear in mind, as well, that, typically, an allergic baby will not only cry, but will also have eczema or diarrhoea. (You can read more on allergies in chapter 11.)

BABY FORMULA

As mentioned above, there have always been women who have not produced enough milk to feed their babies. If there wasn't someone else to take on the breastfeeding, a baby would starve.

At around the turn of the 20th century, the Swedish association Mjölkdroppen (Drop of Milk) was formed in order to offer a clean and safe substitute for mothers who were unable to breastfeed due to a lack of milk, or because they worked and were away from their baby for any reason. The substitute was ordinary cow's milk diluted with water, but it was clean and carefully screened, and many babies survived because of it.

By the 1950s, there had been enough research into the composition of breast milk to establish that diluted cow's milk is not optimal for newborn human babies. It contains more protein than human milk and has a slightly different salt profile. The food industry learned to add and remove substances from cow's milk to create a formula that was quite similar to human milk, known as 'humanised' cow's-milk-based breast-milk substitute.

Breast-milk substitute became so popular in the rich world that it largely displaced breastfeeding, which was seen as rather coarse, old-fashioned, and primitive. All this happened with the blessing of the paediatric health services; it was considered that since there were such excellent products available, breastfeeding could be consigned to the past.

The WHO code promoting breastfeeding, discussed earlier, heavily regulated how breast-milk substitutes could be marketed. This promotion was most effective, and breastfeeding gained popularity in many countries during the 1980s and 1990s. Also, the use of the term 'humanised' to describe breast-milk substitutes has been banned in order to stop anyone believing that they are like human breast milk, no matter how much they have been adapted for the specific purpose. Strange, but true.

Bottle-feeding

If you know from the outset that you only want to bottle-feed your newborn, take bottles and a few teats of different shapes in the smaller sizes to the maternity ward. Make sure it is stated in your pregnancy journal and your birth plan that you want to bottle-feed and not try breastfeeding. Some maternity wards can provide baby formula for you while you're there, and will also have bottles that you can borrow if you don't have your own, but it's best to check this in advance.

Bottle-fed babies need just as much close contact with their parents as breastfed babies. The early skin-to-skin contact is comforting, and the parents can take turns. Make sure you have a bottle of warm formula available when your baby starts to display hunger signals.

A bottle-feeding mother who has just given birth will experience the same changes in her breasts as a mother who breastfeeds: they swell and leak milk. However, the milk production will stop, and the milk in the mammary glands will be broken down into its constituent parts and returned to the bloodstream after a few days. The best way to pass through this stage as quickly as possible is to wear a tight sports bra and never let the baby suckle. You generally won't get mastitis during the first week after birth, which may happen if you were to stop breastfeeding suddenly at a later stage. It can, however, be seriously painful, and NSAID-type painkillers (ibuprofen, diclofenac, or naproxen) may help. There are also special prescription medicines to stop milk production, but they rarely act any more quickly than a tight sports bra and some ibuprofen.

How much formula?

In the very first days, you can give small portions of formula, as babies' stomachs are still small, and their intestines are not used to receiving much food. For most babies, 10–15 millitres is usually enough for these first portions. But if your baby wants more, feed it until it has had enough. Over those first few days you can then work up to full portions, maybe around 60–80 millitres for an average-sized baby who feeds eight times a day. The portions will then continue to increase as the baby grows.

Most babies lose a little weight during the first week, but bottle-fed babies with a good appetite sometimes don't drop very much at all. As a rule of thumb, a baby should be back to its birth weight by the age of ten days. After that, the nurse at the child health clinic will help you to check that your baby is growing properly by weighing and measuring it regularly and plotting a growth chart.

If the feeding is problematic, try changing the teat or the size of the teat hole. Some babies like milk that runs a little faster; others like it slower. Again, the important thing is not the size of the milk portions, but that the baby feeds until full. This ensures good growth.

Preparing formula

There are all sorts of different breast-milk substitutes on the market. The important thing is to choose one you know is approved for sale, and to mix the right amount of powder and water according to the recommendations on the packaging. The complicated instructions on the packaging about boiling the water and then cooling it down are unnecessary, as there are no bacteria to be worried about in places where you are connected to a clean and reliable source of mains water. If you live in the countryside and use bore or tank water, it is a good idea to have the water analysed before you use it for your baby's milk by sending a sample to a water laboratory.

The simplest preparation method (when the water is safe) is to mix boiling water from the kettle with cold water to reach the desired lukewarm temperature (put your finger in the water to check!), and to shake the powder and water in the bottle. Alternatively, you can use a microwave to warm the water in the bottle, then tip in the powder and shake. The temperature is right when you drip a few drops of the prepared milk on the back of your hand and it feels warm but does not hurt. There is nothing to suggest that heating plastic bottles in the microwave is harmful. (If you have heard otherwise, read more about the fear of chemicals and what lies behind it in chapter 12.)

It is not necessary to sterilise baby bottles; regular washing is enough. Any bacteria will die off when the bottles are left to air dry between uses. If you really want to, you can boil the bottle now and then, or sterilise it in water in the microwave. This is not necessary, but it doesn't hurt either. Babies can't ingest any harmful bacteria through their bottle in countries where there are no cholera bacteria or salmonella in the drinking water. However, when a baby drinks from a bottle, their own oral bacteria mix with the milk, and if the bottle is left to stand for several hours, the bacteria will grow, and the formula will smell and taste awful, much the same as when milk goes bad in the fridge. If you're going to travel with your baby to somewhere that doesn't have clean water, you can either boil the water, or pack a supply of ready-to-use infant formula that is guaranteed to be clean. There is also good reason to boil the baby bottles in this situation.

What type of formula should I use?

We suggest starting with the market's cheapest standard formula for newborn babies. Each brand usually has several alternative products suitable for babies of different ages. They are often numbered 1, 2, and 3. You should probably start with no. 1, which is intended for newborn babies, although the differences are so small that you could actually use no. 2 for a newborn baby. Similarly, you can use no. 1 for longer than the baby food manufacturers state, avoiding the need to throw away powder just because your baby has turned six months old.

There are many varieties that are marketed for their health benefits, but these supposed benefits are not supported by reliable evidence. Just because some products are more expensive, there is no good reason for you to buy them (but every reason for the company to sell them, of course). It works out cheapest to buy large tins of powder, but ready-mixed baby formula is very practical. Many babies even accept room temperature formula from cartons, and that's about as easy as bottle-feeding gets! If you're a little more careful with money, a milk powder dispenser can be a smart purchase. You can measure out enough powder for a bottle and place it in the pots, ready to mix with the right amount of water — in the middle of the night, or when you are away from home. For babies with an allergy to proteins in cow's milk (cow's milk allergy), there are special formulas in which these proteins have been broken down enzymatically. (The products will be labelled as containing hydrolysed whey.) If your baby is thriving on standard formula, there is no reason to switch to the more expensive hydrolysed whey products. If your baby cries a lot or has explosive diarrhoea, blood in its poo, or eczema that doesn't respond to treatment, you should look into the possibility of a cow's milk allergy. Bring it up at your maternal and child-health centre to get advice about investigating this further.

CUP OR BOTTLE?

This is a myth that has plagued mothers and babies, and no doubt quite a few fathers as well. It is called 'nipple confusion'. There is a view that a person who breastfeeds her baby, but occasionally wants to give formula, or expressed milk, to supplement her breast milk supply or when breastfeeding is not feasible for some reason, mustn't do so using a bottle, because the baby would not be able to understand the difference between the nipple and the teat. According to this theory, an infant may prefer a teat that has a more rapid flow of milk, and reject the nipple, and this would ruin further breastfeeding. Instead of a bottle, parents are encouraged to give the substitute milk with a spoon or cup — an ordinary cup, not a sippy cup.

The idea of using a cup to feed babies was originally developed to feed babies with a cleft lip or palate, or other facial deformities, and has since become popular in countries with low standards of hygiene, as it is easier to clean a cup by washing and drying than it is to keep bottles clean. Then the idea emerged that using these cups would help breastfeeding mothers. Many paediatric nurses and parents who have tried using a cup find that it is very difficult to get babies to lap milk up like kittens, and attempts at cup feeding often lead to wet clothes, unhappy babies, and parents who feel like a failure.

The Cochrane Institute, an independent organisation for the promotion of evidence-based medicine, has reviewed studies that compare the effects of cup feeding and bottle-feeding on breastfeeding. While there were no studies on full-term babies, the institute found five studies on premature babies.[6] Of those five, four found no better effect from the cup, whereas a Turkish study stated that cup-fed babies were breastfed a little more when discharged from hospital, and at the age of six months. However, the Cochrane Institute had certain reservations about the reliability of this study. No study had investigated what parents or staff thought about the feeding method.

Forget the cup! Use the practical baby bottle or, if you are trying to build up your breast milk supply, you might prefer to use a supplemental nursing system, where a thin silicone feeding tube is connected to a bottle and then taped to the breast, so the baby gets formula through it when it sucks on the mother's breast. This way, the baby has both the nipple and the end of the tube in its mouth, so the breast is stimulated to produce more milk through the baby's sucking, while the baby fills up on the formula coming through the tube.

USE A DUMMY IF YOU AND THE BABY WANT TO

Even the good old dummy was banned by the WHO in their promotion of exclusive breastfeeding. This was due to a belief that a baby with a dummy would get tired from sucking and then not have the energy to feed from the breast. Yet there is no evidence for this theory. On the contrary, existing studies show that the use of a dummy makes no difference in breastfeeding for full-term babies.[7] Among premature babies who are tube-fed because they are too weak to feed themselves, experience shows that those who have a dummy to suck on between and during feeds actually become better at sucking, so the tube feeding can be stopped earlier.

In addition, one study (conducted by Agnes's research team in Gothenburg) shows that the risk of a baby developing eczema or asthma at 18 months decreases if you also suck on the dummy yourself now and then (for example, to clean it after it's been dropped on the floor), compared with rinsing the dummy in water when it gets dirty.[8]

With premature babies who are in the care of the neonatal unit, it may not be entirely safe for you to suck on your baby's dummy and share your mouth bacteria. These babies have an underdeveloped immune system, and are at risk of necrotising enterocolitis (dangerous inflammation of the intestine). It is possible that parents sucking on their baby's dummy could affect this risk, so avoid doing this for the time being, unless you have first discussed it with your baby's doctor.

AVOID BUYING BREAST MILK PRIVATELY ONLINE

The old practice of sharing breast milk has begun to make something of a comeback in recent years. Of course, you can agree to let a friend breastfeed your baby if you trust them and are sure they don't have any infectious diseases, but never order a stranger's surplus breast milk off the internet. For one thing, although it's quite unlikely, that person could have HIV, which is transmitted through breast milk. What is more likely is that the breast milk will contain a few too many bacteria. Hospitals' milk banks perform a bacterium check on all the milk that is donated for premature babies, and it is heated up (pasteurised) to kill harmful micro-organisms. If you don't have milk of your own, it's better to give your baby formula.

IN BRIEF

There are two methods of feeding a baby: by breast or bottle. Breastfeeding provides major benefits in countries with poor water hygiene, but in countries with good water sanitation, baby formula and breast milk are essentially equal in terms of their health benefits. The choice of whether to give breast or bottle, or to combine the two, is up to the parents and, to some extent, the baby. It is no one else's business. If people take it upon themselves to give you unsolicited advice and warnings about how you choose to feed your baby, you may politely ignore them.

CHAPTER SIX

Moving on to solids

Although it may be hard to imagine at the outset, your baby won't always be brought up on milk. Advice about when to begin with other foods, and what those foods should be, varies greatly around the world. In Sweden, advice on feeding is given out with strong conviction, while at the same time the details have varied radically over time. Is salt terribly dangerous? And why can't babies eat leafy green vegetables? Do you dare make the food yourself? Are jars of baby food a bad idea? In this chapter, you will find out when you should begin feeding your baby foods other than milk, what you can do to make the transition to solids as smooth as possible, and whether there are any foods you should avoid giving to your baby.

Starting to feed your baby solids is really your way of introducing them to your own food culture. It may be messy and slow going to start with, but that's the idea. Therefore, it is worth thinking about your own food choices first. As a new parent, you will generally be more than fully occupied with trying to meet your baby's needs. You can easily find yourself not remembering, or not having the time, energy, or desire to feed yourself. The early period, when you are caring for your baby, can be particularly risky if you have a history of dieting or eating disorders.

It is, to some extent, only natural that your own needs will be put to one side, since your baby is reliant on you for everything. But at the same time, it is important that you create space for your own basic needs.

Let us say this loud and clear: you need to eat proper meals — breakfast, lunch, and dinner — at regular times. In the popular Swedish Bamse cartoons, Skalman, the ingenious tortoise, has an 'eat-and-sleep' alarm to tell him when to do both those things.

Here's Skalman with his eat-and-sleep alarm!

A sleep clock may not be an option with a newborn baby at home, but a food clock is a very good idea. Many women who breastfeed get extremely hungry and can't go longer than a couple of hours without food. If you're the type of person who goes on long, long walks with a pram, or attends fitness sessions for mothers at the gym several times a week, you're also going to need a lot of food. If you bottle-feed and are less active, you'll need around the same amount of food as usual, but it can still be difficult to find the time to both prepare and eat a meal. If you have any spare time while pregnant, it's a good idea to cook some meals or buy ready-made meals to store on the shelf or in the freezer so there's always a meal ready in the early weeks.

The vast majority of women will weigh more after giving birth than before their pregnancy. This weight gain is entirely normal and is probably nature's way of making sure you have enough reserves to feed your baby. Women's bodies differ considerably on this score. Some will find the extra weight falling off during breastfeeding, while others will hold onto every last gram of pregnancy fat, whether they breastfeed or not.

The first months with a newborn baby is so demanding that dieting is not recommended. Think 'nine months up, nine months down'. Eat regularly. Get out of the house every day. After nine months, you can think about whether you want to weigh yourself, and if you weigh much more than is recommended for your height, you can consider starting to work on that.

INTRODUCING SOLIDS; THE NUTRITIONAL ASPECT

Now, let's look at the baby's food. There are two important considerations when it comes to feeding a baby: nutrition and allergies. We'll begin with the aspect of nutrition.

Breast milk has naturally evolved to meet a baby's basic nutritional needs during the initial period after birth. But for how long is breast milk alone sufficient for a baby's needs? Up until the mid-1980s, whether a baby was breastfeeding or bottle-feeding, the advice was that they should be given fruit juices from eight weeks to guard against the risk of developing a vitamin C deficiency. Three to four months was considered the right time to introduce proper food, including fish, meat, and vegetables. Since breast milk is low in iron, a delay of six months in the introduction of solids was discouraged, based on the increased risk of iron deficiency.

What then happened was that the WHO advocated extending the time that babies should be exclusively breastfed to the age of six months. The WHO recommendation was part of a drive to reduce the risk of infections caused by unclean water and contaminated food in many countries, as described in chapter 5.

However, there were some paediatricians who feared that the new feeding pattern of prolonged exclusive breastfeeding would mean that certain infants would not get enough iron. A compilation of the available independent scientific studies was undertaken.[1] This evidence suggested that six months of exclusive breastfeeding was likely to be safe, provided both mother and baby had a good nutritional status beforehand, but that it was important to monitor the risk of iron deficiency. The reviewers also pointed out that there weren't enough large-scale studies to entirely rule out the possibility that longer exclusive breastfeeding could lead to nutritional deficiencies.

It has not been proven that six months of exclusive breastfeeding is any better from a nutritional point of view than four months, even though this is the impression you might easily get from reading some authorities' brochures and websites. What the researchers were in fact looking for was evidence that six months of exclusive breastfeeding was worse, and they didn't find any. Subsequent systematic reviews on the subject show more or less the same results: the majority of babies will most likely be fine on six months of exclusive breastfeeding, but with a tendency towards a risk of iron deficiency. Babies who receive solid food from four months of age have slightly better iron levels.[2]

Babies carry reserves of iron from their time in the womb, which is often enough to last them for the first six months. In most cases, breast milk (or formula) is quite good at meeting nutritional needs up to this age. (The one exception is vitamin D, which needs to be given as drops.) However, if a baby is exclusively breastfed for longer than six months, there is a risk of stunted growth and of iron deficiency. At 8–10 months, there is a significant risk of iron deficiency in babies who have not been fed an iron-rich diet. From a nutritional point of view, therefore, you should introduce solid food, preferably rich in iron, such as red meat, at least by the time your baby is around six months old. The problem doesn't arise with bottle-fed babies, because milk formula, and baby cereal porridges are normally enriched with iron.

INTRODUCING SOLIDS: THE RISK OF ALLERGIES

We have covered the nutritional aspect, but there is an equally important consideration when it comes to introducing foods other than milk.
This is the question of when it is best to introduce regular food in
terms of the risk of food allergies. In Sweden and other rich and very
clean countries, the risk of water- and food-borne infections is minimal.
Instead, allergies and similar conditions caused by an overactive immune
system are very frequent — so frequent, in fact, that we dedicate the
whole of chapter 11 to allergies.

It is common for young babies to have a food allergy. There is
uncertainty about exactly how many are affected, but 5–10 per cent of
Swedish babies would be expected to develop some form of food allergy,
and similar figures apply for the UK and Australia. The most common
are allergies to milk, eggs, and nuts. It is, of course, crucial for parents to
know whether it makes any difference to the risk of their baby developing an allergy to eggs, for example, if egg is introduced at one, three, six,
or 12 months.

For quite a long time, parents have been recommended to postpone
the introduction of foods such as eggs, fish, and nuts, in the belief that
this would reduce the risk of their baby developing allergies to these
foods, particularly if there is a history of allergy in the family. The latest
research results, however, suggest that the opposite is true: delayed introduction of foods *increases* the risk of food allergies. Two scientific studies
of the best kind (randomised controlled trials) provide recent evidence
on this subject. In one study, 640 children at high risk of developing a
peanut allergy were randomly assigned to either eat peanut snacks at
least three times a week or to have no peanuts at all until the age of five.[3]
The infants in the study were between four and 11 months old, and had
either severe eczema or an egg allergy, or both, at the start of the study.
In addition, some of them had already developed Immunoglobulin
E (IgE) antibodies against peanuts, which can be a prelude to peanut
allergy. At five years old, the children were tested with double-blind

provocation, which produces a very reliable, objective result. They were given either a small meal containing peanuts, or a meal that looked and tasted the same without peanuts. On each occasion, any symptoms were recorded without anyone (not the doctor, the child, or the parents) knowing whether the child had eaten peanuts or not.

It was shown that consuming peanuts early on dramatically reduced the risk of developing a peanut allergy in the child's first five years. Of those who had no IgE antibodies against peanuts at the start, 0.3 per cent of the peanut eaters developed a peanut allergy, compared with 17 per cent in the peanut-avoidance group. That result represents a 98 per cent decrease in the risk of developing an allergy by eating peanuts from an early age! In the group that had already formed IgE antibodies against peanuts, but had not developed an allergy, the peanut diet cut the allergy risk by 70 per cent. The study clearly shows that you should not delay the introduction of food in the belief that it reduces the risk of allergies.

Another randomised study looked at two groups of healthy babies who had been exclusively breastfed until three months. One group was started on solid food that contained small amounts of peanuts, eggs, cow's milk, sesame seeds, white fish, and wheat. The other group continued to be exclusively breastfed until six months, and were then weaned in the usual way.[4] The families who were introducing their babies to solids were asked to include at least 2 grams of each of the six foods in their baby's meal at least twice a week. But only half of the families who were asked to do this succeeded in this endeavour. The children in these families developed 60 per cent fewer food allergies than the children in the exclusively breastfed group. None of the children who consumed the amount of peanuts prescribed in the instructions developed a peanut allergy, and among those who ate the required amount of egg, the risk of an egg allergy fell by 82 per cent compared with the group of exclusively breastfed babies.

All the infants who were subject to the early introduction of food, whether or not they were given the food in sufficient amounts, were found overall to have a 20 per cent lower risk of food allergies when compared with the exclusively breastfed group. This reduction in risk was not statistically significant, and so we cannot be entirely certain that it really was the early introduction of the foods that protected against allergies. There may be some other factor that distinguishes the families who gave sufficient amounts of the foods to their baby and those who didn't manage to do so. Nevertheless, it is certainly the case that no harm came to the babies who were given solid food from three months.

These two studies suggest that the immune system needs to encounter different foreign proteins via food quite early on in order to develop a tolerance for them. No randomised controlled trials exist that counter this evidence and show that it is better to delay the introduction of particular foods from an allergy point of view.

In every age and in every culture, babies have had all sorts of things put into their mouths right from birth. The following graph is from a study of Pakistani babies who were born in the slums of Lahore in the 1980s.[5] All of the babies were breastfed, but when researchers looked a little more closely at what they were given alongside the breast milk, the variety was striking. Early foods included honey during their first few days, milk (undiluted) from cows and buffalo, regular water (not very clean), and a sort of herb-infused water that stood on a sideboard and fermented for many years, and that the grandmother dripped into the baby's mouth. (In Turkey and Greece, babies are given tea and yoghurt and honey early on, and Eastern European babies have traditionally also been given tea in their first few days.)

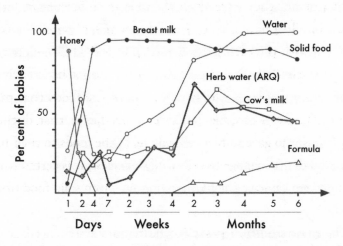

Babies born in the slums of Lahore, Pakistan, in the 1980s received many different things in addition to breast milk from an early age. Source: Adlerberth, I., et al., *High turnover rate of Escherichia coli strains in the intestinal flora of infants in Pakistan. Epidemiol. Infect.* 1998. 121(3): 587–98.

We consider that the practice of giving babies breast milk exclusively for their first six months is likely to be a sidebar in history, with studies showing a steep increase in the risk of allergy from this type of feeding probably helping to bring its time to an end. There is no lower limit for when a baby can begin tasting food. If you want to give your baby tepid tea on the maternity ward because that's what you do in your family, or let your two-week-old baby taste mashed raspberries, you won't be doing any harm; you'll simply be feeding your baby the way humans have always done throughout history. For millennia, mothers may well have been giving their babies little portions of food that they had already chewed themselves, not unlike birds who regurgitate food for their chicks in the nest.

LISTS OF FORBIDDEN FOODS

The official Swedish recommendations on food for young children contain quite a few forbidden foods such as salt, leafy greens, and honey.

The ban on salt is particularly problematic, because it means you either need to buy lots of expensive pots of baby food containing sterilised purée, or make your own salt-free food, which is terribly time-consuming. Extra work is hardly what you need as the parent of a new baby. Just like adults, children who have learned to talk tend to say that food without any salt is horrible. What babies think is anyone's guess, but a suspiciously large number will spit out their first taste of unsalted parsnip purée! Let's have a look at which advice you can afford to ignore, and which advice is worth taking seriously.

Salt — a necessity, even for babies

In Sweden, and in many other countries, parents are advised that babies should consume salt-free food in their first year, and that after the age of one, tiny amounts of salt, gradually increasing, are acceptable. But this is unnecessary advice. With the exception of the very first weeks, babies can handle moderate amounts of salt.

It is often claimed that a baby's kidneys are totally unable to handle salt, and that it is dangerous to give them even the tiniest amount of salt in their food. Scare stories circulate online that babies under the age of one are possibly at risk of kidney failure if you give them the food that the rest of the family eats. The website of Britain's National Health Service (NHS.uk) insists that a parent (usually the mother!) must prepare special salt-free food specifically for her baby.

The kidney function of a baby is, to say the least, a complex subject, and it is clearly difficult for a parent to question so-called authorities who state that infant kidneys are not mature enough to handle salt. Let us try to explain the kidney function of babies with a focus on salt balance.

In its mother's womb, a foetus doesn't need to be able to regulate the balance of salt itself — the placenta takes care of all that. When a baby is born, the kidneys have to take on responsibility for cleaning the blood and balancing out salt and fluid levels in the body. This is done by first filtering the blood through the kidney's network of capillaries (glomeruli), where a large amount of what is known as primary urine is formed. If the baby was to wee out all this urine, it would become dehydrated in no time, but fortunately the vast majority of the water, various salts, and many other substances are sucked back into the renal tubules, which are long, winding pathways within the second part of the kidney. The renal tubules in premature babies have a fairly low capacity to absorb the salt from the urine and reintroduce it into the blood. Premature babies therefore often need extra salt solution in their food to maintain a normal salt and fluid balance.[6]

Full-term newborn babies, on the other hand, have difficulty secreting salt in the urine during their first week if they are fed substantial quantities of salt solution. This was shown by Swedish researcher Anita Aperia in her work on infant renal function in the 1970s.[7] The ability to secrete salt gradually improves during a baby's first year,[8] and it develops more quickly if two–to–three-month-old babies are given experimental breast-milk substitute with a higher salt content than if they are given normal formula with a low salt content.[9] The body naturally adjusts, as it so often does.

Before it was known that really small babies are less able than older children and adults to secrete salt, commercial formula was quite salty — sometimes more than cow's milk, which already contains ten times more salt than human milk. Most infants developed perfectly well on this formula, but it could cause problems if they had a stomach upset. A baby who vomits and has diarrhoea loses a lot of fluid and, in the past, if they were fed a relatively salty formula, or skimmed milk powder from cow's milk, many babies would have developed what is known as hypertonic dehydration.[10] This dangerous condition, in which babies have too little water and too much salt in their blood, can be lethal if not treated correctly.

It is certainly true that feeding newborn babies on undiluted cow's milk — or on a 1950s-style cow's milk-based formula — can be dangerous if they have a stomach upset. But this doesn't mean that it's generally harmful for a four-month-old baby to eat pasta boiled in salted water, or for a six-month-old to eat the family's salted mashed potato or Thai curry. The baby will spend many months mostly consuming breast milk, or a modern breast-milk substitute, with the same salt levels as mother's milk, and the quantity of salt the baby consumes from regular food is highly unlikely to reach levels that pose a danger of salt overload.

One argument that Sweden's National Food Agency puts forward for its salt ban is that you shouldn't get children used to overly salty food because the eating habit might stick for the rest of their lives. They recommend that the whole population should eat less salt to reduce the risk of high blood pressure. But, for one thing, there is some debate about how much impact salt in the diet has on the risk of high blood pressure. And for another, it remains to be proven that people could be so affected by the salt levels in the food they ate as a baby that it would influence their diet as an adult.

The ban on salt consumption is a perfect example of authorities attempting to exploit a window of opportunity during pregnancy and an infant's early years for a broader lifestyle change in the name of public health. We suspect that not many people are going to go to the effort of boiling a pan of salt-free rice for their baby in order to (perhaps) reduce the health burden of high blood pressure and cardiovascular disease in the wider population. But if a parent hears that their infant's own kidneys can't handle salt, they're likely to pay attention. The good news is that a baby's kidneys will not be damaged by the small quantities of salt they get from eating the family's food. If you have a family history of high blood pressure and you want to do everything you can to make sure your baby is not affected at some point in the future, you can choose salt-free baby food — although if the genetic element is strong, avoidance of salt as an infant is unlikely to make a difference. For everyone else, it can be good to know that no harm will come to your baby if they share your family's food or if they taste a crisp or a salty olive. One gastronomic tip is that practically all vegetable purées are much tastier with the addition of a little grated parmesan cheese — try it yourself!

Leafy greens

Another quite common recommendation is to avoid leafy green vegetables before the age of one year for the reason that they are rich in nitrates — substances that can be converted into nitrites by bacteria in the baby's intestine. When absorbed into the blood, nitrites can impair the ability of haemoglobin molecules in the red blood cells to absorb oxygen. This condition is called methaemoglobinaemia.

Babies are sensitive to nitrites before they are three to four months old. They have very little hydrochloric acid in their stomachs, and so more bacteria in the intestine are able to convert nitrates into nitrites. They also retain a little of the foetus's haemoglobin variant, known as foetal haemoglobin, which can possibly be converted into methaemoglobin. After four months, the foetal haemoglobin will have been almost entirely replaced by the adult variant.

The highest levels of nitrates are found in rocket, lamb's lettuce (corn salad), Swiss chard, fresh spinach leaves, and rhubarb. Kale, beetroot, kohlrabi, lettuce, Chinese cabbage, celery, and fennel contain quite high levels of nitrates. Beans, frozen spinach, pumpkin, and aubergine contain moderate amounts. Water from domestic boreholes may contain nitrates from fertilisers.[11] In Navarra, Spain, where the groundwater has high nitrate levels, puréed Swiss chard and the herb borage caused a number of cases of methaemoglobinaemia.[12] Saving prepared purée and giving it to the baby the next day increased the risk.

You don't really have to worry about which vegetables your baby eats. Babies are not usually terribly keen on raw salad leaves. If you avoid homemade purées made from nitrate-containing vegetables for children under three to four months, you'll be safe. If your baby does taste your food before that age, it will be very tiny amounts anyway, which cannot cause methaemoglobinaemia.

Honey — a known but small risk of serious nerve disorder

Honey may contain spores of the bacteria *Clostridium botulinum*, which can grow in the baby's intestines and produce a dangerous nerve toxin. The disorder that then arises is called botulism, and it causes constipation, limpness, and, in severe cases, paralysis of the muscles used for breathing. Infant botulism was often deadly in the past, but with modern intensive care and access to an antidote, mortality rates are now low, as long as the doctor makes the correct diagnosis. Infant botulism is very rare, with only five cases since 1969 reported in Sweden, and just one of those cases is understood to have been caused by honey. In the UK, the first case was recognised in 1978, and fewer than ten cases have been reported since then. The US reports around 100 cases per year, and in Australia 20 cases have been reported since 1991, which is a comparatively high rate. In many of these cases, the babies had been given honey on dummies or directly in the mouth.

Interestingly, honey is something parents in various cultures ritually give to newborn babies. It has all sorts of symbolic meanings that have since been lost to our rationalist culture. It would be straightforward for those with access to a bacteriological laboratory to test samples of honey for clostridium. We would be glad to see bacteriologically tested, guaranteed clostridium-free infant honey appear on the market.

Extra fat in baby food

Your growing baby needs a little more fat in its diet than you do. You can add a teaspoon of butter or oil to your baby's food — or a little whipped cream, if you prefer. Once your baby is eating more than just taster portions, the ratio of one-third vegetables, one-third protein, and one-third carbohydrates with extra added fat is a useful guideline.

Peanut butter, hazelnut butter, and almond butter are recommended as good fat sources that are also highly nutritious. Giving them early has the added advantage of reducing the risk to your baby of developing allergies.

ADVICE FOR MORE PLEASANT MEALTIMES

If possible, let your baby join you at the dinner table right from birth. It can sit on your lap or, once it is able to sit up, in its own highchair. You can offer your baby a lick of your food on a finger or with a spoon, as long as the food is properly mashed up.

In the past, when it was deemed vital for babies to be fed solid food from at least four months of age, there were all sorts of prescribed schedules for what should be given when — potato first! Meat and fish next! It is still commonly believed that fruit purées should be brought into the diet very early on. (Back in the 1970s, fruit juices were introduced by the age of two months.) There is no scientific basis for these rules. Since there is no evidence that one thing or another is better to introduce first, the easiest and most enjoyable approach is just to test now and then whether your baby likes what you are eating.

At three to four months, babies can put their hands to their mouths with greater control, and they start to become more interested in the world around them. At this age, many children show an interest in the food that other people are eating, particularly if they get to sit at the table during mealtimes. Encourage this interest. Let your baby taste new foods and get messy. If older siblings want to feed the baby, let them try, as long as the food is properly mashed up and the little one seems happy.

Some babies love solid food right from the start and quickly increase the amount they want, with feeds from the breast or bottle tailing off at a corresponding rate. Other babies are more cautious, and mostly play with their food. Many of these babies also stick to the breast or bottle for longer. As long as a baby is growing well and its nutritional needs are being met, the mix of milk, formula, and food comes down to individual choice.

Some babies like puréed food, and if your baby is one who does, buying jars or pouches of ready-made baby food is a very practical option. These commercial products are nutritionally balanced, and the food is sterilised — no bacteria can grow as long as the jar is unopened — so you can feel free to try serving your baby food from the jar at room temperature. (We should point out, though, that this will probably be the only sterile food that your baby will ever eat.) Other babies don't like puréed food. They prefer to be able to pick up their food and suck on it, or mash it up in their mouth. These babies tend not to eat large amounts until they get teeth, for obvious reasons.

Eating is fun when you get to eat the things you like. Wherever possible, serve foods that both you and your baby enjoy. It is common for babies under one year to be excited by many different tastes. Make the most of this time, because after one or two years, many, if not most, children will limit their repertoire to pasta, rice, meatballs, fish fingers, sweet corn, and maybe ketchup and peas. There's nothing you can do about this fussiness; it's an almost compulsory (but thankfully not everlasting) developmental stage for many children.

If you're lucky enough to have a baby who likes different sorts of food, try to serve up iron-rich food like red meat a few times a week, or every day. If you don't want to serve meat, include lentils or beans in one meal and dried fruit in another, and preferably introduce iron-enriched porridge at four to six months.

Iron deficiency is the most common nutritional deficiency in babies. Symptoms include tiredness and paleness. If your baby is fussy about food and you are concerned about iron deficiency, go to the health centre and have your baby tested. Once identified, iron deficiency is treated with iron drops.

At all costs, try to avoid making food a battle of wills. Many first babies become the star attraction at meal-times. Their starring role begins when they discover that the adults are entirely focused on getting them to eat. Many parents are terrified that their babies won't get enough nourishment. If they're not big eaters, but they love to be sung to and played with, babies soon realise that they can get their parents to play out fantastically amusing scenes at the table if they only eat something now and then. Don't fall for it! These games are ridiculously hard work and also quite ineffective. Let your baby eat what they want most straightforwardly by allowing them to pick up food while you eat. If your baby wants to be fed by you, then feed them. If possible, avoid having too many fixed ideas and principles about what children absolutely must and must not eat. Children have an enormous capacity to sense what things are emotionally charged, and the ability to exploit such situations.

It is not uncommon for young children to refuse food. Babies who don't eat much can create so much anxiety in parents that it leads to force-feeding. Never do that! Forcing your infant to eat very quickly makes an already bad situation worse, and turns meals into an arena for a traumatic power struggle. It is extremely rare for babies to eat nothing at all. They might eat some cereal porridge and milk, and be happy with that. Since cereal porridge (if industrially produced) contains all the nutrients a baby needs, there is no harm in this feeding pattern.

If by eight to nine months your baby still doesn't want to try any solid foods, talk to the nurse at your child-health centre. They have lots of experience in helping parents with babies who are fussy eaters, as it is quite a common problem in many families. They can refer you for more specialist help if their advice doesn't satisfy you.

WEANING OFF THE BREAST OR BOTTLE

During the first six months, breastfeeding or bottle-feeding is generally the baby's primary source of food. Initially, babies have no daily rhythm at all and need to eat at any time, but they gradually develop a daily rhythm in their first few months. By around four months, babies no longer need to feed at night in order to grow. However, many babies — probably most babies — continue night-time feeding out of habit. If you're lucky, you'll have a baby who sleeps for extended periods at night, even at just a few weeks old, and who is perfectly content without food for that time. But this feeding pattern is not something you can expect or demand from a baby. The more common pattern is that they wake up hungry every three hours or so.

You can continue to breastfeed or bottle-feed for as long as you want, and many parents continue with either method as a sleeping aid or comforter for several years. However, be aware that breastfeeding sometimes leads to a situation where only the breastfeeding mother can settle her infant for the night. It's good for parents if both can do the bedtime routine, and it's good for a baby to learn that one parent can breastfeed them to sleep, while the other gives a bottle or cuddles.

A baby who gets much of their daily food in the form of breast milk or formula is going to wake and want to feed at night. If you'd like a better night's sleep, it can be a very good idea to wean your baby off night-time feeds from around six months. If you're bottle-feeding, take it gradually. Let's say your baby has one bottle of formula at 7.00 pm, one at 11.00 pm, one at 3.00 am, and one at 5.00 am; you could take away the 3.00 am feed first and keep the others. Your baby will probably eat a little more during the day to compensate, although you may not notice

154

that. After a few weeks, you can take away the bottle at 5.00 am or 11.00 pm, whichever works best. Sometimes it is easier to give water to aid the transition for a week or so, and then take the water away.

A baby who is breastfed at night will often fail to understand why it can have the breast at 11.00 pm, but not at 3.00 am. In this case, it's more practical to stop breastfeeding at night altogether. Weaning a baby off night-time breastfeeding, if they really like it, is often a bit of a battle. It may be the first big battle of wills in the family. Take up the fight at a time that suits you. There are likely to be a few nights of loud protest before your baby learns that the breast is no longer on offer at night. Sometimes a bottle of formula in the evening can make the process easier because it leaves the baby really full before bed.

It can help if the non-breastfeeding parent puts the baby to bed in a separate room. When breastfeeding mothers choose to continue settling their baby, they can wear a tight top and bra, and avoid offering the breast. If you're a very sensitive breastfeeding mother, and know that you are likely to struggle with guilt during the weaning process, we suggest you go away for a couple of nights.

IN BRIEF

It's good to make food tasty, fun, and enjoyable to eat. The risk of developing a peanut or egg allergy is very probably reduced if the baby starts eating these foods from the age of three months, and this may also be true for other foods.

There is no nutritional benefit to exclusive breastfeeding up to six months, and after six months breast milk is no longer sufficient as the sole source of nutrition. The risk of iron deficiency in particular means that your baby will need to eat other foods. Make the most of your baby's desire to eat — by all means, give them your own food to try. And a baby's kidneys can handle normally salty food.

CHAPTER SEVEN
Getting some sleep

Few things are as difficult to endure as not getting enough sleep. Since newborn babies have not established a regular day/night sleep rhythm, it is highly likely that, as new parents, you're going to suffer from a lack of sleep. When you get desperate, you may find yourselves searching online for sorts of sleep methods that promise a good night's sleep for your baby and for yourselves. Unfortunately, they rarely deliver on their promises. In this chapter, we consider what does and what doesn't make a difference to a baby's sleep habits, and whether there is anything you can do to avoid the horrible sleep deprivation that affects so many parents of newborn babies. We also explain the most important piece of advice in this book: put your newborn baby to sleep on its back.

We've heard rumours about babies who sleep well after being given a tender kiss on the forehead and then left alone in their cot. In our experience, however, most babies tend to behave differently at bedtime. They sleep well in their parent's arms after feeding and continue to sleep until being placed in their cot — at which point they wake up screaming. A parent picks them up, they drift off to sleep, and the cycle repeats. This isn't particularly surprising. Most young mammals (such as cats, dogs, and rats) sleep together in a heap. They don't have their own rooms with their own cots. And, in reality, that's how things often turn out for humans, too: many homes have a brand-new cot that stands unused and ends up as a dumping ground for clothes, towels, and other paraphernalia while the baby sleeps elsewhere.

The aversion to being left alone to sleep was probably a more useful self-preservation instinct when environmental dangers were greater than they are today. On the savannah, babies who were terrified of sleeping alone would have survived better than those that slept soundly when the lioness leapt out to grab a snack. Because parents and children have evolved together over the course of millions of years, we can also assume that our anguished reaction to a baby's cry has a biological basis. There's no point torturing yourself by trying to follow a particular sleeping method and ignoring your baby's cries if it makes you feel bad. But nor are you a bad person who will cause your child life-long trust problems if you close the door and leave them to cry for a while. Getting your child to sleep isn't some kind of a competition that you will either succeed or fail in — it's more a case of finding your way through an ever-shifting labyrinth.

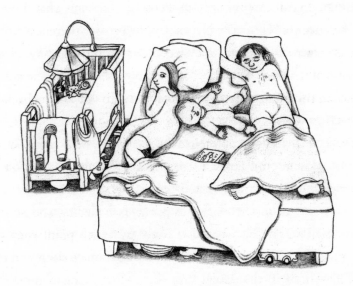

Infants can sleep in many places: in a bassinet; in a cot; in a carrycot; in a pram; in a desk drawer; in a rocker suspended from the ceiling; or on a mattress on the floor. In Finland, many children sleep in cardboard boxes with a mattress and a blanket; since the days when Finland was a poor nation, all families with a newborn baby have been issued with a box containing baby clothing, and parents are encouraged to use the box as a cot for the first few months. Babies can also sleep in bed with their parents, but ideally not during the very early stages. Before the age of three months, there is a heightened risk of sudden infant death syndrome (SIDS), or cot death, if babies and adults share a bed.[1] We discuss co-sleeping below, but first we outline what SIDS is, and how to minimise the risks to your baby.

SIDS

SIDS is the term used when a baby stops breathing and dies without any known illness. This can happen to infants before the age of three months; thereafter, the risk of SIDS is virtually gone. The causes of SIDS are unclear, but it's generally believed that it occurs when a baby's breathing-regulation system stops working.

We now know that the biggest risk factor for SIDS is laying a baby down to sleep on its tummy. However, between the late 1970s and the early 1990s, this was a widely recommended practice.[2] It was thought that if a baby who was lying on its back vomited, there was a risk of its stomach contents entering the lungs and choking the baby. It had also been noted that the tummy-sleeping position worked well for premature babies in intensive care. Consequently, sleeping on the tummy was also recommended for full-term babies at home.

After this recommendation was adopted, the number of cases of SIDS rose steadily. The situation likely worsened when parents were advised not to use dummies. In fact, dummies can reduce the risk of SIDS. (More about that later.)

Today, SIDS is to a large extent preventable, as we have learned from Australian pioneers in this field of research. Dr Susan Beal at the Adelaide Children's Hospital visited more than 500 homes where an infant had died from SIDS between 1973 and 1990. In 1988, she was the first scientist to publish an article clearly showing that being laid to sleep tummy-down dramatically increased the risk of SIDS in infants.[3]

This research finding was replicated in several countries in the following years, and advice about safe sleeping was rapidly produced. Safe-sleeping campaigns spread globally, and in this work, parent's organisations advocating for the importance of this issue were vital. In 1977, Kareene Fitzgerald, who had lost her son Glenn to SIDS, formed the 'Sudden Infant Death Research Foundation Incorporated' (later renamed 'Red Nose') in Melbourne, Australia. Her organisation grew and was rapidly followed by other parent groups across the country. In the late 1980s, safe-sleep campaigns, with the message that babies should be put to sleep on their backs, were launched internationally. These campaigns were extremely effective, with immediate large declines in the number of SIDS cases in all countries where they were launched. In Sweden, the number of infants dying from SIDS in 1990 was 146. In 1992, the campaign came to Sweden and the numbers fell to 40. Since then, they have fallen even more, to 20 a year today.

Safe sleeping

Over the years, many parents have preferred to lay their babies on their tummies, because they have found it hard to get them to sleep for long, and deeply, while lying on their backs. Most babies sleep more easily on their tummies, especially if they are placed in a womb-like 'nest' of covers. However, it is thought that this may be one reason why sleeping on the tummy is so dangerous; the baby sleeps too deeply in a face-down position. Laying your baby on its side is much better than laying it on its tummy, but not as good as laying it on its back, because there is a risk that the baby will roll over onto its tummy.

Smoking increases the risk of SIDS, both if the mother smokes during pregnancy and if the baby is exposed to smoke inside the home. Another factor that increases the risk is the baby sleeping in conditions that are overly warm. You should ensure that your baby sleeps in relatively cool conditions, that their face is clear, and that there are not too many cushions and thick covers surrounding them.

A particularly practical item is a baby sleeping bag, or sleep-suit bag, which takes the form of a romper suit over the upper body and a sleeping bag over the lower body. Babies can't pull these over their faces. Another advantage to the sleep suit is that you can lift your baby up without losing the warmth of its bed, which can be comforting.

Several research studies have found that the risk of SIDS is reduced when a baby uses a dummy, or pacifier, when sleeping.[4] It may be that a dummy in the mouth leaves a gap for air between the baby's head and the mattress. Unfortunately, parents have sometimes been advised not to use dummies due to a fear that they disrupt breastfeeding. In the past, it was thought that babies would have difficulties sucking the nipple if they sucked dummies in between feeding. But there is no scientific basis for this assumption. On the contrary, premature babies with a weak sucking reflex can get better at sucking the breast if they practise with dummies. Feel free to use a dummy if your baby likes it. The usefulness of a dummy varies from baby to baby — some babies always spit dummies out!

We know that there are other factors that can affect the SIDS risk, such as sharing a bed with your baby during the first three months. For reasons that are as yet unclear, it has been shown that this risk is greatest if the parent smokes or has drunk alcohol, or both. Sleeping on a sofa or in a narrow bed raises the risk considerably, as does having large, heavy covers that the baby can be hidden under.

If you don't smoke, have not drunk alcohol, are not overweight, and sleep together with your baby in a large-enough bed, the risk of SIDS is very low (on average, one in 4,400). However, the risk is lowered even further (on average, one in 12,500) if the infant sleeps in their own bed in the parents' room for the first few months.⁵ One obvious problem is that if you lie down at night to breastfeed, it's very hard to avoid falling asleep yourself. A product called a 'baby nest', or a 'baby cocoon', is a separator resembling a soft changing mat with raised sides that a baby can sleep in in their parents' bed. The idea is that it should prevent a sleeping adult from rolling over onto the baby. However, it's not yet clear whether a baby nest makes co-sleeping safer for a baby.

One option is to have your baby sleep on a mattress on the floor. That way, you can feed the baby and lie next to them until they fall asleep, and then sneak away. Even if the baby moves in their sleep and rolls off the mattress, this won't matter. You will probably still find that you fall asleep while breastfeeding, but the total time spent co-sleeping will be less than if your baby sleeps in your bed.

From the age of three months, it isn't dangerous for a baby to share a bed with their parents. This is probably because by then a baby has developed the ability to roll over by themselves, if their airway becomes covered, to maintain their breathing. By that stage, the decision whether to co-sleep or not is just a matter of personal preference.

Breathing monitors

Many parents wonder whether it's safer for a baby to sleep with a breathing monitor close to them. Baby breathing or apnoea monitors are used in healthcare to monitor premature babies when they are moved out of an intensive-care setting. They may also be used for babies who have suffered an apparent life-threatening event, and for the siblings of children who have died as a result of SIDS. There is no clear scientific evidence that breathing monitors protect babies from SIDS, but some parents who have used them and who have been able to resuscitate a baby who has stopped breathing say that they can be useful. On the other hand, there are also examples of tragic deaths where the alarm on the breathing monitor has failed and a child has died in bed, with the alarm still connected.

If you feel safer using a breathing monitor, you can certainly buy or hire one, but remember that you still need to follow the standard advice about babies and sleeping that we have described above — ensure that you lay your baby on its back to sleep and that they are not too warm.

SETTLING A BABY TO SLEEP SUCCESSFULLY

Babies usually fall asleep after feeding from the breast or the bottle. However, as we have said, they often wake up when you try to put them into their bed. We would like to offer a few useful tips on getting your baby to sleep.

Newborn babies are used to a womb that constrains and slows all their arm and leg movements. When they emerge into the open air, many of them are unsettled and a little bit scared by the sensation that they can kick freely. It is generally very calming for a baby to lie in a foetal position with their arms and legs bent towards their body, and to have some resistance against their kicking or arm waving. To enable this position, you can roll up a small towel lengthways into a long sausage shape, and then lay it out in a U-shape around your baby's body (leaving the head free). Swaddling babies in a soft wrap has the same effect.

Babies tend to wake up more when they sleep with their mouths open. Their mouths become dry and uncomfortable, and this can wake them. A baby may sleep better if they breathe through their nose. Using a dummy may help, or you can simply close your baby's mouth by gently pressing their chin.

Many babies sleep well with a calm hand on their head, while some fall asleep much more easily with a gentle, rocking movement, such as a pram that is pushed gently back and forth over a threshold. Find out what works best for your baby.

As mentioned, many babies sleep well after feeding. If so, feel free to use this method. Others sleep well with a dummy in their mouth. If your baby spits it out, try another style of dummy; your nearest well-stocked supermarket will sell a number of different types. You can also try holding a finger on the dummy so that it stays in the mouth until the baby starts to suck, or wobble the dummy gently against the baby's palate, which can trigger the baby's sucking reflex.

Your baby is likely to have a highly attuned ability to know if the person who is putting them to sleep is stressed, sad, or angry. An adult who radiates calmness and security transmits these same emotions to a baby and will be much more successful in getting their baby to sleep than someone who is full of anxiety — perhaps because they aren't able to get enough sleep at night themselves. It is important to try to arrange your parenting so that, as often as possible, a sufficiently rested, calm adult can put the baby to sleep. If there are two parents, share the nights so that you can each sleep better on alternate nights. You can also ask friends and relatives for help. Staying at home and looking after a baby during the day is often more demanding than a paid job. We consider it entirely unreasonable to expect that the parent on parental leave should take full responsibility for the night-time shift as well; the nights should be shared equally.

Sleep patterns

Many parents contact healthcare professionals because they worry their baby isn't sleeping enough. It is practically impossible, however, for healthy babies not to get the sleep they need. There are some rare conditions that hinder a child from sleeping, which we discuss at the end of this chapter. But, in general, the problem is that a baby's sleep pattern is completely different from our own. On average, newborns will sleep for 14 or 15 hours in a 24-hour period, but they wake every two to four hours to be fed. To begin with, a newborn baby doesn't really differentiate between night and day. Sleeping times vary widely, with some babies sleeping for ten hours a day, and others sleeping for 19 hours.

It is usually the parents who have sleeping problems, and it is them we should feel sorry for. They've had a biological clock for the last 20 to 40 years that determines when they are asleep and awake, and it's very hard to change their programming. Adults like to sleep for seven to nine hours per night, ideally in a single stretch. This become difficult when you have to take responsibility for a newborn baby who needs food and human contact every couple of hours, day and night. Some parents are able to doze during the day while their baby sleeps, but many find this hard to do. A few hours of sleep at night are not enough for parents to feel rested.

When you've had your first child and have not managed to get a full night's sleep for three months, it can feel like this will be the situation forever. We are glad to say that it won't be. Although around one-quarter of parents experience so much distress concerning their infant's sleep at the age of three months that they seek some form of help or advice, around three-quarters of nine-month-olds will sleep right through the night. In other words, the constant waking up at night naturally becomes less frequent. As the child grows older, it is more often the routine of putting them to bed that becomes drawn out and causes problems.

Sleeping methods

There are various sleeping methods that aim to teach babies to sleep in their own beds for a relatively long period of the night. Five hours at a time is generally seen as an acceptable target. The methods vary a little, but what they all have in common is that the baby should lie in their own bed in a separate room, and that you shouldn't pick them up immediately if they start to cry. The rationale behind these ideas is that a crying baby is not necessarily unhappy — they might just be tired — and that a baby who is left to cry for a while will get used to sleeping in their own bed.

We found four scientific studies on the subject of sleeping methods. In these studies, parents (usually mothers) were chosen at random to either receive or not receive instructions about what they should do to get their babies to sleep in their own beds. These instructions were all similar, and involved ways of trying to get the babies to soothe themselves to sleep. The parents were encouraged to wait at least five minutes before comforting their crying babies. Three of the studies noted that the sleeping method they recommended did have a positive effect on their child's ability to sleep for longer periods without waking up.[6] In one of the studies, the researchers pointed out that it was hard to get parents to follow the instructions; when it came down to it, most parents just ignored them. The fourth study found no effect resulting from the sleeping method that was examined.[7]

It is worth mentioning that studies which present a positive result for the method being investigated are more likely to be published than studies which do not. It may well be the case that there have been several studies performed around the world that have not been able to show the efficacy of similar sleeping methods, but which have never been published. We simply do not know scientifically whether these sleeping methods work, or not.

How we come to understand children and their need for closeness — as well as their need to learn that they are their own person, distinct from their parents — varies widely from culture to culture. In some cultures, it is considered important to have children sleep in their own beds. In other cultures, babies are carried around for much of the day.

One study compared parents in London and Copenhagen. It found that the English children spent considerably more time alone in their prams, or in their beds, than did their Danish counterparts.[8] It also found that the English parents often waited a good while before responding to their babies' cries, and that they fed their offspring at regular intervals of three or four hours. The Danish parents responded more quickly to their children's cries, interacted with them more, and fed them more often as needed. The researchers measured how much the babies cried, finding that the English infants cried more than the young Danes.

An 'intensive contact' group was formed, consisting of both English and Danish parents who decided in advance to carry or have some other form of body contact with their babies for at least 80 per cent of the day, feeding them frequently and responding quickly to their cries. The babies in the 'intensive contact' group cried approximately as often during the day as the Danish babies had before the intervention, but did not sleep quite as well during the night. An interesting finding was that intensive periods of colic-type crying (see chapter 8) were just as common in all three groups. These results suggest that today's Danish (and probably also Swedish) way of caring for babies results in less crying than earlier, stricter methods, but does not eliminate crying completely, and that carrying and being with babies around the clock does not seem to make them much calmer.

No one has yet proven that 'crying it out' (as it was once called) — commonly called 'controlled crying' in Australia — harms infants. If you manage to follow this method, there's a fair chance that your baby will sleep in its own bed after a few nights. But a lot of parents can't stand the sound of a baby shrieking behind a closed door, and so they give in and abandon the instruction to leave their infant to self-soothe. We can fully understand this response, and we ourselves have never managed to listen to our own children crying without intervening. As we've noted, scientific studies confirm that many parents never succeed in following this method. Feel free to give it a try, and if it works, that's great. But if you can't cope and find it's not for you, don't feel bad.

If you search the internet for 'sleeping methods', you'll come across sites promising that all your dreams will be answered if you just follow their advice. These sites often have active forums where (mostly) mothers congratulate each other on having chosen a successful method. They are happy to welcome new friends into their little community — anyone who wants to use their particular sleeping method. If you want to try these methods (as long as they don't involve babies sleeping on their tummies), you can. If you succeed, you might make some new friends among others who have succeeded with the same sleeping method. But if you 'fail', remember that it's not your fault, regardless of any claims by the 'sleep coaches'. Simply log off and look for friends elsewhere. A final word of warning: some sleeping methods involve the baby sleeping on their tummies, which, as we have explained, is highly dangerous and increases the risk of SIDS. Never try these methods.

YOU NEED AN UNINTERRUPTED NIGHT'S SLEEP YOURSELF

We just have to accept that babies aren't designed to sleep right through the night. What's more, babies continue to need to feed during the night for quite a while. As we've already mentioned, it's the parents — not the child — who need a full night's sleep. Not being able to sleep has a significant impact on everybody's quality of life.

We suggest that you don't count on your baby being able to sleep through the night from an early age. If you have been lucky, congratulations! But, remember, they may start waking up several times in the night again and go through a stage of needing to feed more often. In most cases, it takes many months — in some cases, years — before a baby sleeps all night and allows their parents to enjoy a full night of uninterrupted sleep. You should plan for this period with your own survival in mind. This is one of the reasons why we suggested in the opening chapter that, ideally, both parents should be at home for the first two months.

If one parent is breastfeeding, their partner should take all the other night-time duties (including changing nappies and playing with a child who doesn't understand it's the middle of the night), particularly during the first month or so while the nursing parent is recovering from pregnancy and childbirth. If one of you experiences depression or any other mental-health disorders, it may be worth the other parent taking on more of the night-time duties, because sleep deprivation can easily trigger depression and make it harder to deal with such problems. A lack of sleep can also increase the likelihood of anxiety.

If there are two parents and you bottle-feed, you can each take responsibility for alternate nights, or half the night, or whatever arrangement suits you. Even those babies who are exclusively breastfed can be bottle-fed by the other parent, using expressed milk. Another alternative is to use formula at night from time to time, or even on alternate nights, so that the nursing parent can get some sleep. This strategy requires having a breast pump to hand in case the nursing parent wakes up with engorged breasts when the baby isn't hungry.

One useful strategy is to set up a spare bed in another room to which one parent can escape for an undisturbed night's sleep. You can spend alternate nights sleeping in the other room, or half the night, or whatever suits you. Having both parents lying awake and exhausted is a lose–lose situation. If the mother is breastfeeding, the other parent must, of course, then bring the baby to the mother, but it's nice for her to have a break from changing nappies and putting the baby back to bed. If you're a single parent, we strongly recommend asking anyone and everyone for help. Invite friends and relatives to stay with you, or arrange for the baby to stay overnight with them so that you can catch up on sleep.

What to do if your baby wants to continue breastfeeding at night

We often hear fantastic tales about babies who feed less and less frequently at night of their own free will, and eventually stop completely. In our experience, this tends to be a rather rose-tinted view. Breastfed children have no real reason to stop feeding at night; having a quick snack and then going back to sleep is both practical and comforting from their point of view. But in the end, long periods of broken nights can bring even the most pro-breastfeeding parent to breaking point.

If you decide that you want to stop night-time feeds, one option is to sleep in a separate room or to go off on a break for a couple of days. Another approach is to sleep with the baby, but to wear a tight-fitting bra and a top. The baby may well cry and protest a lot the first night, and a little less the following night, before settling down after three or four nights. Giving the baby an evening bottle of formula during this period may reassure you that your baby is not hungry — it's just that they are used to being able to feed little and often.

What to do if you are not coping

Sometimes parents end up so exhausted due to a lack of quality sleep that they and the baby end up in a vicious cycle. The baby cries, the parents get desperate, and the child cries even more. In the past, families would sometimes be sent to a clinic for a couple of nights in such cases. A nurse would put the child to bed, and the parents could sleep. Such sleep clinics, which aim to help parents change their babies' sleeping patterns, as well as offering some respite, are still available in some countries such as Australia, but not in Sweden nowadays, where the number of hospital beds has been reduced so dramatically that there are barely enough for seriously sick children. Specialist sleep consultants who come to your home and help you devise a plan for training your toddler or baby to sleep, and provide follow-up support, can often be very effective and worth the investment.

If you end up in such a desperate situation that you feel you can't cope, you should absolutely seek help, whether from a clinic, a sleep consultant, or from a friend or relative. Let somebody else look after the baby for a night, or from time to time, until you've managed to catch up a little on your sleep.

Sometimes parents are driven so mad by a screaming child and a lack of sleep that they lose all sense of reason and shake the baby. When a baby's head is flung back and forth it can cause a cerebral haemorrhage that results in the baby losing consciousness, and can lead to permanent brain damage. Whatever you do, never shake a child. If you are desperate and feel you can no longer cope, place the baby on the floor or safely in its cot, and leave the room. You can even shut the door. Leaving a baby to scream alone in a room won't kill them, but shaking them might. Seek help by calling a friend, a family member, or a helpline. Phone your clinic and request an emergency appointment so that you can explain how you are feeling, and get advice on how to break the cycle of exhaustion.

Child-free evenings or sleeping in?

Unfortunately, babies don't sleep for 12 hours at a time. It's unrealistic to expect both a child-free evening from eight o'clock onwards and then a lie-in until eight o'clock the following morning. Once they're a few months old, some babies might sleep for a total of six to eight hours during the night, with a couple of interruptions to feed.

Decide which is most important to you: a bit of peace and quiet in the evening, or the chance to sleep in. The price you pay for a child-free evening is often a very early morning; if you've put your baby to sleep at eight o'clock, they may wake up at two, three, or four in the morning. Getting up that early is not a pleasant experience for a tired parent. It may be better for you to keep the baby up with you until midnight, and hope that they sleep until seven or even eight o'clock. The best thing for parents to do is to discuss what you both want beforehand. Just remember that having adult time together in the evening and then sleeping until a reasonable hour in the morning is impossible during the first six months — and sometimes it takes considerably longer than that. If there are two of you, we recommend splitting sleeping and night-time childcare for the first few months, rather than trying to have adult time together. You'll get plenty of chances to spend evenings together in future, but if you or your partner are sleep deprived for months on end, your relationship won't be particularly healthy.

The one good thing about babies' sleep compared with other people's is that they are generally entirely insensitive to noise, light, and activity, and can continue sleeping under the rowdiest of circumstances. It sometimes seems as if they prefer to sleep among people who are talking and getting on with various activities, rather than waking up in their own bed in a quiet, darkened room. If your baby sleeps well in your arms and resists being put to bed, a good solution may be to spend an evening on the sofa holding the baby until your own bedtime. A sleeping baby is rarely disturbed by its parents chatting, watching television or a film, or whatever you choose to do.

If you get bored at home, or start to get cabin fever, and your baby will sleep in a carry-cot or a pram, you can take the baby with you to meet up with a friend, go out for dinner, or go for a walk. The other parent can stay at home and catch up on some sleep.

ILLNESSES THAT LEAD TO POOR SLEEP

Healthy babies sleep for short periods and wake frequently, and many babies find it hard to sleep without being close to their parents' bodies. If your baby is growing well, is content while awake, and experiences sleeping problems characterised by frequent waking and difficulties sleeping alone, there is no reason to suspect any illness.

If, on the other hand, your baby seems to suffer pain when being put down to sleep, this may be a sign of illness. If the symptoms appear suddenly — particularly in connection with a cold — an ear inflammation is one likely cause. If your baby is otherwise healthy, eats well, and doesn't have a fever, you can give them infant pain-relief medication, and contact your clinic the next morning. However, if your baby is younger than two or three months, and is lethargic, has a temperature of more than 38°C, or isn't feeding properly, always seek emergency help.

If your baby seems to regularly suffer pain when being placed down, this may be an indication of painful acid reflux (the stomach contents regurgitating into the throat). And if your baby finds it hard to settle down, cries a lot, and has diarrhoea and/or red, spotty, dry skin, they could have an allergy to cow's milk. In either case, contact your GP and book an appointment with a paediatrician for an examination.

A baby that coughs a lot during the night may have a cold or, if the cough lasts a long time and is troublesome, bronchial asthma. If your child coughs during the night and experiences disturbed sleep for more than three weeks with each cold, book an appointment with a paediatrician. If your child snores a lot and wakes up frequently during the night, their sleep problems may be due to an enlargement of the lymphoid tissue behind the nose. This is a fairly common infant condition, which can be investigated and treated by an ear, nose, and throat (ENT) specialist.

IN BRIEF

A baby's sleep rhythm tends to be its most troublesome characteristic and the most problematic aspect of early parenthood. There's no right or wrong way to deal with sleep patterns — babies sleep for much shorter periods than adults want to, and they wake up several times in the night wanting to feed, leaving their parents exhausted. It can be therefore worthwhile using a spare bedroom so that one parent can sleep, and setting up a schedule for sharing the night-time shifts so a lack of sleep doesn't become too much of a problem for one or both parents. One piece of sleep advice is vital: lay your baby on its back when sleeping, and ensure that there aren't cushions and covers around its face that could disrupt its breathing.

CHAPTER EIGHT

Poo, vomit, crying, and colic

As a parent of a newborn, you need to help your baby with everything, even their most intimate hygiene. When you are changing nappies up to eight times a day, your baby's poo — its consistency, smell, and appearance — becomes of greater interest to you than you could ever have imagined. That's why in this chapter we go through what baby poo can look like and what the different types of poo can tell you. You will also become familiar with your baby's vomit, so it's useful to learn why they do it and when it might be a problem that requires action. You'll also learn more about babies' crying, what colic is, and how you can survive with a truly colicky baby.

POO

For much of our lives, the colour, consistency, and other qualities of our excrement is a strictly personal matter. But as the parents of a newborn child, you are responsible for the baby's wellbeing, including changing its nappies, and the question crops up time and time again: is this poo normal? Let's take a closer look at the full colour scale for baby poo.

In the womb

Ideally, an unborn baby should not poo while in the womb. During pregnancy, the foetus doesn't eat anything by mouth so it doesn't produce much poo, but the liver produces bile, which is secreted into the intestines and mixes with cells from the intestinal mucosa. Together, this forms a thick, dark green-black mixture called meconium. Some babies excrete meconium into the amniotic fluid during birth. This indicates that a baby is stressed, and requires particular attention, because it is not healthy for a baby to lie in, and breathe in, its own meconium. Once the baby has been born, however, the meconium should be expelled within a few days. Nine out of ten healthy babies poo out their meconium during the first day of their lives.

The colour of the poo

Breastfed babies' poo is sticky, yellow or green, and granular, and it often smells a bit sour. Yellow and green poo is completely normal. If babies are fed with formula, their poo will vary in colour, form, and smell. It will normally be browner than the poo of breastfed babies, and more like adult poo. The colour of poo comes from pigments in the bile from the gall bladder that are released into the baby's intestines. The purpose of bile is to dissolve the fat in food, much in the way that dishwashing detergent is used to break down grease. The pigments come from a red substance, haemoglobin, in the red blood cells, which is converted into a yellow compound, bilirubin, and excreted via the bile. Bile is a bright green-yellow colour, but as it makes its way through the infant's intestines the pigments are modified by intestinal bacteria and turn greener, or browner.

The particular shade of a baby's poo is not particularly important, as long as it's coloured. If the poo is very pale, beige, or a very light yellow, this can be a sign of the rare disease biliary atresia, in which bile can't be secreted into the intestines due to a malformation of the baby's bile ducts. It is important to detect and treat this condition as early as possible. You should contact a paediatrician if your child's poo is very pale for several days, and, if possible, take a soiled nappy in a plastic bag as a sample.

How often should babies poo?

Ninety-five per cent of all babies poo between five and 40 times a week. However, there are some differences in habits between breastfed and bottle-fed babies.

Babies that are exclusively breastfed poo five times a day on average, but this can vary considerably between individual babies. Constipation is unusual among exclusively breastfed babies. If your baby is exclusively breastfed and only poos every three or four days after extensive straining or after being helped, you should tell your child health nurse. Babies that are fed with formula tend to poo less often, from a few times a day to once every other day. They also experience constipation more often than breastfed babies. A constipated baby poos less often than every other day, often after considerable straining.

A baby who remains constipated for several days will begin to feel ill. They may vomit and stop eating normally. In this situation, it is important to seek help from your GP or child health nurse. In the first instance, diluted prune juice or an over-the-counter laxative, such as lactulose, is the usual suggested treatment. Severe constipation in a baby can be a sign of an illness that needs to be investigated and treated.

Diarrhoea

If your baby's poo becomes looser, watery, or much more copious and much greener than usual, this is called diarrhoea. Sudden diarrhoea is often due to a gastroenteritis virus. When an infant has diarrhoea it is important to ensure that they do not become dehydrated from loss of fluids. Give your baby their usual food, breast milk, or formula — ideally, a little more often than normally. If your baby becomes lethargic, is unable to eat, or stops urinating, contact the emergency department.

Babies under the age of six months are particularly sensitive to dehydration, so do not hesitate to seek medical help if your child has diarrhoea and becomes tired or stops urinating.

In some cases, diarrhoea is caused by an allergy. If your baby is not lethargic and is otherwise well, you can continue to look after them at home, but if diarrhoea lasts for more than a couple of weeks, seek advice from your child health clinic.

Blood in your baby's poo

Blood in a baby's poo is often due to an allergy to cow's milk. A single streak of blood isn't a problem, but if this happens several times you should contact a paediatrician. Copious intestinal bleeding is unusual for a baby, but if your baby's faeces repeatedly contain a lot of blood you should go to an emergency paediatric clinic. The same advice applies if your baby has smaller amounts of blood in its poo and is pale, tired, in pain, unwilling to eat, or is otherwise not its usual self.

VOMIT

All newborn babies vomit. Vomiting has three main causes. First, the cardia (the valve between the stomach and the oesophagus) has not yet developed, and allows the stomach contents to pass back up through the oesophagus. Second, the child only eats liquid food, which can come back up more easily than solid food. Third, babies consume large amounts of food relative to their body volume and the size of their stomach. It is hard for the stomach to process a lot of food at once, and it can easily overflow.

Some babies vomit a lot, especially after feeding. If your baby is one of these, it's simply a matter of having plenty of small towels to lie over your shoulder when you carry your baby, and lots of clean baby clothes, as they will need to be changed frequently. Buy second-hand clothes if you are not given hand-me-downs; they'll be vomited on and repeatedly laundered soon enough. Sometimes it is better if the baby is held in an upright position after mealtimes, or seated in a reclined cradle or a car seat, because gravity will help to keep the food down.

As long as your baby is putting on weight and the vomiting doesn't seem to be causing pain, there's no need to seek healthcare advice. If you use formula, special thickeners can be added — ask about these at your child health clinic. They might work, but they certainly don't in all cases. Usually it's just a matter of waiting until your baby's habits change. The situation often improves dramatically when a child starts eating solids, but some vomiting may remain. As an infant reaches 18 to 24 months, the cardia usually becomes more developed, and the vomiting finally stops.

If vomiting causes pain

Children tend to have much less hydrochloric acid in their stomachs than adults, which is why baby vomit doesn't smell nearly as bad as adult vomit. But if vomiting is causing your baby pain, it may be because the vomit contains so much acid that it is damaging the lining of the oesophagus. Contact your GP or a paediatrician for advice — you may be prescribed medicine to help neutralise the vomit. However, this will not reduce the frequency or volume of the vomiting.

Blood in the vomit

If a breastfed baby has blood in its vomit, first check the nursing parent's nipples. The appearance of blood is frequently caused by the baby swallowing blood from cracked or sore nipples. This isn't harmful for the baby, but the mother will need help healing her nipples for her own sake. Blood in the vomit can also be due to a small sore in the lining of a baby's throat, which is completely harmless. However, if your baby's vomit contains large amounts of blood, you should contact the emergency department.

Projectile vomiting

Regular vomiting may be copious, but it doesn't have a lot of pressure behind it. If, however, your baby's vomit spurts out with enough force to hit the wall, or someone sitting a metre away, you should contact the emergency department. Projectile vomiting could be due to pyloric stenosis — a thickening of the muscles around the pylorus, which separates the stomach from the small bowel. The condition affects around one in 500 babies, and becomes apparent between the ages of three weeks and three months. The cause of the condition is unknown. It is important to detect and treat pyloric stenosis, as the vomiting can result in dehydration. A doctor will carry out an ultrasound examination of the baby's stomach to see if the pylorus is thickened. The condition can easily be treated with an operation whereby a small incision is made in the baby's abdomen and the thickened muscle is cut away.

CRYING AND COLIC

All babies cry quite a lot, especially during their first few months. A summary of the studies carried out in different countries shows that babies cry for an average of two hours a day for the first six weeks, falling to just over an hour a day by the age of three months.[1] This probably sounds like a lot of crying. As mentioned previously in chapter 7, it has been found that Scandinavian babies cry about half as much as their English counterparts. This finding has been interpreted to mean that the Scandinavian approach to parenting babies — trying to comfort them when they cry, feeding them more often than every three or four hours if hungry, and maintaining a lot of body contact — results in less crying.

What is colic?

Babies with colic cry more than other newborn babies. The term 'colic' is commonly used when a baby cries for at least three hours a day, on at least three days a week, for at least three weeks, but is otherwise healthy and puts on weight normally. Colic tends to start when the baby is a couple of weeks old; it peaks at five to six weeks, and then gradually subsides. After the age of three months, most infants no longer suffer from colic. For this reason, the condition is sometimes known as 'three-month colic'.

Around one in five families report that their baby cries excessively — in other words, that the baby suffers from colic.[2] Colic mostly occurs in the evening, and is more common among first-born children than among their siblings. Colic is also more common among babies whose siblings have also had colic than among babies with no other cases of colic in their family. Bottle-fed babies don't have more colic than breast-fed babies; some studies even suggest that they have less.

It is usually assumed that colic relates to the alimentary tract, because colicky babies behave as if they are in pain, and often pull their legs in towards their tummies. However, there is no evidence for this theory. Instead, researchers have found that those who suffer from colic as babies develop migraines later in life more often than others.[3] Colic may be the paediatric equivalent of a migraine — a particular type of headache associated with sensitivity to sound and light, and a feeling of nausea. A colicky baby may have a headache and react to pain by appearing to have a stomach ache, or it may have an equivalent 'headache' in its stomach. Colic seems to be associated with a period when the nervous system has not yet matured, and before the baby has established a daily rhythm where sleeping and waking are controlled by the hormone melatonin. By the age of around three months, many babies can tell the difference between day and night, and it is around the same time that colic usually disappears.

Colic can easily become a vicious cycle. The baby cries inconsolably, the parent despairs and becomes exhausted, and then the baby finds it hard to settle down and cries all the more. There was a time in Sweden when crying babies were admitted to hospital for a couple of nights to take the strain off their parents. There are now fewer places at paediatric hospitals, and babies who are not ill are rarely admitted. The responsibility for helping parents of colicky babies lies with friends and family. Ensure that you get support: if you need a break, ask friends or relatives to look after the baby for a couple of nights a week. And make sure both parents share the night-time responsibility for a colicky baby — you can't cope alone and keep your health intact!

What helps with colic?

In spite of the many methods for dealing with colic that have been trialled, it cannot be said with certainty that any method has shown better results than a placebo (a treatment that has no actual effect, or a 'sugar pill').[4] In studies of colic, around 30 per cent efficacy is typically achieved in the group that receives the fake treatment. There are two reasons why the placebo effect may be so strong in the case of colic. First, colic disappears spontaneously with time, even without treatment. Remember that colic normally lasts for a maximum of five or six weeks and has almost disappeared within 12 weeks. If treatment is introduced at six weeks of age, say, and lasts for three weeks, many cases of colic would resolve spontaneously during that time. The second explanation is that parents relax when they believe their child has been given active medication, thereby breaking the vicious cycle of exhausted, distressed parents, causing even more crying in their child.

Massage and colic drops are among those treatments that have shown no better effect than a placebo. The only harmless treatment that has demonstrated a greater effect than a placebo in certain studies is probiotic *Lactobacillus reuteri* drops (sold in different territories under various commercial names — ask your pharmacist for advice) They have been shown to reduce the crying time compared with similar non-lactobacillus drops in four of five conducted randomised controlled trials.[5] However, in the fifth trial, infants cried more with lactobacillus supplementation, although this difference did not reach statistical significance.[6] There are also probiotic drops with other bacteria on the market. None of these have been tested for efficacy in clinical studies, so we don't know if they help against colic.

Manipulation by a chiropractor or an osteopath has been used for infantile colic, and in some small non-blinded studies parents who knew their infants had been treated for colic with these methods reported less crying afterwards.[7] However, all these studies were of very low quality, thus no certain effect on colic has been shown. In addition, chiropractic or osteopathic manipulation are not without risks, so these interventions are not recommended. Nor does acupuncture have any greater scientifically proven effect than a placebo, but a number of private acupuncturists offer treatment for colic. Acupuncture in infants has a lower risk for side effects than chiropractic or osteopathic manipulation, which makes it a better choice if you want to try something more than probiotic drops.

Fennel extract has been shown to work on colic better than a placebo in two small studies. However, Sweden's National Food Agency advises against its use, as no safety studies have been carried out on fennel use in children, pregnant women, or breastfeeding women. There are two case reports of breastfed infants who got severe side effects when their mothers consumed more than two litres of fennel-containing herbal tea a day, so it's not unreasonable to suspect side effects could occur if you give your baby fennel extract. The drug dicyclomine, which acts on the nervous system, may be effective against colic, but is definitely to be avoided. It has many seriously harmful side effects, including cramps, breathing problems, and coma. Some babies have even died as a result of this medicine, which was deregistered in Sweden in 2008. Whatever you do, don't buy dicyclomine (also known as dicycloverine) abroad or online to give to a colicky baby.

Cow's milk allergy?

There has been an endless discussion about whether certain cases of colic may be a sign of a cow's milk allergy. Formula contains cow's milk proteins, but even breastfed babies can develop an allergy to cow's milk. If a breastfeeding mother drinks cow's milk, her breast milk will also contain cow's milk proteins. If you suspect that a cow's milk allergy may be the cause of your baby's colic symptoms, book an appointment with a paediatrician. They will be able to help you decide whether it's worthwhile trying a hypoallergenic bottled breast-milk substitute (which does not contain any intact cow's milk proteins and cannot produce allergic symptoms), or whether a breastfeeding mother should avoid all foods containing cow's milk. If this helps, you can continue the baby on a diet free of cow's milk for a few months and then try re-introducing it. As a rule, babies who are allergic to cow's milk tend to grow out of their allergy after a couple of months, or sometimes years.

No study has been able to show that babies who suffer from colic would generally be better off if their mothers cut out milk or other foods. No one derives much pleasure from experimenting with restrictive diets; they can end up making you feel exhausted and grumpy. Many trials have been carried out in which women have avoided certain types of food during pregnancy and breastfeeding, with no reduction found in the risk of childhood allergies.[8] Our basic advice is to eat and drink whatever you want while breastfeeding, and concentrate on sharing your parenting duties so you don't reach the end of your tether due to a crying baby.

Surviving with a colicky baby

Scientific studies into colic can be summarised with the observations that colic is a common condition among babies during their natural development, and that it is probably due to their nervous system not yet being fully formed. There is currently very little that can be done about this difficult situation. The best thing you can do is to conserve your energy to cope with a period of colic, and ask others around you for support. Put in earplugs, or listen to music through headphones. Don't think for one moment that your baby's colic is your fault, and remember that it will pass.

If at any time you feel that you can't cope with the crying, simply put your baby down on the floor or in a cot, and walk away for some minutes. This won't harm your baby, and it's completely normal to be unable to put up with listening to endless wailing. Call someone and ask for help. It's much better for your baby to cry alone for a while than for you to shake them in frustration or panic, or harm them in any way.

IN BRIEF

All colours are normal for a baby's poo, except white-beige and blood red. All babies vomit to some extent, and you only need to seek medical advice if vomiting seems to cause your baby pain or if your baby is projectile vomiting. Colic, or shrill screaming, is tough for both the baby and their parents. Lactobacillus drops may possibly help to reduce the baby's discomfort. Remember that the colic will pass, and be sure to share the parenting — in good times and in bad.

CHAPTER NINE

Infections

How many times have you read that you should consume vitamin C, drink spinach or kale smoothies, or do something else entirely to 'boost your immune system'? Most of this advice is nonsensical, and, for some reason, popular-health gurus love talking about the immune system, despite having a very vague understanding of how it works. You don't need to look far to find disinformation about a child's immune system — it's everywhere! Claims that children are unable to fight off bacteria and viruses, and need to be wrapped in cotton wool, are not true. Yes, children contract more infections than adults, but not because there is anything wrong with their immune systems. On the contrary, their immune systems are in a training phase, building up immunological memory so that they can avoid infections in the future. In this chapter, you will learn how the immune system works, and how it functions in children.

During pregnancy, a baby is protected against most infections. It is physically protected by the amniotic sac in the womb, and the placenta acts as a barrier between the mother's blood and that of the baby. Only a few contagions — mainly viruses, such as rubella — are able to be transferred from the mother to the baby in the womb.

Babies are born into a world filled with viruses and bacteria, and maybe the occasional fungus or parasite. Children are able to cope with most of these threats from the start, thanks to their highly developed immune systems, which have evolved over the course of millions of years to fight off bacteria, viruses, fungi, and parasites (collectively known as microorganisms).

Bacteria and fungi exist on everybody's skin and mucous membranes, where they don't do us any harm. However, from time to time they find their way into our bodies. These incursions trigger violent activity in our immune system, resulting in symptoms such as fever, pain, and swelling. These bodily responses to an offending microorganism produce what is known as a bacterial or fungal infection.

Viruses are, essentially, a bunch of genes (either in the form of DNA or RNA). They don't have a life of their own, and can only sustain themselves by invading our cells, where they replicate and direct the cells to produce new viruses that, in turn can infect new cells. As with bacteria and fungi, the presence of foreign invaders in the form of viruses inside our cells triggers the activation of our immune system, leading to fever and other signs of infection.

Antibiotics (medicines that kill bacteria) have existed for less than a century. Antivirals (medicines that kill viruses) have only existed for around 30 years, as have medicines to combat fungal infections. Before the advent of medicines that kill different types of microorganisms, all we had to fight infection with was our immune system. Because infections have been a very common cause of death throughout human history, the immune system is one of the most important systems in the body. Without it, humans would not have survived as a species. It is extremely rare to be born without a functioning immune system — this only occurs in around two per 100,000 births, equalling fewer than 10 babies a year in Australia, and fewer than 20 babies a year in Great Britain. A somewhat greater number are born with less severe immune deficiencies, but the vast majority of babies are born with a robust immune system that is ready to take on whatever microorganisms it encounters.

The immune system is made up of two parts: the innate immune system and the acquired immune system. As the name suggests, the innate immune system is fixed and functioning from birth. It includes cells that can eat bacteria and fungi that have invaded the body. This process goes unnoticed, as it involves low numbers of invaders that are calmly and quietly eliminated. The innate immune system also protects against viruses. When white blood cells encounter viruses, they produce large quantities of substances called interferons, which instruct all cells to stop forming new viruses. The innate immune system needs no training in order to function.

THE ACQUIRED IMMUNE SYSTEM — OR WHY YOU ONLY GET CHICKENPOX ONCE

The other part of the immune system — the acquired immune system — needs training in order to recognise and destroy bacteria, viruses, and parasites. The main players in the acquired immune system are a group of white blood cells called lymphocytes, comprising T and B lymphocytes. Each lymphocyte recognises a single foreign structure, much in the way a key only fits one lock. The foreign structure may be found on a virus or a bacterium, on a food substance, in a cat's saliva, or in birch pollen, to mention just a few examples. Lymphocytes are like the world's biggest bunch of keys, ready to open any lock in the world that presents itself. They swirl around in the blood, looking for the specific structure that they can react against.

At birth — before the immune system has encountered any bacteria or viruses — there are only a few individual keys that fit each lock. When an infant's immune system encounters a microorganism such as a chickenpox virus for the first time, it will start producing tens of thousands of copies of the key (lymphocytes) to fit the lock for the chickenpox virus. This process takes a week or two, after which there are plenty of lymphocytes that recognise this particular virus.

B lymphocytes form antibodies — 'labelling' molecules that enter the bloodstream, where they circulate until they find the microorganism on which they fit. The antibodies label the chickenpox virus so that it is quickly identified and eliminated by other parts of the immune defence. A virus cannot enter the body's cells if it is covered with antibodies blocking the molecules the virus normally uses to enter a cell. T lymphocytes are expert at recognising microorganisms — particularly viruses — that have hidden themselves in the body's cells. Cells that are infected with a virus display small parts of the virus on their surface so that the immune system can recognise the infection. Once T lymphocytes recognise that a cell is infected with a virus, they will kill the cell, because it is better to lose some cells than to let the viral infection spread from cell to cell and eventually kill you.

The troublesome symptoms experienced by a child during infection — fever, tiredness, swelling, and muscular pain — are signs that the immune system is working actively in the body. Generally, after a few weeks, the battle between the immune system and the virus is over and the infant is healthy again. It takes time for an infant to return to health the first time they encounter a certain virus, because their immune system has to mass-produce the keys to fit each particular lock before the virus can be eliminated from the body. But the next time the same virus appears, the reaction is lightning fast, because the child has lots of the right keys.

For example, once children have had chickenpox, chickenpox antibodies will be found in their blood for many years to come, because antibodies continue to be produced long after the infection is gone. If chickenpox reappears, the antibodies will deal with the virus immediately. And even if the antibodies have dwindled after many years, there will be memory cells available to produce more antibodies of the same kind.

Some of the lymphocytes that have taken part in the immune defence will be converted into these memory cells. They are extremely persistent and circulate around the body, checking to see if the chickenpox virus makes another appearance. As soon as the virus re-appears, the memory cells get to work and fight the virus. The response happens so quickly that neither you nor your child will notice that a foreign invader has entered the child's body. Immunological memory explains why adult parents can look after a child who is covered in chickenpox spots without getting a single itchy spot themselves. It's fantastic when it works! There are only two ways to acquire an immunological memory, or immunity against a disease: through being infected by it, or by being vaccinated. against it.

Fever

Fever is diagnosed when an infant feels unusually warm and has a measured temperature higher than 38°C. It is a sign that the immune system is working; it is not harmful in itself, even if the temperature becomes very high. Therefore, there is no need to medicate a child to reduce a fever. If the child is in pain, you can give them appropriate doses of paracetamol, which has the side effect of taking away fevers.

However, fever in the very young should be taken seriously. For the first few months of their lives, babies can't easily express how they feel. They become dehydrated more easily than older children, and are also at greater risk of contracting serious infections. Babies under three months with a fever should be examined by a paediatrician the same day. Paediatricians can often quickly determine whether a situation is dangerous, sometimes by taking a blood sample, but usually through their extensive experience in examining healthy and sick babies. With older children, it is more sensible to wait out the fever for a few days unless the child is particularly lethargic. If there is a good explanation for the fever (such as a cold or gastroenteritis), a child's immune system will usually be equipped to fight the infection.

The mother lends the baby her immunological memory

Newborn babies have an excellent innate immune system, but they have not as yet acquired any immunological memory. As babies have not encountered any bacteria or viruses in the sterile womb, their acquired immune system has not formed any antibodies or memory cells that can respond very quickly to such threats. Fortunately, nature allows babies to borrow antibodies from their mothers to provide temporary initial protection. This protection happens in two ways: during pregnancy, antibodies are transferred from the mother to the baby via the placenta; breastfed babies also receive antibodies with the mother's milk.

There are different types of antibodies. The most commonly found antibody in the blood is called immunoglobulin G (IgG). During pregnancy, IgG antibodies are pumped from the mother's blood into the baby's bloodstream. The IgG pump starts working mid-pregnancy, and the baby gets more and more IgG the longer the pregnancy continues. At birth, a baby actually has higher blood IgG levels than its mother. However, a baby born in week 24 will have a much lesser amount of IgG than a baby born at term. This is one of the reasons for the sensitivity of very premature babies to infections. The IgG antibodies are gradually broken down in the newborn's body, but during the first two or three months they provide fairly good protection against many infections, provided that the mother has previously had these infections or has been vaccinated against them. If she hasn't, she will not have antibodies against these particular bacteria or viruses.

Many mammals lack our ability to pump IgG from mother to baby during pregnancy. Calves and piglets are born without antibodies, leaving them extremely vulnerable to infections. They need their mother's colostrum (the first milk) in order to fight early infections The colostrum from cows and sows contains IgG antibodies that are absorbed in the intestine and help their calves or piglets to defend themselves against contagions.

Human milk mostly contains immunoglobulin A (IgA), which is not absorbed into a baby's blood. Instead, IgA in human milk binds to bacteria and viruses in a baby's throat and intestines, making them unable to attach to the baby's mucous membranes. This makes it harder for bacteria and viruses to enter the body and cause infections. The IgA antibodies provide particularly powerful protection against two types of infection: bacterial diarrhoea (such as that caused by *Salmonella*, *Shigella*, or *Campylobacter*) and bacterial sepsis (blood poisoning). Bacterial diarrhoea is extremely common in countries where people don't have access to clean water, and where poor sanitation leads to contamination of both water and food by faecal bacteria. These bacteria are very rare in high-income countries like Sweden, the UK, and Australia, although *Campylobacter* can sometimes be found in raw or incorrectly prepared chicken, and *Salmonella* may be found in eggs and other foods.

Blood poisoning (sepsis) occurs when bacteria enter the bloodstream via the intestine, the mouth, the urinary tract, or the skin, resulting in an extremely dangerous infection throughout the body. Sepsis is relatively common among newborn babies in poor countries, with 1–2 per cent being affected. In high-income countries, sepsis is about fifty times less common; in Sweden, only one in 4,000 newborn babies contracts sepsis — mainly premature babies. The protective role of breast milk against sepsis is one of the reasons why, since the 1970s, premature babies in Sweden have been given their own mother's expressed milk or milk from a milk bank. Another reason is that breastfeeding reduces the risk of necrotising enterocolitis, a serious intestinal inflammation that can affect premature babies.

In addition to providing protection against bacterial diarrhoea and sepsis, breastfeeding also has some effect against respiratory infections and possibly against rotavirus infections. It is hard to know whether the effect is due to breastfeeding itself. Mothers who breastfeed generally have a higher level of education and smoke less, which are factors linked to a reduced risk of infections. However, as we have said previously, in high-income countries with good hygiene standards and very few serious infectious diseases, there is generally little difference between breastfed and bottle-fed babies in terms of the child's general health.

Why do newborns become more seriously ill from infections than older children?

As we have explained, a newborn baby's immune system is well developed, even though it lacks its own immunological memory. Despite this protection, infectious diseases requiring hospital treatment, such as respiratory infections and gastroenteritis, are more common during the first few months than later in a child's life. Of course, this is not to say that serious infections are common among newborns; only that they are more common than among older children.

Respiratory infections that would merely be an inconvenience for adults can present serious problems in newborns. Their airways are much narrower, and it is easier for them to get blocked with mucous. Newborns also have weak respiratory muscles and are not good at coughing up mucous. This is the main reason why infection with respiratory syncytial virus (RSV) — a common-cold virus that we all catch from time to time — affects around one in 100 newborn babies so badly that they need hospital care.

Newborns are more susceptible to fluid imbalance, and can become dehydrated more easily than older children and adults. Dehydration often occurs when babies have gastroenteritis, but also when they have a respiratory infection, which causes them to breathe more quickly, resulting in increased moisture evaporation. Dehydration leads to tiredness, which may mean that the baby doesn't drink and ends up in a vicious cycle of dehydration.

The most important treatment for infections in babies is often to clear the nose so they can breathe, and to feed them, either from breast or bottle. If the baby is unable to feed, they will be fed in hospital through a silicon tube that is inserted into the nose and down into the stomach.

In rare paediatric conditions such as bacterial blood poisoning (sepsis), and the equally rare — but extremely dangerous — meningitis, the initial signs are often vague and diffuse, and include tiredness, weak sucking, and sometimes fever. In both these conditions, early treatment with antibiotic or antiviral medication is important to reduce mortality and complications. Many babies with fever are treated for a day or two with antibiotics or antivirals until doctors are able to rule out any dangerous underlying cause. For these reasons, you should take your baby to the emergency department if they are younger than three months old and have a temperature of more than 38°C. Even more importantly, go to the emergency paediatric clinic if your baby is unusually lethargic and unable to feed as usual, even if they don't have a fever.

Is it safer to stay indoors?

In Sweden, parents of babies are regularly advised to stay at home and indoors — throughout the entire winter season at least — to avoid their baby contracting infections. This advice is not based on medical evidence. First, it is only respiratory infections that children risk contracting when they are in contact with other people. Blood poisoning, urinary tract infections, and meningitis cannot be transmitted via the air, but are usually caused by bacteria present in the mother's or the baby's own intestines, throat, or skin, or by the herpes virus, which can be transferred from the mother's vagina. For the first few months, the baby will be protected against certain diseases, including measles and chickenpox, through IgG antibodies received from the mother during pregnancy, providing that the mother is immune to these viral agents.

Measles is spread through the air. It is such a severe disease, with potentially devastating complications, that we recommend keeping unvaccinated children out of reach of the measles virus. Fortunately, measles vaccination has led to a situation where the virus is not normally spread in Sweden, Australia, and New Zealand. In the UK, large outbreaks have occurred, with long measles-free intervals in between. When no measles virus is spreading in the population, it is safe for infants to mix with other people. If an outbreak occurs, it is wise to keep an unvaccinated infant away from crowded public places such as public transport and shopping malls.

However, if your baby is diagnosed with congenital heart disease, severe immunodeficiency, or metabolic disease, or if they were born extremely preterm and have just come home from a prolonged hospital stay, it may be sensible to keep them a few metres from other people, even when indoors; for these babies, a cold virus could result in a life-threatening condition. In such cases, ask your paediatrician for individual advice.

For all other babies, the risk of contracting respiratory infections in public places or on public transport is very low, and a common cold is not usually dangerous, even for a newborn. Microorganisms that can cause more serious problems, such as whooping cough bacteria (pertussis) and RSV virus, tend not to infect a baby in a pram. One research study shows that a person has to hold and be extremely close to a baby to pass on a RSV infection.[1] Babies tend to catch RSV infections or whooping cough at home, usually from a snotty older sibling who brings it home from preschool, or from a parent with a persistent cough.

Staying at home all the time with a baby may be risky for a parent and, by extension, for their baby. New parents can find themselves in a fragile mental state, as social isolation is a known risk factor for mental ill health and is also an early symptom of depression and anxiety disorder. Having a parent with depression is much worse for a baby than having a common cold. A reasonable level of precaution would be to prevent someone outside the immediate family who has a heavy cold from snuggling up with the baby, but otherwise we would encourage you to socialise, and to take your baby out and about.

If a baby has older siblings, there is no sense in trying to control the minimal risk of contagion within broader society, when most infections are spread within the family and there is no real way of avoiding them. You could, in theory, isolate an older sibling from other children, but this is not recommended. To be told that they are unable to spend time with their preschool friends for the baby's sake is beyond what most average three-year-olds can cope with mentally. And looking after a newborn baby and an hysterical three-year-old who misses their friends is much more than most adults can cope with without losing their sense of humour! It is also important to remember that having an older sibling is one of the best-documented protective factors against allergies (see chapter 11), and it is probably the older sibling's habit of bringing infections home to the baby that provides this protective effect. We understand that it's not easy for parents when a baby has a cold, but it's not dangerous. Dangerous infections are rarely spread to a baby in a pram when a parent visits a café, library, or shop.

STARTING DAYCARE OR PRESCHOOL: TRAINING CAMP FOR THE IMMUNE SYSTEM

As we have explained, a newborn baby has no immunological memory. The greater the number of infections to which an infant is exposed (and the more vaccinations they receive), the greater the number of infections they will be protected against by acquiring immunological memory. Young children normally have six to eight viral infections a year, while adults might get only two or three. Bearing in mind that there are hundreds of different viruses that can cause a common cold, we'll have been exposed to maybe half of them by the time we reach our twenties. On average, by that stage, we'll already be immune to half the viruses we encounter, and will therefore only catch half as many viral infections.

Since almost all viral infections occur in the winter months, it's completely normal for a young child to have a cold almost half the time during these months. This doesn't mean there's anything wrong with their immune system; they're still building up their own immunological memory so as to avoid catching many infections later in life. There is no particular time by which children become 'immunologically mature' and more resistant to colds — it's just a matter of how much they've trained their immunological memory.

Before their child starts daycare or preschool, we recommend that parents draw up a plan for who will care for the child when it's sick. After all, illness will certainly happen, especially during the first winter season of out-of-home care. Just as we believe you should share your parental leave equally during your first year with the baby, we also believe parents should share the care of a sick child equally. Make a plan in advance so you can avoid fraught negotiations about who has the most important meeting or the most boring job, or who generally feels the hardest done by when it comes to allocating childcare. You could take responsibility for alternate days, or allocate odd and evenly numbered weeks between you, so you can book in important meetings when you know you won't be responsible for looking after a sick child. Try to pick some method of sharing the care that allows you to avoid last-minute negotiations.

Children with chickenpox can be cared for by healthy grandparents who aren't at risk of being infected. However, it's sensible not to inflict colds and gastroenteritis on the older generation, especially if they're not in the best of health. Just like babies, grandparents risk being hit harder by infections than a baby's parents.

FEAR OF GERMS

For some reason, a fear of germs is incredibly common today. On the evidence, this seems strange, because very few people in Sweden or comparable countries would know someone who has suffered from a deadly infection. It may have been reasonable to be scared of bacteria centuries ago when many people died from infectious diseases; but in the 21st century, infections represent a minimal threat to our health. A fear of germs is highly irrational nowadays.

Some people think that they can catch an infection by touching a handle, by sitting on a seat on public transport, or by using a mobile phone that someone else has used. The good news is that these fears are completely unfounded. Despite what you may read on click-bait news sites, there's no risk at all that you can catch an infection from the regular skin bacteria you might find lurking on a public handrail, a mobile screen, or a dirty keyboard.

If you fear germs, you'll naturally feel a strong urge to protect your child from them. You might start boiling dummies and bottle teats to sterilise them. This is unnecessary extra work. Sterilisation is important in a maternity ward where premature babies are cared for, or if you're on holiday in a country with unclean water, or if a warning has been issued about an outbreak of waterborne contagion in your local drinking water supply; otherwise, there is no need to boil dummies or bottle teats.

If you give in to an irrational fear of germs, you may find that you are adopting more and more rules and are starting to develop irrational behaviours. You might start carrying hand sanitiser around in your handbag and insisting that people sanitise their hands before holding your baby. You might not want your child to crawl on a dusty café floor, or to suck its fingers when they haven't been recently washed. You might start trying to persuade your partner to be more wary of germs, too. This kind of behaviour doesn't help your child.

It's a good idea to try to combat anxieties that you may develop about other people's bacteria. Challenge your fear by sharing drinking glasses and spoons with others. Pick up the sandwich you dropped on the floor, and eat it — the bacteria on your kitchen floor are no more dangerous than the ones on your desk top. If these challenges make you particularly anxious, you probably have more than a mild fear of germs. These fears can develop into a phobia, so if you find yourself excessively worrying about germs, a psychologist who specialises in cognitive behavioural theory will be able to help you. The highly troubling condition of obsessive-compulsive disorder (OCD) can sometimes manifest itself through an excessive fear of dirt and bacteria. Fortunately, OCD can be treated successfully by psychiatrists and psychologists.

IN BRIEF

Common infections aren't something that parents of young children in high-income nations generally need to worry about. Harmful infections such as meningitis and blood poisoning do occur, but they are rare and are not spread in public places or between people. Children have excellent immune systems that need to be trained through contact with people and animals. If you have a fear of germs, try to challenge your fear rather than encouraging it with control behaviours, hand sanitiser, or excessive hand-washing.

CHAPTER TEN

Vaccination

No single medical intervention has been as important for children's health as vaccination. Childhood vaccination has saved billions of lives, and is one of the most important factors behind the decrease in childhood mortality worldwide.[1]

Despite this, there is some vocal and active opposition to vaccinations, especially online, and it's not always easy to know whose advice to trust. In this chapter, we describe current immunisation programs for children, and the diseases they protect against. We delve a little into the history of diseases that used to be commonplace and often deadly, but today are almost forgotten due to the effectiveness of vaccinations in their eradication. In chapter 2, we discussed which vaccines are safe for pregnant women. Here, we discuss the safety of vaccinations generally, and emphasise the importance of vaccination for individual children, and for the general community.

For most of human history, infections have been the most common cause of death. Young children have been the most vulnerable to deadly infections, but infections have killed people of all ages. We can see this pattern in in the following illustration, which reproduces 1786 church records from the Swedish town of Sipoo.

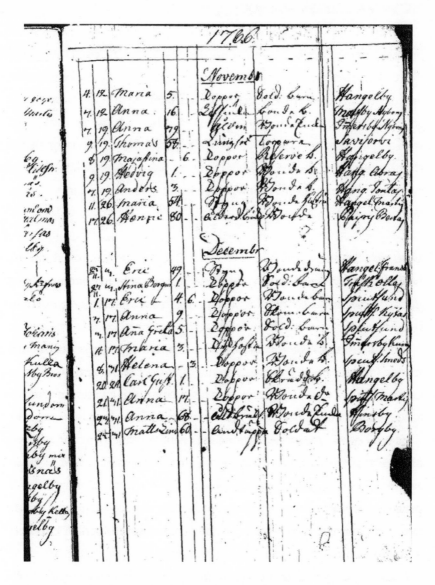

Sipoo parish records, 1786. Maria, aged five, Maja Stina, aged six months, Hedvig, aged one, Anders, aged three, Stina, aged one, Erik, aged four, Anna, aged nine, Anna Greta, aged five, Helena, aged three months, Carl Gustaf, aged one, and Anna, aged 17, all died from 'pox' (*koppor* in Swedish), now usually called smallpox. Source: http://www.digiarkisto.org/sshy/index_eng.htm.

HOW VACCINES WORK

Vaccines are designed to induce a long-lasting immune response to protect against certain bacteria or viruses. In order to achieve this protection, the main ingredient of a vaccine needs to be either a micro-organism or molecules with identical structure as parts of the microorganism recognisable by the immune system. There are two main types of vaccines: live and non-live. Live vaccines contain living microorganisms that cannot cause disease in an immunocompetent host, while non-live vaccines do not contain live microorganisms — thus they cannot cause disease in any host.

Live vaccines

Live vaccines can be of two types: related species and live-attenuated. In the first type, a related microorganism, which does not cause real illness, is used in the vaccines to protect against dangerous disease-causing microorganisms. Examples of this include the cowpox virus that Edward Jenner used as vaccine against smallpox, and the Bacillus Calmette Guérin (BCG) strain, a relative of the tuberculosis bacterium that is used to vaccinate millions of children against tuberculosis.

The second type of live vaccine uses weaker versions of the original microorganism to produce a vaccine. A virus can be attenuated by culti-vating it for a long time in a laboratory until it loses certain genes that would cause disease. Live-attenuated vaccines offer good immunity, but the problem is that they often can't be given to those with an impaired immune system, such as children undergoing treatment for cancer, or who have a serious congenital immunodeficiency. Even attenuated vac-cine strains that are harmless to the rest of us can make these children seriously ill.

Non-live vaccines

Non-live vaccines can never cause infection; therefore, they can be safely given to individuals with an impaired immune system. They can be produced in different ways: some are whole microorganisms that are killed in the laboratory (also called inactivated vaccines); others use parts of the outer membranes or capsules of a microorganism, either in a pure form or molecularly tied to a protein that activates the immune system. For diseases where microorganisms produce toxins that cause symptoms, the vaccine might be a variant of the toxin that does not cause disease (a toxoid). Vaccines of this type often contain an adjuvant, which is a substance that is added to stimulate the immune defence to more readily form an immunological memory against the content of the vaccine.

Vaccines have been used successfully against a range of diseases and conditions that would otherwise represent a serious threat to children's health.

CHICKENPOX

Chickenpox (varicella) is an extremely infectious viral disease that almost all children contract in countries such as Sweden where the vaccine is not included in the national immunisation program. Most will suffer from a slight cough, fever, and itchy blisters, and some will experience many blisters in the mouth and throat, making it painful to eat and drink, or in the genital area, causing difficulty in urinating.

Complications from the varicella virus are common. The most prevalent complications include ear inflammation and bacterial infection of the blisters, while the spread of the virus to the lungs and the brain is less common but more serious. Blood poisoning caused by bacteria getting into damaged blisters is another dangerous complication.

After the initial infection, the varicella virus lies dormant in nerve cells. As long as the immune system remains healthy and swift-acting, it can keep the virus in check and inactive. However, if the immune system is weakened by illness or age, there is a risk that the virus in the nerve cells will be re-activated and manifest as shingles, a condition with painful, localised skin blisters.

For several decades, there has been an effective live vaccine against chickenpox that is available either in combination with the measles-mumps-rubella (MMR) vaccine or as a stand-alone vaccine. The chickenpox vaccine is not included in the public vaccination program in Sweden or in the UK, in contrast to many other countries — such as Australia, New Zealand, the US, and Germany — where it has proven highly effective. One reason why some countries have been reluctant to introduce the vaccine is a fear that vaccinating small children will increase shingles disease in the elderly. The reason for this fear is based on the hypothesis that if a child contacts varicella, their immune response towards the virus will be boosted, and this will protect them against shingles in later life. Another reason is that varicella is considered a relatively mild disease. That is true in most cases, but not all, as with many of the vaccines in national immunisation programs.

DIPHTHERIA

The old Swedish name for diphtheria — strangulation disease — tells us why we are lucky to have a vaccine for diphtheria. The diphtheria bacteria live in the throat, secreting a toxin that causes a severe inflammation which damages its lining and produces a thick grey-white coating called 'pseudomembrane'. This coating looks like leather, and indeed the word diphtheria is derived from the Greek word for leather. The pseudomembrane can block the throat and prevent breathing. The bacterial toxin also spreads through the bloodstream, and can attack nerves and the heart. Even with today's modern treatments, 5–10 per cent of those who are infected will die. Children under five and adults over 40 have an even greater risk of dying from diphtheria, with the mortality rate standing at around 20 per cent.[2]

The diphtheria toxin is a protein. Medical research has produced a version with no toxic effect — a toxoid that is so similar to the original toxic protein that it induces the production of antibodies in vaccinated children to protect them from the toxin. The diphtheria vaccine gives almost complete protection against this deadly disease, but unfortunately diphtheria has not yet been eradicated globally. WHO reported 4,530 cases in 2015. In Australia, there were 21 diphtheria cases in the five-year period 2013–18, including the death of an unvaccinated 20-year-old man in 2018. No vaccinated person has died from diphtheria in Australia in more than 20 years. It is extremely important to continue vaccinating against diphtheria in order to prevent new epidemics.

INFLUENZA

The influenza (flu) virus spreads across the world in annual epidemics, and comes in four types: A, B, C, and D. In human populations, the epidemics arise from the A and B types. Influenza A is divided into different subtypes, and as the virus mutates readily, new subtypes are formed continuously. Influenza B usually has two different lineages, Influenza B/Yamagata and B/Victoria, named after the places in which they were first isolated.

Influenza spreads mainly through the inhalation of saliva droplets expelled by coughing and sneezing. After an incubation period of one to two days, the disease produces a high fever, coughing, malaise, muscle pain, a sore throat, and a runny nose. Otherwise healthy people who contract the flu usually stay in bed for a week or so, and then go back to work feeling a bit tired but otherwise well. For infants, elderly people, pregnant women, and people with chronic health conditions, influenza may take a severe course, developing into pneumonia or encephalitis. Many influenza cases are also complicated by bacterial infections such as middle-ear infections or bacterial pneumonia.

Vaccines against influenza can only be targeted at the subtypes that spread in any given year. But as these subtypes vary from year to year, people have to have a new flu shot every year to ensure maximum protection. There has been a recent improvement in influenza vaccines, whereby tetravalent vaccines, which protect against the four strains of virus (the two B lineages and two A subtypes) have replaced earlier

PARENTHOOD THE SWEDISH WAY

trivalent vaccines that protected only against three strains. The standard flu shot is an inactivated injectable vaccine, but a live nasal spray vaccine is also on the market and is recommended for child vaccination in some countries.

Seasonal influenza is therefore a major cause of illness that also contributes to deaths in the population, which is why annual vaccination is recommended and funded for at-risk groups in the national immunisation programs of Australia, New Zealand, and Sweden. In the US, vaccination is recommended for everybody above six months of age. In the UK, in addition to medical at-risk groups, an annual influenza vaccination program for children two years and older is currently being introduced. Even though annual influenza vaccinations have not been included in the funded national programs in other countries, no country recommends against such vaccinations, even if you are not part of an at-risk group. If you live in one of these countries and want to give yourself or your child even better protection against infectious diseases than is offered through the national immunisation program, the addition of a yearly influenza vaccination is a good start.

HEPATITIS B

Hepatitis B is a blood-borne virus that can cause acute or chronic liver inflammation, cirrhosis, and cancer of the liver. Most people who carry the hepatitis B virus are asymptomatic, and they might not know they are carriers. The prevalence of hepatitis B varies globally from less than one in 200 Caucasians to more than one in 10 people in Sub-Saharan Africa, south-east Asia, and Pacific Islands populations. In Australia, hepatitis B is more common in Aboriginal and Torres Strait Islander populations.

Newborn infants may contract hepatitis B from their infected mothers during delivery. Small bleedings during labour, and contact with maternal secretions with live virus in the birth canal, can transmit the virus. Babies in Australia are routinely given the hepatitis B vaccine soon after birth. In the UK and Sweden, the vaccine was introduced in the national immunisation programs in 2017.

The vaccine against hepatitis B is highly effective, and the WHO has long recommended that all countries should include hepatitis B in their vaccination schedules. This practice would eventually stop the circulation of the virus in humans. Even in populations where hepatitis B is uncommon, it is wise to immunise all infants, as you cannot predict who will cut themselves on a used needle or have unprotected sex with a hepatitis B-positive partner later in life. When everyone is immunised we are all protected.

HIB

Older paediatricians sometimes recall, with a note of terror in their voices, the condition of epiglottitis (inflammation of the epiglottis) that once affected preschool children and could cause a blockage of the airways in a matter of hours. They vividly describe children arriving on stretchers, a look of panic on their faces, sweating with fever and drooling saliva that they were unable to swallow. Today, all young doctors still learn the importance of delaying the examination of a child's throat, or otherwise causing them anxiety, until a tube is inserted into the airway to reduce the risk of them not being able to breathe at all and dying in the emergency room.

However, children with severe inflammation of the epiglottis are nowadays very rarely seen in emergency paediatric clinics in Sweden, or in other countries with a vaccination program against *Haemophilus influenzae* type B (or Hib). Hib is a bacterium, and is not related to the influenza virus that causes flu. Apart from causing epiglottitis, another common presentation of Hib disease in children is meningitis.

In Australia, before introduction of the Hib vaccine, annual attack rates in most populations was between 40 to 60 per 100,000 in children under five years of age, with epiglottitis as the most common presenting symptom. In indigenous populations in the Northern Territory, however, rates were tenfold higher, and the most common presentation was meningitis. In Sweden, the annual attack rate was 50 to 65 per 100,000 children under five, and in the UK it was 21–44 per 100,000.

Hib vaccination programs were introduced in the UK in 1992, and in Sweden and Australia in 1993. They have been a pure success story. Before the introduction of the vaccine, each year around 1,500 children under five years of age in the UK, 600 in Australia, and 200 in Sweden suffered from epiglottis infections, meningitis, or blood poisoning caused by Hib, and a number of children died. Today, there are only a few individual cases per year.[3] The Hib bacterium is still spread within many other countries, so it is important to continue to vaccinate all children.

Many variants of *Haemophilus influenzae* are commonly found in normal throat flora and at the back of the nasal passage of young children. These variants are not the type-B variant, but are other bacteria that lack a capsule and don't cause life-threatening diseases of the type described above. Non-encapsulated *Haemophilus influenzae* is a common cause of green nasal catarrh and ear inflammation, and the vaccine does not protect against these symptoms.

MEASLES

Worldwide, measles kills more than 100,000 children every year. The measles virus spreads through the air, and is one of the most contagious diseases we know of. In an unvaccinated population, almost all children will catch measles during childhood. The disease often manifests in symptoms such as coughing, conjunctivitis, rash, and fever. A third of those who contract measles experience some kind of complication — usually a middle-ear infection, diarrhoea, or pneumonia. In one in 1,000 cases, infection by the measles virus affects the brain (encephalitis).

In a well-nourished population with high-standard healthcare, such as in Australia or Sweden, one in 500 people who contract measles will die from it. Among survivors, some will experience a complication that returns several years after the original measles infection in the form of serious, increasing brain damage, cramps, and ultimately death. This condition is called subacute sclerosing panencephalitis (SSPE), and there is no effective treatment for it. The risk of developing SSPE is highest for children who contract measles before one year of age, where the risk, according to the latest research, may be as high as one in 600 infants. The only way of preventing SSPE is by preventing measles infection, especially in young infants.

A measles vaccine has been available since 1963, while the combined MMR vaccine was introduced in Australia in 1975, in Sweden in 1981, and in the UK in 1988. The vaccine is highly effective; only small, containable outbreaks now occur in countries with good vaccine coverage, such as Sweden and Australia, and they are due to travellers who contracted the disease abroad. MMR vaccine is scheduled at 12 and 18 months in UK and Australia. If an infant is at high risk of contracting measles, as during an outbreak, an extra vaccine dose can be given at six months of age.

Because there are so few people without immunity, the virus cannot spread among the population; this phenomenon is known as herd immunity. Some 93–95 per cent of the population must be vaccinated in order for herd immunity to operate; if fewer are vaccinated, there will be outbreaks (a collection of cases of an infection contracted from a single infected individual).

In many countries, including the UK, vaccine refusal has reduced the vaccination rate below this point, and measles outbreaks and even epidemics (larger outbreaks) are commonplace. In Australia, confirmed cases of measles were at a five-year high in 2019, when 78 cases were diagnosed in the first three months. Although a worrying increase, the number is small compared with the large epidemics seen in the last few years in Europe, with 27,000 cases and 71 deaths in 2017 and 2018. Most cases have been seen in unvaccinated individuals, not least in infants too young to be vaccinated. Countries with historically low vaccination rates in the whole population, or in parts of the population — such as Germany, Greece, Italy, Romania, and France — have been particularly afflicted.

The risk of measles infection remains present in many countries where vaccine coverage is not high enough. For example, about 60,000 people in the western Pacific region are infected with measles every year. If you are heading abroad with young children who have not yet been vaccinated against measles, you should definitely consider having them vaccinated. If they are below six months of age and therefore too young to be vaccinated, check the measles situation in your destination before you go. A travel vaccination clinic is a good place to start. The European Centre for Disease Control provides up-to-date information about European outbreaks. If there is a current outbreak in your destination, ask yourselves if your trip is so important that you are willing to risk your child contracting measles, with a one-in-500 risk of death, and an additional one-in-600 risk of SSPE disease and death later on.

MENINGOCOCCAL DISEASE

Meningococci are bacteria that are known to cause especially severe meningitis and septicaemia in people of all ages, but small children are the most vulnerable. The bacteria are spread through close physical contact, and outbreaks have been common in adolescents and young adults who meet in places such as summer camps and college campuses. Septicaemia and meningitis caused by meningococci are known to develop very rapidly — one person out of 20 with such a disease dies, even with intensive care. Of the survivors, one in five will suffer permanent disabilities such as limb amputation, hearing loss, and brain damage.

Meningococci have capsules (as do pneumococci), and there are six distinctive variations, or serotypes (A, B, C, W, X, Y) that cause the vast majority of meningococcal disease worldwide. For a long time there was only a vaccine against type C, which was included in the UK national immunisation program between 1999 and 2017. Presently, there are two vaccines: a group B vaccine, and a group ACWY vaccine. Both are non-live vaccines, and provide excellent protection against meningococcal disease caused by those particular variations. In Australia, the ACWY vaccine is included in the national immunisation program, and in the UK, both the B vaccine and the ACWY vaccine are included.

MUMPS

Mumps is a viral disease whose most common symptoms are fever and sore, swollen salivary glands. It is unpleasant, but generally not harmful if contracted as a child. However, when boys and men contract mumps after puberty, 15–30 per cent experience testicular inflammation (orchitis). In some rare cases, bilateral orchitis has been associated with infertility, but in most cases, fertility is preserved. When adult women contract mumps, around 5 per cent develop inflammation in the ovaries, which has been associated with infertility and premature menopause in some women. Mumps disease in early pregnancy is associated with an increased risk of spontaneous abortion. Around 4 per cent of mumps cases are complicated by pancreatitis, often in a mild form, and 1–10 per cent develop meningitis. Encephalitis and deafness are rare complications. Since the inclusion of the mumps vaccination in the combined MMR vaccine in the national immunisation programs in most high-income countries, mumps has become a rare disease. Unfortunately, the vaccine does not provide perfect protection against mumps, and large outbreaks have occurred in many countries, including the UK. Including a second MMR dose in immunisation programs is thought to enhance protection against mumps, even if the primary reason for doing it is to protect our populations against measles.

PNEUMOCOCCAL DISEASE

Streptococcus pneumoniae (pneumococci) are bacteria commonly found in young children's normal throat flora. Our nose and throat flora contains millions of bacteria that don't make us sick and are transferred to other people in droplets of saliva or mucous — typically through sneezing, coughing, toy-sharing, or kissing.

But pneumococci also cause illnesses, from very mild infections to life-threatening diseases. Mild infections caused by pneumococci are often mild or acute middle-ear infections, or mild cases of pneumonia. Pneumococcal pneumonia may also be more severe, and most severe infections are septicaemia (blood poisoning) and meningitis, which are called invasive diseases because the bacteria invades parts of the body, such as blood, fluids, and tissues that are normally free from infection. Children below two years of age, and people above 65 years, are more susceptible to invasive pneumococcal disease than older children and adults. People with untreated HIV, or who have sickle cell disease, or are without a spleen are at the highest risk for invasive disease.

The pneumococcus is surrounded by a thick, slimy layer (a capsule) that prevents white blood cells from capturing and eating the invading bacterium. Antibodies are needed to get rid of the capsule, but the problem is that there are around 100 different types of capsules. Some occur less commonly, and not all capsule types have the same ability to cause infection. The vaccine used for children currently contains 13 capsule types. In the vaccine, the capsules are joined with a protein to produce a better immune response, because children's immune systems are not good at forming antibodies against the capsules in a pure form.

The capsule types chosen for the vaccine are those that most often cause serious diseases, while the less harmful strains found in normal flora are not affected. Since the introduction of the vaccine in childhood immunisation programs, the number of children contracting invasive pneumococcal disease has decreased significantly. In the UK, more than 43,000 children have been saved from severe pneumococcal disease from 2002 to 2015, thanks to pneumococcal vaccination.[4]

In most countries, a decrease has been seen even in non-vaccinated age groups following the general introduction of the childhood vaccine. The reason for this is that vaccinated infants and toddlers no longer transmit these bacteria to their parents and grandparents, indirectly protecting them from disease. The strains of pneumococcus included in the vaccine have almost disappeared from the throat flora, although pneumococci with other capsule types have increased.[5] While these weaker strains are less likely to cause disease, pneumococcus diseases cannot be eradicated unless researchers manage to develop a vaccine against all pneumococci types.

POLIO

The polio virus causes diarrhoea, and is transmitted to others by ingestion, just as with other gastroenteritis viruses. In most people, a polio infection presents as an uncomplicated gastroenteritis or respiratory-tract infection; in some, it is asymptomatic. But in some children the virus enters the nerves and spinal cord. The virus itself and the immune response against it leads to the destruction of nerves and to paralysis. In the worst case, the respiratory muscles are also affected, and the disease can prove fatal.

Polio epidemics were a regular occurrence in Sweden up until 1953, when a major outbreak caused more than 3,000 cases of paralysis. Two effective vaccines were developed against polio in the 1950s: an inactivated Swedish vaccine and a live, weakened vaccine from the USA. Sweden began a mass vaccination campaign against polio for all ages in 1957. The number of cases fell rapidly, with 64 cases reported in 1961 and only four in 1962.

The most recent — and, we hope, the last — case of polio in Sweden was reported in 1977.[6] Since polio has not been eradicated globally, the polio vaccine is still included in Sweden's child vaccination program. Australia has been officially polio-free since 2000, and it was declared eradicated in the UK in 2015. Inactive polio vaccine (IPV) is included in the vaccination schedule for children in Australia and in the UK because of the risk of people travelling to or from the few countries where polio still exists.[7]

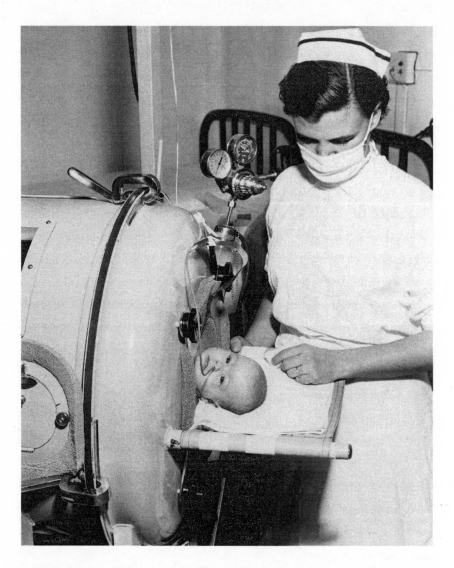

A baby with polio being cared for in an iron lung. The iron lung, an early version of a respirator, was designed in the 1920s and used during the polio epidemics of the 1940s. It was an airtight tank with a set of bellows one end. When the bellows were compressed, the pressure inside the tank rose, the patient's lungs were compressed, and the patient breathed out. When the bellows were expanded, the pressure inside the tank fell, the patient's lungs expanded, and the patient breathed in. In this way, natural breathing was replicated despite the paralysis of the respiratory muscles.

ROTAVIRUS

Rotavirus — one of several viruses causing gastroenteritis or stomach bug — is highly contagious, and is the most common cause of severe vomiting and diarrhoea in infants and young children. It spreads through physical contact, and is easily spread in daycare facilities and within families. In populations with good nutrition status and health-care access, rotavirus infections result most often in some weeks of taking care of a sick child, and a substantial number of children needing rehydration therapy in a hospital. Serious complications are uncommon, but very occasionally rotavirus has caused meningitis and severe dehydration with electrolyte balance disturbances, which may be fatal even in high-standard-care settings.

In malnourished populations with water-hygiene problems and scarce access to healthcare, rotavirus disease is responsible for many deaths among infants and small children. There, rotavirus vaccine is an important life-saver.

The vaccine against rotavirus is a live-attenuated vaccine given in drop form to children in two or three doses at four-week intervals. To minimise the risk of side effects, the final dose must be given before the age of around six months.

The vaccine provides around 90 per cent protection against rotavirus disease, and is included in immunisation programs in Sweden, Australia, and the UK.

RUBELLA

The rubella virus produces cold-like symptoms, with joint pain and rashes. The symptoms are mild in both children and adults. However, if a pregnant woman is infected with rubella, there is a risk that her foetus will be harmed. If she contracts the infection during the first eight weeks of pregnancy, there is an eight-in-ten chance of her baby being born with birth defects — most commonly associated with the brain, the eyes, the inner ear, and the heart. The risk that a child will develop diabetes is 100–200 times greater than for a child whose mother has not been infected with rubella.[8] Studies of adults who were affected while in the womb during a rubella epidemic in New York in 1963–65 showed that one-third were able to function well, one-third lived at home with their parents and were able to cope with adapted work tasks, and one-third needed around-the-clock care due to their severe medical problems.[9] Worldwide, it's estimated that more than 100,000 children are born each year with rubella-related defects.[10]

If you've never met anyone with rubella, it is because most high-income countries introduced effective vaccination against the disease decades ago. Australia began vaccinating 12-year-old girls against rubella in 1971, and Sweden did so in 1975, with the intention of protecting them if they were to become pregnant. However, rubella remained just as common until boys were also vaccinated, which occurred in Australia in 1989. Subsequently, the high rate of vaccination created herd immunity, with the result that rubella is extremely rare in Sweden today, and Australia has been almost free of rubella since 2014. (In 2014, the Australian notification rate was 0.1 per 100,000 people, with 17 notifications.) The WHO announced in October 2018 that Australia has eliminated rubella. However, elimination does not mean eradication. Outbreaks may still occur, so it is important to continue vaccinating children to prevent the spread of infection to pregnant women. Rubella is rare in the UK nowadays — most cases occur in people who come from countries that don't offer routine immunisation against the disease — but there are occasionally large outbreaks. One of these occurred in 1996, when close to 4,000 cases were reported in England and Wales.

SMALLPOX

Smallpox is one of the world's most deadly viruses. It is airborne and highly contagious, and leads to death in at least eight out of 10 infected babies, and in around half of infected adults. There is no cure for the infection, and blindness or unsightly scarring can affect those who survive it.

However, today there is no need to worry that your baby will contract smallpox, and for that you can thank the 18th-century British physician Edward Jenner.[11] Jenner saw the potential significance of the conventional farming wisdom that milkmaids very rarely caught smallpox. The reason they were protected was that they were exposed to cowpox during milking. Cowpox is a virus closely related to smallpox that affects cows instead of humans. The milkmaids were catching a very mild infection from the cowpox, with symptoms showing as just a few pustules on their hands. However, their immune systems were stimulated by their exposure to cowpox, forming an immune defence that was also effective against the closely related smallpox virus.

In an early experiment, in April 1797, Jenner took fluids from pustules on a milkmaid's hands, scratched the forearm of an eight-year-old boy, James Phipps, and rubbed the pus into his skin. The boy suffered a mild fever, some swelling of the lymph glands in the armpit, and a few days of tiredness. When Jenner then exposed Phipps to the contents of smallpox pustules three months later, the boy remained healthy. Jenner coined the term 'vaccination', derived from the Latin word for cow — *vacca* — and within just a few decades the practice of smallpox vaccination had spread around the world.

The first vaccination in Sweden took place in 1801, and in 1816 a new law decreed that all children under the age of two had to be vaccinated. Subsequently, smallpox epidemics became considerably rarer; 1895 marked the first year in which no one died of smallpox in Sweden. In 1978, Janet Parker, a medical photographer at the University of Birmingham, contracted smallpox in a laboratory where she worked. Her mother also developed the disease. They survived, and were the last people to be infected by the smallpox virus. By 1980, the whole world was declared smallpox-free by the WHO. Today, the smallpox virus only exists in frozen form in laboratories, and we hope that it will never rear its ugly head again.

Today, almost 40 years after the eradication of smallpox, it is the only disease we have succeeded in completely eradicating. We have come close to fully eradicating polio, and, at the time of writing, this disease is only spread in three countries: Afghanistan, Pakistan, and Nigeria. In these places, vaccination campaigns have been met with violent resistance — from the Taliban in Afghanistan and Pakistan, and from Boko Haram in Nigeria.

TETANUS

Tetanus is caused by a toxin from soil-borne tetanus bacteria. If a person is not vaccinated against tetanus, small cuts can become contaminated with infected soil. The tetanus toxin causes muscle cramps, resulting in extreme stiffness of the neck, difficulty in swallowing, lockjaw, and respiratory, calf, and abdominal muscle-spasms. Seizures, fever, and sweating are also common symptoms. Cramps of the respiratory muscles lead to death in around 10 per cent of cases, even with modern medical treatments.

Newborn babies have antibodies that are transferred from the mother during pregnancy, and so are protected by the mother's vaccination against tetanus until their first injection at three months. In many poor countries, however, mothers are not vaccinated and cannot transfer antibodies to their babies. Unprotected babies are vulnerable to neonatal tetanus caused by an infection of tetanus bacteria through their umbilical stump. Tens of thousands of babies die every year from this disease in countries with poor sanitation.

Tetanus is rare in Australia. It occurs at any age, but mainly in older adults who have never been vaccinated or were vaccinated more than 10 years previously. Between 2008 and 2011, 12 cases of tetanus were reported in Australia, and one death from tetanus was recorded.

As these bacteria live in soil, eradication of tetanus through vaccination is therefore impossible, so we will always need to be individually protected. Children who have completed their full vaccination schedule do not need additional tetanus injections, even if infected soil has got into a cut. However, children who have not completed the full schedule may need purified antibodies against tetanus if they have been exposed to a risk of infection, and urgent medical attention should therefore be sought if they get soil into cuts and grazes.

WHOOPING COUGH

Whooping cough (pertussis) bacteria cause a long-lasting cold with severe coughing fits. The coughing can result in a child being short of breath, vomiting mucous, and losing consciousness. Few things are as distressing as watching on helplessly as a baby has a choking fit. The infant panics, becomes sweaty, is unable to breathe, and turns grey-blue, while all you can do is wait it out. These severe choking fits often persist for three or four weeks. Older children and adults who contract whooping cough do not typically suffer from these extreme choking fits; they just have a cold, with a lot of coughing, for a period of six to eight weeks.

In recent years, 700–800 cases of whooping cough have been reported annually in Sweden, but the unreported figures are probably higher. There were 20,106 notifications of whooping cough in Australia in 2016; about one in 33 notifications were of infants under 12 months. In New Zealand, there has been an outbreak of pertussis since October 2017, with more than 4,500 cases reported by March 2019.

The main problem with whooping cough is that it spreads across the general community and can infect babies who are too young to have the vaccine and who are also at the greatest risk of developing the most severe symptoms. The vaccine provides protection against whooping cough in most cases, but only for a few years. After this period of protection, children and adults may contract whooping cough again, and spread it to unvaccinated babies. It is important to test family members with a persistent cough to see whether they have been infected by pertussis bacteria. Babies under six months who have been exposed to whooping cough should be given preventive antibiotics.

Vaccine researchers and policy-makers are working on ways to improve the protection of the very youngest babies from pertussis infection. The re-vaccination of all immediate family members has been tried, but this approach has had little, if any, effect. Giving women a booster vaccination during pregnancy appears to be a promising approach, because the increase in their antibody levels is transferred to their baby to provide better protection at birth. This booster vaccination is, as we have already mentioned, recommended in the UK, Australia, and New Zealand. If your prenatal healthcare provider does not offer you the vaccination, ask for it yourself.

Experts agree that babies should be given the first dose of the pertussis vaccine early; it is scheduled at six weeks in New Zealand, and eight weeks in Australia and in the UK. Do not delay the dose! Even if the vaccine currently in use is only moderately effective and does not always prevent illness, the first dose does provide good protection against the most severe effects of the infection that can lead to death.[12]

NATIONAL IMMUNISATION PROGRAMS

National immunisation programs exist in all countries, and are tailored to protect populations against as many severe diseases as possible. The programs are quite similar in most high-income countries, with some small variations. Recommendations for immunisation programs are made by the WHO, and the national programs are developed by public-health experts.[13] The professionals who participate in this development are not allowed to have any financial interests in the vaccine industry.

The number of vaccinations and the intervals between them needed to ensure a good immune response differ between different vaccines, and the national programs are constructed to give maximum protection from all vaccines with as few doses as possible. When new knowledge is acquired from research results, the schedules are revised accordingly. It is therefore wise to follow the national program exactly as it is offered to your child, as it will reflect current scientific knowledge about effective and safe vaccination.

Some parents feel anxious about subjecting their young children to multiple vaccines, and about whether their children's immune systems are sufficiently developed to handle so many vaccines at the same time. The answer is clear: children's immune systems can manage this perfectly well. In fact, their immune systems are better activated by a mixture of vaccines than by a single vaccine. Another advantage is that, this way, the child does not need as many injections. Most vaccines contain aluminium to activate the immune system, and repeated doses of vaccines containing aluminium can lead to an irritating but harmless side effect in the form of itchy skin. Fewer injections reduces the risk of this reaction. You could postpone vaccinations for your child, or let them have just some of them, but remember that if you choose not to follow the national program, you will be taking a less-studied vaccination path whereby vaccines may be less effective.

Aluminium, formaldehyde, and mercury in vaccines

As mentioned above, some non-live vaccines contain a tiny amount of aluminium as an adjuvant, which is needed to activate the immune system for the vaccine to work. Many parents feel uneasy about the idea of injecting aluminium into their children, but large studies have been done on potential side effects, and the only one that has been shown to occur is the contact allergy mentioned above. The amount of aluminium is so tiny that a child ingests more aluminium in two days of drinking infant formula than they get from each vaccination.

In the production of some inactivated vaccines, viruses are killed using formaldehyde, a chemical that is toxic not only to viruses, but also to humans when in high concentrations. Despite efforts to wash away as much formaldehyde as possible during this process, there are measurable traces of formaldehyde left in such inactivated vaccines. However, the doses are extremely low. A new bookshelf from IKEA will cause a larger exposure through the release of formaldehyde in the air during its first weeks in a new home than a vaccine gives to a child. No side effects of these traces (neither in vaccines, nor from IKEA furniture) have been noted.

Historically, a mercury-containing preservative, thiomersal, was used in some vaccines given to children. Parents questioned this use, and research confirmed that the preservative was an unnecessary component of vaccines. It was ultimately removed from most vaccines, and most countries now use thiomersal-free and thus mercury-free vaccines in their national immunisation programs. We should also mention that no side effects were ever noted from thiomersal use in vaccines — they were simply proven unnecessary.

SIDE EFFECTS OF VACCINES

All effective medicines have side effects, and naturally this applies to vaccines. However, in order for a vaccine to be included in national immunisation programs, it must be extremely safe and well documented.

The vaccines in the national immunisation programs

The vaccines against diphtheria, tetanus, pertussis, polio, Hib, hepatitis B, and pneumococcal disease are inactivated, and no serious side effects have been noted for these vaccines — millions of doses of which are administered annually worldwide. Harmless side effects include mild pain and redness at the site of the injection, or grumpiness and fever on the first day after the vaccination. These reactions signal that the immune defence is starting to be activated. In some uncommon cases, the redness is greater, and the swelling may remain for a few days.

One particularly frightening (but entirely harmless) side effect seen in around one in 10,000 vaccinated children is called a hypotonic-hyporesponsive episode. This side effect was more common after vaccination with an old type of pertussis vaccine (whole-cell pertussis vaccine), but has even been described following other vaccinations. Nobody knows why it happens. On the day immediately after a vaccination, a child may become completely limp and unresponsive. This condition remains for a few hours, but then passes and the child returns to normal. If your child does become unresponsive following a vaccination, call an ambulance so that the episode can be investigated at a hospital.

The MMR and chickenpox vaccines are live vaccines and can cause a mini-disease, which is mild and not contagious. After an incubation period of a week or two, the vaccinated child may develop a slight fever and rash. The MMR vaccine can also result in mild joint pain. There have been cases of children experiencing febrile seizures (which are harmless, but uncomfortable) in connection with fever following a vaccination.

People with significantly reduced immune systems, such as those with a serious congenital immunodeficiency, or children undergoing treatment for leukaemia, should not be vaccinated with live vaccines; their low resistance can lead to them suffering from the disease instead of being protected against it.

Rotavirus vaccine

The most common side effect of the rotavirus vaccine, which is a live-attenuated vaccine, is a mild case of gastroenteritis with a slight fever, feelings of sickness, perhaps a little vomiting and mild diarrhoea.

There is a known serious side effect called intussusception, whereby part of the child's intestine folds into an adjacent part of the intestine, a bit like when the shaft of a sock is turned inside out. Intussusception can also occur in children who have not been vaccinated, but rotavirus vaccination increases the risk somewhat. Between one and six in every 100,000 vaccinated children are thought to suffer from intussusception as a result of vaccination.[14] The symptoms of intussusception are periods of shrill screaming and abdominal pain, interspersed with symptom-free intervals and sometimes also bloody diarrhoea. If intussusception is left untreated, the child will become increasingly tired and listless. If your child shows these symptoms, go to your hospital's emergency department, where intussusception can be readily treated.

Influenza vaccines

Narcolepsy (sudden sleeping illness) has been described in association with ASo3-adjuvanted pandemic influenza vaccines, predominantly in the Scandinavian population and particularly in children. These vaccines were not used and are not available in Australia.

Narcolepsy is a sleep disorder that involves a complete loss of daily rhythm. Sufferers can sleep at any time of the day, but might not sleep at all during the night. Most have a ravenous appetite and episodes of cataplexy, which means that they collapse when they experience strong emotions such as laughter. Narcolepsy is thought to be due to the immune defence attacking the brain cells that produce the hormone orexin (also known as hypocretin), which regulates sleep and wakefulness, as well as hunger and satiety.[15]

It is believed that narcolepsy can be triggered by infections. In particular, H1N1-type influenza, or swine flu, has been linked to an increased risk of children developing narcolepsy. In China, the number of cases of narcolepsy increased dramatically around six months after the 2009–2010 swine flu epidemic. Vaccination against swine flu was very uncommon in China, and these cases were probably caused by the influenza itself. Narcolepsy only affects people with a specific set of immune defence genes, but the vast majority of people with these genes do not contract narcolepsy.

The first reports of a swine flu epidemic came from Central America, and stated that almost half of those affected — mostly young adults — died. Based on this information, large quantities of vaccine were hurriedly produced that could quickly be tested on relatively small groups of people and then recommended for the entire population. Around half the Swedish population chose to heed the vaccination recommendations. It then turned out that using a particular swine flu vaccine, Pandemrix, increased the risk of narcolepsy more than the risk of contracting the condition from the swine flu infection itself. Other swine flu vaccines did not come with the same increased risk, and it is still not known what component of Pandemrix caused the heightened risk. It has been speculated that it was because the vaccine contained squalene. Squalene is an adjuvant (like aluminium in the vaccines included in the national program) that is used to give the vaccine a stronger effect. However, the same adjuvant was also used in another swine flu vaccine that did not increase the risk of narcolepsy.

There is no known increased risk of narcolepsy from any swine flu vaccines other than Pandemrix, nor from the regular seasonal flu vaccines or any other vaccines. Vaccination against seasonal flu is currently only recommended in Sweden for children if they have an increased risk of becoming particularly seriously ill. The authorities in the USA take a different view, recommending seasonal flu vaccination for everyone over the age of six months. In Australia, influenza vaccine is recommended for all children, and certain groups — such as Aboriginal and Torres Strait Islander and medically at-risk populations — are vaccinated annually.

We know that vaccination against swine flu caused cases of narcolepsy. With hindsight, we know that the influenza epidemic turned out not to be as serious as had been imagined and that there was no need to vaccinate so many people. However, the unfortunate case of the Pandemrix vaccine should not be used as an argument against vaccination in general; the vaccines included in the public child-vaccination program and many other vaccines have been tested on millions of people, and the side effects are much less common and less dramatic than the risk of serious illness and death from the infections they protect against. But this case study does serve as a reminder of how important it is for the public vaccination program to be continuously evaluated, and that the safety requirements for vaccines must be extremely high.

THE PREVENTION PARADOX: WHY VACCINATE WHEN THE DISEASES ARE NOT PREVALENT?

In societies where deadly epidemics are a frequent occurrence and where infectious diseases are a real threat to life, parents queue up to vaccinate their children. Certain side effects from the vaccines are considered acceptable if they are clearly milder than the torments caused by the disease.

When a vaccination program is effective, the situation changes. When almost everyone has been vaccinated, the disease does not have the chance to spread. If 98 out of every 100 people are vaccinated with an effective vaccine, and an infected individual meets an average of five people, the likelihood that one of them will be unprotected is low (10 per cent). If the infected individual does meet an unprotected person who is infected, that person must in turn find another unprotected person to infect, and so on, in order for the disease to continue to spread. Where there is a population with a high rate of coverage with an effective vaccine, the disease soon dies out. As previously mentioned, this is called herd immunity or community protection.

Herd immunity also protects those who are unvaccinated. This is why we can wait until Swedish babies reach the age of 18 months, and Australian babies reach 12 months, before vaccinating them against measles, leaving them unprotected for a year or more, even though the protection from their mother only lasts for a few months. Since measles is neither spread in Sweden nor Australia, the child is not at risk of being infected.

The community-protection principle is of crucial importance for a small but vulnerable group of children (and adults) with serious immunodeficiency, such as children with leukaemia or other cancers, whose treatment erases the memory cells in the immune system. These people cannot be vaccinated with a live-attenuated vaccine because it can cause disease in individuals with an ineffective immune defence. However, if the vast majority of the population are vaccinated, the disease no longer circulates within society, and those who would be otherwise vulnerable survive.

But when we no longer see a disease, when not even our parents can tell us how they feared polio and diphtheria, then obvious questions arise. Are vaccinations important? Are they worth the risk of side effects? These are important questions. To answer them requires in-depth, up-to-date knowledge about diseases and how they are spread globally, the side effects of vaccines, and the significance of herd immunity in terms of public health.

VACCINATION HESITANCY AND ALTERNATIVE FACTS

Around 97 per cent of Swedish parents choose to vaccinate their children in accordance with the national immunisation program. This is one of the highest vaccination rates in the world, which is probably in large part due to our excellent paediatric nurses, who instil great confidence in parents. Australia also has excellent vaccination rates. The nation-wide immunisation rates for five-year-olds was 94.6 per cent in 2018, which was the highest figure on record.

Of the small minority of parents who do not vaccinate their children, most lack confidence in the system, and some choose to delay vaccination for various reasons. There is also a small proportion who actively campaign against vaccination. The anti-vaccination movement is global, with a strong online presence, operating websites that appear trustworthy and that quote from what are often real scientific articles to legitimise their theories. However, if you take the time to read these articles, you will find that they don't support the anti-vaccination argument at all. The content of these websites is usually a combination of articles about real vaccination side effects (such as narcolepsy as a result of Pandemrix), and a wealth of conspiracy theories about why 'the public health authorities' are trying to trick us into global child vaccination.

Vaccinations and autism — a widespread falsehood

One of anti-vaccination activists' favourite claims is that vaccination — and the MMR vaccine, in particular — causes autism. These fears were ignited by a long-discredited article published in the respected British medical journal *The Lancet* in 1998, which claimed that a new syndrome consisting of autism and inflammatory intestinal disease might have been caused by vaccination. As a result of the widespread reporting of this article, up to 10–15 per cent of parents in North America and in several European countries chose not to give their children the MMR vaccine. Consequently, these countries, which had previously been almost measles-free, experienced measles outbreaks. Vaccination coverage has remained high in Sweden and Australia, where major measles outbreaks have been avoided. In the UK, anti-vaccine activists have been much more influential, and large outbreaks of measles have occurred.

The author of the article in *The Lancet* was Andrew Wakefield, a British medical practitioner who was later revealed to have a financial interest in taking action against the vaccination industry on behalf of parents. The article was exposed as fraudulent research, and *The Lancet* subsequently withdrew the publication.[16] Although Wakefield was struck off the medical register, he continues to promote his anti-vaccination message in the US. Since then, several major, reliable studies have investigated whether the MMR vaccine causes autism. The results are unanimous: there is no demonstrated link between vaccines and autism.[17]

IN BRIEF

As we have already said, not all advice you will come across that is provided by paediatric healthcare spokespersons, and other healthcare authorities, is based on science. The good news is that no other field is as strictly evidence-based as the national immunisation programs. The effectiveness and safety of public vaccines is constantly monitored, and no vaccine is added to the schedule unless there is a thoroughly satisfactory safety margin. Vaccinations are medical interventions that save many lives every day. By following your national immunisation program, you can provide your child with excellent protection against seriously dangerous diseases. Do it.

CHAPTER ELEVEN

Allergies: the immune system's phobias

Allergies are incredibly common in Sweden and in other high-income countries, and they are the topic of eager discussion. What are they? How dangerous are they? Is it possible to protect your child against them? Interest groups, politicians, and health services all have their points of view, and it's easy to become confused by contradictory messages. Is it good or bad for a child to grow up with a household pet? Should you, and your baby, avoid gluten or milk? Should you stop infants from eating strawberries if they develop a red rash around their mouths? Few of these questions have a simple answer, which is why we've included this comprehensive chapter on allergies in children, and on what today's research can tell us.

WHAT ARE ALLERGIES?

No one is born allergic, but children can show signs of allergy from as early as just a few weeks of age. Several generations ago, allergies were an unknown concept. Very few of today's elderly citizens are allergic, and neither were they allergic as children, but around a quarter of young people today have been found to have allergies.

When someone is afraid of something that is harmless, it's called a phobia. You could, using the same reasoning, describe allergies as the immune system's phobias. The immune system is designed to recognise dangerous microorganisms, be activated by them, and fight them. That fight results in symptoms such as a congested or runny nose, coughing, and fever. Things get complicated when some people's immune systems respond to completely harmless substances as if they were dangerous microbes. For example, when their immune system attacks milk molecules on the mistaken basis that they come from a hazardous parasitic worm, allergic symptoms appear — such as a runny nose and a swelling of the airway — that to some extent resemble those of an infection. This reaction occurs despite the fact that the milk itself is harmless and doesn't intrinsically require a defence response.

The scientific definition of allergies reads: 'Immunologically caused hypersensitivity to harmless foreign substances.' In other words, allergy sufferers are hypersensitive to something that other people don't have a problem with, as a result of which their immune system reacts to it and produces allergic symptoms. There are different sorts of allergies, depending on which part of the immune system has developed a phobia. Let's start with the most common, which is caused by immunoglobulin E (IgE) antibodies.

The IgE antibody: the villain of the allergy drama

Antibodies are the immune system's first line of defence. They recognise and tag substances they identify as harmful, and they are an important part of our immunological memory. Different kinds of antibodies have different properties, and they activate the immune system in different ways. In the case of allergic disease, IgE antibodies are the most important. An allergic child's immune system produces large quantities of IgE antibodies against one or more substances that the immune system has incorrectly decided the child needs 'protecting' against. A substance that triggers an individual's allergic reaction, such as a protein in eggs, milk, or grass pollen, is called an allergen.

When someone with an egg allergy eats an egg, proteins from the egg are absorbed in the intestines, and the allergen makes its way into the bloodstream. The process is the same for everyone, but someone with an egg allergy will have produced IgE antibodies against the egg allergen. In the tissues of the body near the blood vessels, certain cells — mast cells — are ready to defend the body. In people with allergies, the mast cells are covered with IgE antibodies, and in the case of the egg-allergic individual, these antibodies are directed to recognise egg proteins. When these antibodies detect their allergen, the mast cells are activated and emit large amounts of histamine, a substance that enlarges blood vessels, causing them to leak fluid that swells the surrounding tissue. Dangerous physiological responses in an allergic reaction include contraction of the musculature of the airway.

Allergic reactions can affect different parts of the body

The allergic reaction can appear in different organs. On the skin, it can take the form of hives (a red, swollen rash with white centres similar in appearance to the rash you get from contact with stinging nettles), or eczema (thickened, dry, red, and itchy skin). A runny nose (hay fever), often in combination with watery eyes and wheezy or whistling breathing (asthma), are also common symptoms of allergy. If the allergic reaction occurs in the alimentary tract, it manifests in the form of vomiting and diarrhoea.

The most dangerous allergic reaction of all happens if mast cells are activated throughout the entire body. All the blood vessels then widen and start to leak fluid, resulting in a drop in blood pressure. Children can also experience swelling of the mouth and throat, causing breathing difficulties, and sometimes their entire skin surface will be covered with blotchy hives. This severe allergic reaction is called anaphylaxis. Anaphylaxis can be life-threatening, and requires immediate medical attention. Thankfully, the majority of allergic children never experience an anaphylactic reaction, and in most cases there is no need to worry that this will happen.

THE ATOPIC MARCH: ALLERGIES AT DIFFERENT AGES

Allergies that are due to the child producing IgE antibodies are called atopic allergies, or sometimes simply atopy. Their manifestations change during childhood according to a particular pattern, known as the atopic march. This often begins with eczema and/or food allergies, and progresses to asthma and hay fever when the child is of school age.

Eczema

The most common type of atopic allergy among babies is atopic eczema. It can appear at the age of just a few weeks. The skin becomes dry and itchy, and a child's sleep may be disturbed by the discomfort. The condition tends to start on the cheeks, but may spread to the entire body. In children who are a couple of years old, atopic eczema is often localised to the creases of the elbow and the knee. Atopic eczema can sometimes indicate a food allergy, but in most cases it is not possible to identify the actual trigger of the immune system's reaction. If you suspect that your child has eczema, contact your GP, or a child-health centre, or a paediatrician. As a general rule, they will recommend that you apply cortisone cream to reduce the immune reaction in the skin until the eczema has healed. When a child has scratched at the eczema and caused a bacterial infection, antibiotics may be needed.

A daily generous application of softening creams is required as a preventative measure between eczema flares. If the eczema is severe, a doctor will normally test for allergies to egg and milk, which are the most common food allergies that appear at this age.

Food allergies

Allergies in young children are usually to certain foods, or, more accurately, to proteins in these foods. The symptoms manifest in the alimentary/gastrointestinal tract as vomiting or diarrhoea, and/or on the skin as hives or eczema. The most common infant food allergies are to cow's milk and eggs. Later on, allergies to fish, nuts, and peanuts are common. (Despite their name, peanuts are not related to hazelnuts and other true nuts. Instead, they are more closely related to soya beans. Nor are almonds nuts; some people are allergic to almonds, but this is not regarded as a nut allergy.)

It is not easy to determine whether your child is allergic, or what sets off their allergy. Proper investigation requires the help of a healthcare professional. The usual process involves excluding possibly allergenic food from the child's or the breastfeeding mother's diet, and then monitoring for improvement. If the symptoms do improve, the food is reintroduced, and if the symptoms worsen again, an allergy has been identified. IgE antibodies against egg and cow's milk are some-times measured by taking blood samples or a prick test, whereby a drop of egg or milk extract is placed on the skin and the skin is pricked with a needle in the middle of the drop. Even a positive test result doesn't necessarily mean that the child is allergic, but it can support a diagnosis.

If you believe your child is allergic to certain foods, it may be worth asking your doctor to organise what is known as component testing, which involves blood tests that can differentiate between IgE antibodies formed against closely related foods. Component testing can be used to predict whether your child is at risk of experiencing a severe (anaphylactic) reaction to soya, peanuts, or hazelnuts, for example, or whether the risk is negligible. If your doctor is not familiar with the relatively new process of component testing, and your child is found to have a nut allergy, you need to ensure that your child is referred to a paediatrician with knowledge of allergies who can carry out the comprehensive testing.

Most children with nut allergies are only allergic to a few types of nuts and can eat others. If your child suffers a life-threatening reaction to a particular nut, a full assessment is obviously needed, and allergy tests must be ordered and interpreted by a knowledgeable doctor for accurate advice about which nuts to avoid, and which could be considered for a provocation. A 'provocation' means eating a controlled amount of the food the child is suspected to be allergic to in a healthcare facility to see if any allergic reactions occur. Sometimes parents will instinctively exclude all potential allergens, for safety's sake, if their child has, say, an unexplained rash. However, this extreme approach is not a good idea for a number of reasons. First, avoiding a large number of foods makes everyday life difficult. Second, it is probably completely unnecessary. What's more, research shows that there is a greater risk of children becoming allergic if they avoid a food they can tolerate than if they eat it regularly. (We have written more about this research in chapter 6.) The immune system works like the brain when it comes to phobias: the more we avoid what we fear, the greater the phobia becomes. Instead, before you take matters into your own hands, you should consult your paediatrician. There are sound procedures for investigating suspected food allergies, and your path will be easier if the condition is investigated correctly from the outset.

If a child has a known allergy to a food, the current treatment is to exclude the food from the child's diet. How careful you have to be in avoiding the food, and for how long, depends on the severity of the child's symptoms. Ensure that you are given clear guidelines by the child's doctor. A child who has had a life-threatening anaphylactic reaction must, of course, be protected much more carefully against the food in question than a child who has had eczema or an upset stomach due to the same food. Good allergy care also involves regular re-examination of the allergy diagnosis. We know that children will outgrow many allergies, and re-examination maay mean that a child doesn't need to continue with a restricted diet unnecessarily.

Asthma

Allergic asthma is generally first seen when a child is of preschool or school age. In the case of asthma, the immune system produces antibodies against some protein that is common in the air. These IgE antibodies bind to mast cells in the airway, and on inhalation, the allergen can adhere to the IgE antibodies. The mast cells are then activated, resulting in a swollen airway and difficulties in exhaling. Typically, the child's breathing is accompanied by whistling and wheezing sounds. An attack of asthma is generally caused by inhalation of pollens or dander from animals. Physical exertion usually brings on asthma symptoms if the asthma is not managed sufficiently.

Many young children develop a cough and experience breathing difficulties when they catch a cold. This is sometimes called bronchial asthma. However, this condition does not necessarily mean that your child is allergic — only that their airway is narrow and swollen due to infections. In children who do not have allergic asthma, the whistling in the chest usually goes away once the child grows and the diameters of the airway increase.[1] In children with an allergic disease, the asthma does not taper off with age, and the wheezing and coughing can occur during periods when the child does not have a cold.

If your child has breathing difficulties, regardless of the cause, you need to seek emergency care. To see whether a child has difficulties breathing, it is wise to undress the child on the upper part of their body, then watch them breathing. If breathing is calm and does not seem to bother the child, everything is okay. On the other hand, if your child looks like they have just run a marathon, with rapid breathing, their belly going in and out for each breath, and the skin between their ribs drawn in on each breath, it is time to go to a hospital — in an ambulance if the hospital is a long distance away. There your child will receive acute anti-asthmatic medication and, if needed, oxygen therapy until their breathing is calm again.

After an asthma attack, a child will receive asthma medications they

234

can use at home, to minimise the need for emergency visits. In addition to the bronchodilators given in the acute situation, the treatment for asthma consists of an anti-inflammatory medication to heal the lungs and relieve the inflammation.

Hay fever

Hay fever symptoms are located in the upper airways, in the nose, and the eyes. A swollen, runny nose and red, watery eyes are typical hay fever symptoms, and in many cases they are accompanied by an unusual tiredness. The allergens are the same as those that trigger asthma: airborne proteins from cats and horses, or pollen proteins from grasses and trees that are common in the surroundings. In Australia, most pollen allergens are from introduced species of trees, and from introduced grasses that are produced in vast quantities and can be blown over long distances.

In the case of hay fever with itchy eyes, antihistamine tablets from a pharmacy are usually effective. Treatment is also available in the form of nasal sprays or eye drops. These medications are available over the counter, and if the appropriate dose relieves your child's symptoms, there is no real reason to seek healthcare advice. If symptoms are more severe and persist despite use of over-the-counter antiallergic medications, or if they are accompanied by coughing or episodic breathing difficulties, it is time to seek medical advice.

The IgE antibody is specific to a particular protein. Sometimes the same protein, or a closely related one, may be present in both pollen and certain foods. Those who are allergic to birch pollen usually also react to foods such as hazelnuts, apples, celery, or peanuts. As a general rule, this phenomenon, which is called cross-reactivity, rarely produces dangerous allergic reactions — just red lips and itching in the mouth.

Allergies to bees and wasps

Around one in 100 children are allergic to bee or wasp stings. The allergic reaction will produce hives all over a child's body. In serious cases, a sting can cause anaphylaxis. Seek medical attention immediately if your child experiences such a reaction.

All children react with swelling, redness, and pain around a bee or wasp sting, even if they are not allergic. This is a reaction to the toxin in the sting; it can be painful, but is not normally dangerous. Medical attention is not required after a local reaction to a bee or wasp sting, with one important exception: if your child is stung inside the mouth, seek immediate medical attention or call an ambulance, because a child's airway can swell up and prevent them breathing.

FOOD ALLERGIES THAT ARE NOT CAUSED BY IGE ANTIBODIES

Food allergies that are caused by IgE antibodies against proteins in food manifest themselves in the form of fast-acting symptoms such as vomiting, swelling around the mouth and throat, or as hives, and possibly asthma.

However, there is also a type of food allergy that is not caused by IgE antibodies, but probably by IgG antibodies (the most common type of antibody found in blood circulation, which are created and released by plasma B cells), or T lymphocytes, or by both. In this case, the symptoms will be more gradual in onset and may include stomach pain, constipation or diarrhoea, and poor weight gain. These symptoms do not become apparent immediately after the child has eaten the food to which they are allergic, but appear perhaps a day or so later. The delayed onset of symptoms means it is more difficult to ascertain the cause of the allergy. One-third of all cow's milk allergies and some soya allergies are of this type.

Non-IgE mediated cow's milk allergies almost always disappear when the child is a few years old, and the child does not carry any greater risk than other children of subsequently acquiring atopic diseases such as asthma and hay fever. A diagnosis is made by carefully excluding the suspected allergen from the child's diet for a set period of time and observing whether the symptoms disappear, after which the allergen is reintroduced and any symptoms are monitored. Again, this is not a process you should experiment with yourself; it's easy to get confused with symptoms and uncertainties. Contact a paediatrician to investigate if your child has gastrointestinal symptoms and is not gaining weight well.

'ALLERGY TESTS' CAN'T PROVE THAT A CHILD HAS AN ALLERGY

You may see offers for 'allergy tests' at clinics and online. The term 'allergy tests' is misleading because these tests can't reveal whether or not a child is allergic. Instead, they show whether a child has IgE antibodies against various allergens, which is called being 'sensitised'. We reiterate that the definition of an allergy is having allergic symptoms to something that is not actually harmful. The presence of antibodies in a child's system is not a symptom and, hence, is not evidence of an allergy.

It is pointless finding out whether a child has been sensitised to something if they don't exhibit any symptoms. Sensitisation without symptoms is very common, and should not be treated. There is no research which suggests that a child should avoid a substance to which they have been sensitised. On the contrary, the important, reliable study we reported on in chapter 6 shows that children who have been sensitised to peanuts, but are not yet allergic to them, have a good chance of avoiding developing an allergy if they eat large quantities of peanuts. Conversely, the same group of children are at a significant risk of developing an allergy if they avoid peanuts altogether. Carrying out tests unnecessarily can lead to restricting certain foods, therefore increasing the risk of the child becoming allergic. Avoid these tests!

We would like to issue a particular warning: never test your child for sensitisation to dogs. This test is so bad that it doesn't tell you anything meaningful at all. Nevertheless, this pointless test is the reason why plenty of people believe they are allergic to dogs, even though they don't have any symptoms when they meet dogs, and are therefore not allergic, by definition. Unfortunately, this test is included in many standard test regimes, and thousands of people in Sweden have been told they are allergic to dogs even though they aren't. Also, bear in mind that such tests only measure IgE antibodies, and so allergies that are not caused by IgE cannot be detected by them.

AN ALLERGY TO FURRY PETS DOESN'T EXIST

Many people believe they are allergic to both cats and dogs because someone has talked about 'allergy to furry pets'. However, this is an inaccurate term. Allergies to animals have nothing to do with their fur: if you're allergic to cats, you're allergic to a particular cat protein called Fel d 1.[2] This protein is formed in the skin, and is present in the cat's tears and saliva. Hairless cats have just as much allergen as those with fur. It is only found in cats, and not in dogs, horses, or rabbits.

A dog's most common allergen is called Can f 1, a protein present in the dog's blood, mucous membranes, and saliva. Again, this allergen has nothing to do with fur. From an allergy point of view, it is therefore completely pointless dwelling on whether particular breeds of dog have long, short, or wiry hair, or whether or not they shed their hair.

It is well known among doctors who work with allergies that cat allergies are very common, as are allergies to horses, whereas it is far less common to be allergic to dogs. But many people incorrectly believe they're allergic to dogs because they're allergic to cats, and the doctor has talked about an 'allergy to furry pets', as if all animals with fur and hair have something in common. From an allergy point of view, they don't. In fact, most people who are allergic to cats have no allergy to dogs or any other furry animals.

WHY DO SO MANY CHILDREN DEVELOP ALLERGIES NOWADAYS?

Back when 20 per cent of babies died before their first birthday, usually from infections, there were almost no allergies. Hay fever was first described in 1819 by the physician John Bostock, who himself was the first known allergy patient. He had noticed that his eyes became aggravated and his breathing became strained in the spring, but that these symptoms eased with a change in season— only to return the following year. He called this new condition 'summer catarrh', and asked his colleagues to search through their patients' records to try to find other people with similar symptoms. After ten years of diligent searching, he was able to identify a total of 23 cases from the whole of England. Doctors noted that those suffering from the condition included neither poor people nor farmers, which seemed strange considering that almost all diseases affected the poor more often than the rich. The name of the condition was later on changed to hay fever, as it appeared in late spring and early summer, during the particular time of year when hay was harvested.

Slowly but surely, cases of the new condition grew in number during the 20th century. The collective term 'atopy' was coined in 1923 to describe the group of diseases including asthma, hay fever, and eczema, which, it was noted, appeared within a single individual, or often within a family. Following World War II, allergies became fairly common in the prosperous parts of the world, and between 1970 and 1990 allergy cases (asthma, hay fever, and atopic eczema) tripled in wealthy nations such as the UK and Sweden. In poor countries where there are many infections and high rates of infant mortality, allergies remain very rare. However, as populations prosper, and fewer people suffer from infections, allergies are on the increase. Atopic allergy is the most common chronic disease among young individuals in Sweden, and in other high-income nations with Western lifestyles.

The hygiene hypothesis

Today, the idea that dominates research into the causes of atopic allergy is called 'the hygiene hypothesis'. This hypothesis was first presented in 1989 by the British scientist David Strachan, who studied adults with hay fever in relation to their childhood environments. Strachan's research showed that the more siblings an individual had, the lower their risk of developing hay fever. The risk was also lower if their parents had a lower level of education.[3] As Strachan pointed out, it is a well-known fact that children in large, poor families have many infections,[4] and he proposed that these early infections train the immune system in some way to act as effectively as possible. Without this early training, the immune system might overreact to completely harmless substances that we breathe in or eat on a daily basis. As a side note, Strachan also demonstrated that there was a somewhat elevated risk of suffering from hay fever among those who were breastfed rather than bottle-fed, but that this was not a decisive factor.[5]

Many studies support Strachan's hygiene hypothesis. However, we still don't know exactly which infections provide protection, or whether it is simply the effect of having a normal flora containing many bacteria. Studies of Italian soldiers who grew up under a wide range of very different circumstances — ranging from poor parts of southern Italy to the prosperous north of the country — show that those who have had the type of gastrointestinal infections that spread under poor hygienic conditions have fewer allergies as adults.[6] Certain studies also show a protective effect from common respiratory infections, but this finding is not consistent.[7] Some studies have demonstrated a certain protective effect from having many different bacteria in the intestinal flora as a young baby.[8] The transfer of oral bacteria from parent to child when a parent 'cleans' a dummy by sucking it is also thought to provide some protection.[9] However, despite almost 30 years having passed since Strachan presented his hygiene hypothesis, we still have not established which microbes are needed to train the immune system, or exactly what training the immune system needs.

Thorough studies have been conducted to determine whether vaccinations lead to more allergies, and no link has been made. Don't believe anti-vaccination activists who insist that the measles vaccine causes allergies.

One finding that has been demonstrated in many different countries is that growing up on a farm is the best way to avoid allergies.[10] This is particularly true for children on small, family-owned dairy farms. Children spending time in the cowsheds, the mother working in the cowsheds during pregnancy, and the child drinking farm-fresh milk have all been shown to be protective factors.

HOW CAN WE REDUCE THE RISK OF ALLERGIES IN CHILDREN?

In summary, we know of three lifestyle factors that are certainly associated with a low risk of allergies: growing up in crowded conditions with a poor standard of housing; being born into a large family with many older siblings; and living on a farm.[11] It is the environment in early life — the first months and the first year — that has the greatest impact on the risk of a person developing allergies. Studies of children who live on farms, for example, show that most of the protective effects conferred by living in a farming environment are obtained during the first year of life; if they move to a farm after that age, the protective effect is weak or absent.

No one wants to return to the living conditions of a century ago, with outside toilets, and poor food and water hygiene, which resulted in many gastrointestinal infections, even if fewer allergies. Today, very few children are fortunate enough to grow up on a farm surrounded by animals, and it is hardly sensible to buy a farm just to protect your future children from allergies. Even if those who drink farm-fresh milk have been found to have fewer allergies, we cannot currently buy unpasteurised milk that is tested for dangerous bacteria, so it is not advisable to give young children unpasteurised milk.

Reducing the risk of allergies through contact with people and animals

However, you can still try to ensure that your child's immune system gets a little training by introducing it to other people and, ideally, to animals. And don't try to protect your newborn from older children. The best thing is to ensure that children without siblings also get to meet other children. Don't worry if your child catches a cold — every infection goes towards training the immune system. Bear in mind that this training must take place early on, not when the child is older.

Most of us don't have many opportunities to come into contact with farming life. However, even ordinary cats and dogs offer allergy protection, albeit not as effectively as cattle on a farm.[12] Growing up with pets halves the risk of developing allergies, and the greater the number of cats and dogs in the household, the greater the protection — it's sort of a 'mini-farm' effect. Interestingly enough, exposure to animals offers even better protection for those children who have allergies in their family and are at a higher risk of developing allergies.[13]

Of course, the problem is that if there are already members of the family with an allergy to cats or dogs, finding a suitable pet becomes more difficult. Remember that dog allergies are much less common than cat allergies, and that many people with cat or horse allergies have no problems with dogs. Don't worry if you've had a positive prick test result; this doesn't necessarily mean you're allergic.

Reducing the risk of allergies by offering food

It seems that one important way of reducing the risk of a child developing allergies to various foods such as nuts, peanuts, milk, fish, sesame, and soya is to introduce these foods into the child's diet early on. In chapter 6, where we discuss food for infants, we describe new studies that have shown how the risk of food allergies seems to be lower if the infant is given taster portions of food from the age of three to four months. It is important to give children different types of food early on, because their immune systems need to be exposed to harmless foreign substances in order to develop a tolerance to these proteins. Eating a protein is normally the best way to develop an immunological tolerance to it, which is the opposite of an allergy.

Allergy specialist Professor Gideon Lack has a theory that if children are allowed to ingest peanuts they become tolerant; but if, instead, they get small doses of peanut protein through their skin, the risk of them developing an allergy increases. Peanut protein may be found in oils, shampoos, or ointments, or transferred by skin contact with someone who has eaten peanuts. It only takes minuscule amounts of protein to sensitise an individual, so even these types of exposures are enough to promote sensitisation in the child.

We know that a child needs to eat a relatively large amount — a couple of grams — of a particular protein to develop tolerance to it. It has been observed in animal studies that giving tiny doses actually increases the risk of developing an immune response and a later immune overreaction, equivalent to the allergic reactions in humans. A taster portion should therefore be a proper spoonful, not just a tiny pinch, and it is also important to give the child the protein regularly.

COELIAC DISEASE

Another type of allergy is coeliac disease, in which it is not IgE antibodies, but IgG antibodies and T lymphocytes that react to the protein in a food, causing intestinal symptoms. The body reacts to the presence of a protein — or, more accurately, a group of proteins — called gliadin, or gluten, that is found in three commonly consumed types of grain: wheat, rye, and barley (but not in oats). If someone with coeliac disease eats wheat flour, thereby ingesting gluten, antibodies and T lymphocytes in their intestinal mucosa will react to pieces of the gluten protein (peptides), and the immune reaction will damage the mucosa.

For those who don't have coeliac disease, gluten is not in the least bit harmful — just as grass pollen isn't harmful to those who aren't allergic to it, and cats aren't harmful if you don't have a cat allergy. Various myths suggest that gluten in itself is unhealthy, and that it's worth eliminating it from your diet, even if you don't have coeliac disease. This has not been scientifically proven.

Coeliac disease is found in all countries, and affects around 1–3 per cent of children in high-income countries. Coeliac disease may appear during the first year of life, as the child starts to consume cereals, but it will often appear later on. The most common symptom is poor growth, initially in terms of weight and then height. Affected children may suffer from stomach pain and constipation, and sometimes diarrhoea. Many have few or no symptoms, and coeliac disease may not be diagnosed until a teenager is tested because of their anaemia.

Investigation and treatment

A particular variety of the HLA-DQ gene (either HLA-DQ2 or DQ8) is needed in order to develop coeliac disease, but many people have one of these gene varieties without necessarily having the condition. If a close relative has the condition, the risk of having coeliac disease is considerably higher compared to not having a history of the disease in the family.

It is best to allow a healthcare professional to carry out an investigation for coeliac disease. For children over the age of two, there is an excellent blood test that measures the level of transglutaminase antibodies (TGA) in the blood. A reliable diagnosis is made, either with a combination of two highly elevated TGA values or with tissue samples from the small intestinal mucosa. If the results are normal for a child who eats gluten, coeliac disease can be ruled out. The test is less reliable for children under the age of two, and additional tests and investigations are sometimes needed.

Home tests for coeliac disease are available, but we advise against using them for your child. If you do use such a test and the results are positive, there is a high likelihood that the child has coeliac disease, but you must then contact a doctor for an actual diagnosis and instructions on managing the disease. On the other hand, if the test is negative, you can't rely on it, as it only measures the presence of IgA-type transglutaminase antibodies, which some people can't produce. For people who do not produce IgA antibodies, alternative methods must be used to rule out coeliac disease — exactly which methods are appropriate vary, depending on clinical history and findings.

In a hospital lab, the two tests are always carried out simultaneously. If the child is too young or does not eat much gluten, the test can also be negative despite the child having coeliac disease.

A child with coeliac disease should always have an assigned paediatrician and dietician. The treatment is a gluten-free diet throughout life.

Can coeliac disease be prevented?

Can anything be done to reduce the risk of a child developing coeliac disease? Coeliac disease is becoming increasingly common within the general population, and Swedish infants have a higher risk of contracting the disease, compared to French, German, and US children, despite a similar proportion of the children having the HLA-DQ risk genes discussed above. Unfortunately, we don't know which lifestyle factors affect the risk of coeliac disease, and so we are unable to do anything to prevent it yet. Whether you breastfeed or not, and for how long, does not affect the risk of the baby developing coeliac disease; neither does the age at which you introduce gluten into their diet. However, one study shows that the amount of gluten you feed your child plays a role: feeding large amounts of gluten during the first two years of life increases the risk that the child with the HLA-DQ risk genes will contract coeliac disease. Vaccinations do not increase the risk, but one German study reports an increased risk of coeliac disease if the child was delivered by C-section.

LACTOSE INTOLERANCE IS NOT AN ALLERGY

Both human milk and cow's milk contain lactose, or milk sugar. Milk sugar is composed of two simple sugar molecules: galactose and glucose. Lactose is broken down into galactose and glucose in the intestines, with the help of the enzyme lactase. Congenital lactase deficiency is an extremely rare genetic disorder. Children who are born with this condition cannot produce lactase at all, as a result of which the lactose remains in the intestine and the child suffers from severe diarrhoea from the first week of life. Diarrhoea can prove fatal, due to dehydration. However, the diarrhoea disappears when the baby is given special lactose-free formula.

Except in the case of this extremely rare condition, everyone in the world produces lactase in the intestine during the first years of their life. This fact is obvious, otherwise we would not be able to survive on either breast milk or formula, which contain milk sugar. Among much of the world's population, the ability to break down milk sugar gradually decreases from around the age of five, and children increasingly experience upset stomachs and flatulence from drinking milk. If children take lactase enzyme tablets, they are perfectly able to consume large quantities of milk, and there is often a certain residual degree of enzyme activity that allows small quantities of milk to pass unnoticed.

However, for those of us with Scandinavian, Dutch, or British origins, it is most common to retain the ability to produce lactase throughout our lives. This ability means that even adults can drink milk without having diarrhoea — a major advantage for survival in colder parts of the world where cow's milk has been a valuable dietary addition for thousands of years. In southern and western Europe and north Africa, a varying proportion of the population can tolerate cow's milk, while most adult Asians are lactose intolerant.

It isn't dangerous for a lactose-intolerant person to consume lactose

In contrast to allergies (including coeliac disease), where sufferers need to avoid the allergen, no short- or long-term harm can come from a lactose-intolerant person consuming large quantities of lactose. It's simply unpleasant having an upset stomach and being gassy.

There is no reason to give babies lactose-free products, as babies can tolerate lactose. Lactose-free products are not healthier in any way, only more expensive. In contrast to coeliac disease, a cow's milk protein allergy, or other food allergies, you don't have to be particularly careful if your child is lactose intolerant, but you can try sticking to a level of lactose that avoids discomfort. If your child is lactose intolerant, it's worth knowing that hard cheeses and yoghurt are usually fine to eat.

Lactose-intolerance tests are rarely meaningful

There's no point taking blood samples from babies to test for lactose intolerance, because these are gene tests designed to indicate the likelihood of tolerating lactose as an adult. Despite this lack of suitability, many such blood tests are carried out by doctors, who must either be lacking in knowledge or are not using the knowledge they have. Babies worldwide tolerate lactose regardless of which genes they have, and it is not until school age that lactase production slowly disappears. If a baby reacts to cow's milk, this may be due to an underlying intestinal disease, a cow's milk allergy, or something else, and must be investigated by a paediatrician.

Testing is not particularly meaningful for most older children or adults either. If members of your family tend to get an upset stomach when consuming milk after they are school age, they almost certainly have a lactose intolerance and would be wise to avoid the quantities of lactose that cannot be tolerated without it becoming a social inconvenience. Remember, though, that this is not a disease; lactose intolerance is experienced by about 70 per cent of the world's healthy population.

IN BRIEF

Allergies are very common, and coeliac disease is not entirely uncommon. Both are immunological diseases that should be investigated by a doctor. Fortunately, we have much better allergy medications now than we did 30 or 40 years ago, although coeliac disease requires life-long treatment with a gluten-free diet. Lactose intolerance, on the other hand, is not something you need to worry about with babies. Don't buy unnecessary, expensive lactose-free food for babies, and steer clear of costly home tests for allergies, coeliac disease, or lactose intolerance. They rarely provide you with the clear information you need. Consult your doctor if you have concerns.

CHAPTER TWELVE

Harmful or harmless?

As a new parent, you're responsible for the life of a helpless newborn baby. There is no more terrifying thought than that of your baby being harmed in some way, either as a result of your actions or as the victim of external events. You don't need to look far to find claims about potential harms, and one way of handling this situation is to try to avoid whatever you've been told could be harmful. However, apart from being an impossible way to live, avoidance generally increases fear and anxiety. We therefore recommend a different approach: protect your baby from real dangers, and let them explore the rest of the world while you watch them grow. In this chapter, we tease out the differences between dangers and fears: which risks you can minimise; which harms you can prevent; and what is out of your hands. We also discuss the difference between facts and beliefs, and why it is that scientists and paediatricians can so seldom guarantee that something is completely harmless, while influencers and random non-professionals feel free to deliver 'medical' advice at a pace that is hard to keep up with.

FACT OR BELIEF?

For us, as medical scientists, facts are always either true or false. It's true that a heart pumps blood around the body, and false that babies will be born with a blood-red birthmark if their mother looks at a fire while pregnant. Other questions, such as whether pink baby growsuits are cute, or whether God exists, are a matter of opinion or belief. They can neither be scientifically proven to be true or false, nor are they facts. Science and research are tools we use to identify facts. In the biological sciences, researchers formulate hypotheses about different ways in which the body functions, based on the facts that are already known and accepted. The scientific process then tests these hypotheses, and only the ones that are proven to be true are counted as new facts. Then researchers begin again on formulating new ideas and theories, which in turn are put to the test, and so the process continues. This is a slow process, especially when many hypotheses in an area are hard to examine in scientific experiments, or when several hypotheses are proven to be false. To formulate a belief, or matter of opinion, on the other hand, might be done faster than you are even able to write the belief down.

Before the internet, a journalist fact-checked information before it was spread by newspapers, radio, and television. Journalists would put questions to researchers as experts in their field, and aimed at publishing facts as facts, and opinions as opinions. In quality newspapers, facts and opinions were clearly separated. At least, that's how it was in free societies; in totalitarian states, the government controlled the media and decided what would be presented as a fact.

In the internet era, professional journalists find themselves in a situation where they produce only a tiny part of all the information that is available to media consumers. Anyone can produce a podcast, blog, or YouTube video, and whoever is most charismatic gets the most followers. Self-appointed experts make pronouncements about complex medical issues with a certainty that a professor or doctor would never claim. Sometimes, it is not easy for a journalist to distinguish between a self-appointed expert and a scientist claiming to have expertise on health or medical issues, especially as a professional influencer is always more accessible to a journalist than a physician or professor who is fully booked with patients, research, or educational tasks.

As well, all sorts of organisations — such as pharmaceutical companies, research institutes, hospitals, and individual researchers — have vested interests in promoting their 'discoveries', and are well versed in packaging their revelations to the media. One of the results of this are daily reports, especially on commercial television and in tabloid newspapers, of medical 'breakthroughs'. As journalists never want to be second with the news, there is a high risk that a new opinion or belief presented as a fact by a self-appointed authority with millions of followers, or by an organisation trying to drum up business or government support, will be transmitted as a groundbreaking piece of news, even by semi-serious journalists.

In the background, the traditional print media are under enormous financial pressure, with readership plunging and advertising budgets being spent more and more on Google and Facebook rather than on advertisements in newspapers. As a result, journalists are being made redundant in large numbers, and those that remain have less and less time to critically review the accuracy of what they're writing about. Taking up this slack are internet trolls who spread their opinions in every comments forum available, day in and day out. Some of these trolls pursue an underlying agenda, while others just seem to enjoy picking a fight. Some are human, while others are a piece of code — a bot designed to spread an idea or a belief that their creator found meaningful.

All this has meant that the fact-checking capacity of the mass media has mostly disappeared — and suddenly, you, as a citizen and new parent, have needed to sort out by yourself what is true or false. However, since we wrote the Swedish edition of this book in 2015, a shift has emerged in this area. Serious newspapers have begun to use paywalls to get their readers to pay for digital content, with very good results. With digital subscriptions, media budgets have risen, and more journalists have been employed. If you wish to access factual information, getting one or more digital subscriptions to high-quality newspapers is a very good idea. In addition, Google now includes 'trustworthiness' in its algorithms for some areas, including the medical fiueld. This does not yet work perfectly, but it is definitely a step in the right direction.

We suggest you limit your internet searches for health symptoms to trustworthy sites containing fact-checked articles intended to educate people about health issues. When evaluating a new site, try always to check its credentials. What organisation has created and maintained the site, and why?

Pregnancy, Birth and Baby is a national helpline, video, and website service provided on behalf of the Australian government's department of health. The NHS in the UK has an equivalent site: *Your pregnancy and baby guide*. The goal of the Australian department and the British NHS is to promote health in their respective populations, and their intention is therefore to help people understand symptoms, treat what they can treat themselves in a medically sound way, and search healthcare at an adequate level when needed. That is a good starting point for delivering high-quality advice. You can also count on these organisations to have fact-checked their articles rigorously before publication.

Separating fact from opinion is always important, but for expectant or new parents it can be a matter of survival. If, at this sensitive time of life, as well as having to look after your helpless baby, you have to listen to the self-appointed experts and prophets of doom telling you how to keep yourself and your family safe, your daily life could become dominated by the task of trying to dodge each and every potential risk.

An increased level of worry in new parents may well have evolutionary roots: a two-year-old child with parents who are a bit anxious is more likely to survive than a child with more confident and relaxed parents who leave them unsupervised close to water. The flipside of this increased inclination to worry is that anxieties and obsessions with no protective function are also more common in new parents. We believe that concentrating on extreme risk-minimisation is a flawed strategy, as it is impossible to eradicate all risk in all situations. It is also well known that avoiding something you are afraid of will increase worries and fear. Modern cognitive-behavioural therapy interventions for anxiety are always based on this fact, and a core component in them is exposure to whatever causes the anxiety. It's better to challenge your own anxieties, and look at them as dispassionately as possible.

WHY DO RESEARCHERS AND DOCTORS KNOW SO LITTLE?

In previous chapters, we have repeatedly stated that there is still a lot that is not known about pregnancy, birth, and babies. No one knows exactly why a pregnant woman gets morning sickness, or the best way to treat it, or what causes colic. How can so much remain unknown, when the world is full of scientists?

Where the scientific community hasn't reached a conclusive answer to a certain question, there are two possible explanations (or sometimes a combination of both). The lack of knowledge can be explained simply by the fact that a certain area hasn't received sufficient research. Such is the case for many questions that concern exclusively female biology, such as pregnancy, and perineal functions after giving birth. Research demands money, and to secure research funding, the state must decide that the topic deserves to be researched; a fund must exist to raise money for particular research; or pharmaceutical companies must see opportunities to make money by developing a new drug. We hope that there will soon be a 'perineum fund' to donate to, and we look forward to governments presenting strategic research initiatives focused on morning sickness or colic. It's high time for more such research.

It is sometimes the case that despite much research having been focused on a subject for a long time, and with great energy and rigour, no conclusive results have been reached. Perhaps none of the various hypotheses have stood the test of time. For example, no one knows exactly what causes autoimmune diseases (diseases in which our immune system attacks our own body), even though many thousands of scientific papers have been published on the subject. And no one knows what gives rise to schizophrenia, or what exactly is going on in the brain when we suffer from depression, even though these are diseases that affect millions of people, at an immense cost to society.

The human body is endlessly complicated, and we only understand a fraction of its functions. And while we have relatively good knowledge about certain parts of the body, such as the heart, we know much less about how the brain works. When something goes wrong with the body, we know even less about how and why it malfunctions.

WHY ALL THE NEW AND CONTRADICTORY ADVICE?

Before a new medication can be launched, extensive research is required to show that the medication is effective against the disease to be treated and that it does not produce any harmful side effects. Medical history has taught us that not all severe side effects are detectable in pre-launch clinical studies, which is why safety assessments continue even when new medications are on the market, including the reporting of side effects to the drug-safety authorities. It is well known among doctors that a new medication is always more risky to prescribe than an older, well-documented one.

The same rigour is not applied to health advice, which is why the advice fluctuates so much. Take the feeding of infants as an example: we are variously told that babies should move on to solids by at least three months of age, or that they should be breastfed until six months, then eat taster portions from four months; maybe soon we'll be back to being told that babies should start on solids at three (or perhaps four) months. As we have explained in chapter 6, there is no gold standard starting-point for infant feeding, and there never has been. You would expect sensible advice to reflect this variability and the need to be flexible. This has not been the case: advice on infant feeding is most commonly presented as a non-negotiable obligation.

The way this advice changes is rarely due to firm knowledge pointing in one direction and then new knowledge showing something entirely different. It's much more common that those who offer the advice use flawed knowledge, and supplement facts with opinions and guesswork. This generalisation is by no means confined to internet trolls and bloggers; public agencies and medical groups are often guilty of padding the facts with opinions and beliefs as well.

For those of us who strive to understand the scientific evidence in a particular area and to fully read up on the scientific literature, it's rarely necessary to completely change our understanding of how the world works when new knowledge appears. In fact, if we continue to read and research, our understanding will deepen and broaden all the time. Of course, we gain new knowledge constantly, but that doesn't mean we throw away the old knowledge if it's the result of proper research. After all, Einstein's theories didn't disprove Newton's laws; his new laws complemented the old ones. Researchers tend to know a lot about their particular area of expertise, but they also have daily practice in reading other research, thinking critically, and putting together facts from different fields in order to gain a better understanding of complex problems. But it's not realistic to expect most parents of young children to be researchers, so let's look at some of the research together.

WHAT DO CHILDREN REALLY DIE OF?

Since the very worst fear of a parent is that their child will die, we're going to start by looking at what actually kills children in high-income countries. Our analysis is based on Swedish statistics, but the basics apply to high-income countries generally. In low-income countries, the picture is different. In societies where adequate sanitation and nutrition does not reach a substantial share of the population, malnutrition and infectious diseases will kill a large number of children before their first birthday. When countries start to function better — for example, when internal conflicts are resolved or a working government is formed — child mortality successively decreases as more and more people get access to sufficient nutrition, clean water, and vaccinations. When access to basic obstetric care is added, maternal mortality drops rapidly, and with basic neonatal care, the number of children dying neonatally will decrease.

The two categories that stand out as causes of death in children up to the age of four in high-income countries are congenital disorders and diseases, and neonatal diseases. The third most common cause of death is sudden infant death syndrome and similar conditions, including, in older children, unexpected and sudden deaths with no identifiable cause. Then there is a step down to deaths due to cancer and diseases of the nervous system, and then a further step down to deaths due to infectious diseases, with only seven deaths attributable to these diseases in Sweden each year. A tiny number of children die in road traffic accidents, or from drowning, choking, fire, or violence by another person.

Before we consider which of these causes of death you can have any control over, we suggest that you linger for a moment on the fact that only seven out of half a million children under the age of five die from infections in Sweden each year. The majority of the children who die from infections have other serious underlying illnesses, such as brain damage or cardiopulmonary diseases. This means that you can rationally set aside any worries that your child risks dying from exposure to other people, eating soil, or licking a dirty floor.

Congenital disorders and diseases

Congenital disorders and diseases are the most common cause of death in children aged 0–4. Many children who die early in life have deformities or malfunctions in one or more of the body's organs. Some of these abnormalities are not compatible with life outside the womb, such as being born without a major portion of the brain and skull (anencephaly), or with a severely malformed heart. Other congenital diseases affect basic metabolic functions: for example, a baby may be born with an inability to digest certain nutrients in breast milk, such as amino acids or fatty acids. Faulty breakdown-products, some of which may be toxic, are formed in these children. If discovered early on, some (but not all) of these conditions can be managed with a special diet to exclude the particular nutrient that the child cannot metabolise. These conditions are very rare. Most babies in high-income countries are screened for a large number of such diseases in the first few days after birth.

Serious congenital disorders and diseases often, but not always, have a genetic or hereditary origin. Other causes may include foetal infections (such as the Zika virus or rubella, which are fortunately rare in Australia) or foetus-harming drugs (including epilepsy drugs, thalidomide, which is now used to fight certain forms of cancer, and the anti-acne drug isotretinoin). If your child has an abnormality, the doctors will try to determine the cause. Whatever the conclusion, it's important to remember that there are no lifestyle factors, either before or during pregnancy, that either protect against or cause lethal birth defects. In many cases it's impossible to identify exactly why a baby is born with a deformity. Each individual case is extremely sad and often difficult for the parents to handle, but it's important not to bear any guilt for something over which you've had absolutely no control.

Neonatal risks and diseases

The second most common causes of death in children aged 0–4 occur at the time of birth and the period immediately after birth. The most common problem is that the baby fails to breathe properly. The baby doesn't need to breathe in the womb because the placenta provides a constant supply of fresh, oxygen-rich blood. At birth, a baby has to switch to breathing on its own, which requires the blood-flow to be redirected so that it passes through the lungs. Sometimes, that automatic switch fails to operate. In most cases, this is because the baby is born much too prematurely. The risk also increases if the birth has been difficult and the baby has received insufficient oxygen through the umbilical cord. In rare cases, a breathing problem can affect term or post-term babies after a normal birth.

Another neonatal risk occurs when a baby has pooed in the womb and afterwards draws the meconium inside its lungs. This can cause a very severe pneumonia known as meconium aspiration, which needs the highest-level neonatal intensive care for treatment.

Infant mortality at, or shortly after, birth is minimised through good neonatal care. In Australia, three in every thousand infants die during their first month of life. In Sweden, the figure is two in one thousand, which is one of the lowest mortality rates in the world. By contrast, in countries such as Angola and Pakistan, around fifty infants in every thousand die during their first month of life. Most of these deaths could be prevented by simple and effective medical interventions, such as assisting newborn babies to start breathing, keeping them warm, and giving extra food to those babies who need it.

SIDS

If we had written this book in 1990, our table of the causes of death would have looked quite different. In that year, 500 children in Australia died of sudden infant death syndrome (SIDS). Since then, the mortality rate has dropped substantially so that 130 infants per year die from SIDS, equal to one in three thousand babies. This rate is comparable to many Western countries, but still higher than in Sweden, where only 16 infant deaths were attributable to SIDS in 2014 (one in 7,000 babies). What has made such a difference in the SIDS rate over time? It is the practice of laying babies on their back to sleep, as described in detail in chapter 7.

Cancer

In the majority of cases, no one knows why a child contracts cancer. In some cases, a child is born with a gene that increases the risk of developing cancer at a young age. If there is a history of childhood cancer in your family, we recommend that you contact a genetic counsellor for advice. If you seek the advice before pregnancy, there may be the option of carrying out screening or a pre-implantation genetic diagnosis. If the baby has already been born, the geneticist can often carry out an investigation to establish the child's risk of developing tumours. In a high-risk case, a program of check-ups may be recommended to detect tumours in good time. In a best-case scenario, early screening may show that the child has not inherited the gene linked to other cases of childhood cancer in the family and does not have an increased risk of cancer.

A child's diet — whether they eat soil and gravel, suck felt-tip pens, eat sweets with artificial colourings, enjoy burnt sausages, or drink fizzy drinks — and whether or not they suck on plastic toys or enjoy cheap bubble baths — does not affect the risk of childhood cancer.

Childhood cancer treatments are tough for children, and some have long-term side effects. Nevertheless, many children return to normal lives after some months of hospital treatment and a few years of follow-up treatment. This is particularly true of acute lymphoblastic

259

leukaemia (ALL), the most common type of childhood cancer, which currently has a survival rate of more than 90 per cent.

Diseases of the nervous system

When you think about severely ill children, it is likely that you will conjure up an image of a bald, smiling child with a drip, in a hospital bed. Childhood cancer is a visible disease, and many parents let their relatives, friends, and acquaintances follow their child's progress through social media.

Children with severe diseases of the nervous system are not as visible in social media, but their diseases are generally not possible to cure and often lead to a life with disabilities. Sometimes, they result in a very short life; other times, the children reach adulthood. In some cases, the disability is confined to motor skills, with intellectual and language skills unaffected. In other cases, all brain functions — motor, language, and intellectual functions — are affected.

There are many types of diseases and injuries that affect the nervous system badly. Some, such as spina bifida or brain malformations, are congenital. Babies may also suffer a stroke early in life, or, as mentioned above, have their brain damaged due to oxygen deprivation (asphyxia), either prenatally or during birth. Some suffer a virus infection (such as rubella, Zika virus, or cytomegalovirus) in the womb. Regardless of the cause of nervous-system disease, the symptoms resemble each other, and these children will often be given a diagnosis of cerebral palsy. Others may have genetic disorders leading to an accumulation of toxic metabolites in their brain. These children may develop some skills early in life before the accumulation becomes too severe and they start to lose their skills. Children showing any signs of losing their motor, language, or social skills should always be evaluated by a paediatrician promptly.

There are some measures you can take to help protect your children from severe nervous system disease: attend prenatal screening tests, have prenatal check-ups, and give birth with skilled attendants and foetal monitoring in place. Make sure you are vaccinated against rubella, and avoid travelling to areas where you risk being infected by the Zika virus. Realistically, this is all you can do. If your child is diagnosed with a nervous system disease, co-operate with your child's medical team, make sure you get all the practical support you are entitled to from community organisations, and try to get support from your family and friends. Life as a parent to a disabled child is in many aspects more challenging than life as a parent to a healthy child. But several things are common, not least that sharing responsibility for a child always makes life much easier.

Infectious diseases

Infectious diseases are a very rare cause of childhood death in high-income countries. In the few cases where children die from infectious diseases, there is usually an underlying cause, such as a serious heart problem or a disease of the nervous system, that prevents the body's defence system from working. In some cases, an infection is a complication of premature birth.

A small number of previously healthy children occasionally suffer from a virulent case of meningitis or blood poisoning that claims their lives. It is impossible to predict who will be affected by these extremely uncommon deadly infections, and other than to vaccinate against certain viruses and bacteria, there is nothing parents can do to reduce the individual risk.

Infant mortality due to infectious diseases has fallen dramatically in high-income countries during the last hundred years, for three reasons. The most important factor has been a general improvement in living standards, with clean water and sewerage, better housing, and better food-handling controls. While at least 20 per cent of Swedish deaths were due to infectious diseases in 1865, this figure had fallen to around 1 per cent by 1930, despite the fact that antibiotics had not yet been discovered. Having access to clean drinking water and wholesome food clearly protects against death from infections; a malnourished, dehydrated child is much more likely to die from an infection than a well-fed child with access to clean fluids during a period of illness.

The second reason is the introduction and expansion of national immunisation programs (see chapter 10). The most significant way you can reduce the risk of your child dying from an infectious disease is to follow your national immunisation program and avoid travelling to countries where a particular disease has spread before your child has had a vaccination. If you have a baby that is sick, and so tired that it is unable to feed, you need to seek medical care so it can be helped with feeding, and antibiotics, if necessary.

The third reason for the decline in deaths from infectious diseases is the development of antibiotics. Treatment with antibiotics saves lives in the case of serious bacterial infections such as pneumonia, pyelonephritis (infection of the kidneys in conjunction with urinary tract infection), meningitis (infection of the protective tissue surrounding the brain), osteomyelitis (infection of the skeletal bones), and blood poisoning.

If your child is highly susceptible to infections and has an underlying condition such as pulmonary disease following extremely premature birth, heart problems, serious physical disabilities with weak cough and swallowing reflexes, a serious congenital immunodeficiency, or a serious metabolic disease, it may be sensible to avoid attending parent and toddler groups during a gastro outbreak or the colds-and-flu season. Talk to your child's doctor for individual advice. However, if your child is otherwise healthy, it is important for you all to mix with other people, even if there is a risk of gastrointestinal or respiratory infections. This is because the child's immune system needs to be trained, and this can only happen through infections or vaccinations (see chapters 9 and 10.. Do not listen to fear-mongering about the dangers of young children encountering bacteria and viruses, or risks in socialising with other people and animals. Children are built for these things!

Road traffic accidents

In Australia, around 20 children aged 0–14 were killed annually in the 2001–10 period in motor vehicle accidents. Of these, around seven per year were killed by a vehicle moving around a home, a so-called driveway death. Traffic accidents are approximately twice as common in Australia (5.4 deaths per 100,000 people) than in Sweden (2.8 per 100,000) and the United Kingdom (2.9 per 100,000). New Zealand has 40 per cent more fatal traffic accidents compared to Australia (8.4 per 100,000), and the US has twice as many traffic deaths as Australia (10.6 per 100,000). These figures show that society can do a lot to reduce traffic deaths, if enough effort is put in.

Over recent decades, Sweden has implemented very active traffic-safety programs that have helped to save many lives, including young lives: the 1975 seatbelt law; the 1988 law that stipulated the use of a booster seat for children shorter than 135 centimetres; improvements to car-safety features; and the addition of central reservations to main roads. Today, it is so unusual for children to die in traffic accidents in Sweden that the risk would be almost zero if the laws relating to the use of seatbelts and booster seats were followed, and if children never travelled with a drunk driver or were never left unsupervised near roads and driveways.

Accidents that kill children in home driveways are entirely preventable. Make it a routine to check where your children are before you start your car, especially if there are bushes or other areas where small children may hide close to where the car is parked. You could also make it a routine to call home when you are a few blocks away, so that whoever is at home can make sure that children are not in the driveway area.

Drowning

An average of 30 children under the age of five have drowned in Australia each year for the past 10 years. This can be compared with three Swedish children under the age of five who die each year in Sweden as a result of drowning. There are approximately three times more children in Australia than in Sweden, which means that the risk of a child drowning is three times higher in Australia than in Sweden.

Most of the Australian children who drown (65 per cent) do so in a private swimming pool. Almost all (82 per cent) are between 12 and 35 months of age, most (65 per cent) are boys, and most of them fall into the water accidentally. If you own a pool, you must ensure that young children cannot have access to it unless they are accompanied by an adult. If your neighbour has a pool, talk to them about pool safety and make sure your child cannot go unaccompanied into your neighbour's garden. This is what fences with locked gates are good for. The children who drown generally manage to get access to the pool area because either a fence or gate is faulty, there is no fence, or a gate has been propped open.

Children must never ever be left alone close to water, and older children should never be given the responsibility for guarding younger ones. A person given the responsibility of watching a child swimming must be capable, in an emergency, of diving into the pool to fetch the child, and swimming to the side of the pool while holding the child's face above the water. It's best by far for you to be in the pool yourself with a young child while they are playing and if you are helping them to learn to swim.

Drownings can even happen when several adults are present at a beach or a swimming pool, when each adult assumes that someone else is watching the children. If there are several adults present, decide who is supervising the children, and take over from each other in shifts, with the understanding that the person on lifeguard duties will not take their eyes off the children even for a second. Drowning can happen very quickly. A child who gets water into their lungs can't shout, and in just a few minutes brain damage will be severe and often fatal. If a child disappears under the surface of the water, it's not easy to know exactly where they are if you haven't been watching them all the time.

It doesn't take a lot of water for a small child to drown. Although nine out of 10 drowning accidents occur in home swimming pools, 6 per cent occur in portable pools. Infants can also drown in the bath-tub. Never leave a child alone in the bath — even a very shallow bath, and not even for a very short while. A bath seat or ring cannot prevent an accident. Don't leave water in the bathtub, because a little child can fall in.

Choking

A couple of children under the age of four die each year in Sweden from choking, either on pieces of food or as a result of their airways being obstructed by small toys or other small objects.

A typical choking situation occurs when a child runs, jumps, or falls down with a small piece of food or a toy (such as a Lego brick or a marble) in their mouth. During these activities, the reflexes that protect against choking are out of action, and the small object can get stuck in the child's airway. With a bit of luck, the airway will not be completely blocked, the child will have a coughing fit, and the object will be coughed up. If the object isn't ejected immediately, call the emergency services and request an ambulance.

If the object completely blocks the airway, the child will fall silent, turn blue, and start to panic. You need to help the child eject the object. If the baby is less than a year old, place them on their stomach on your left forearm and hold onto the baby's chin and lower jaw for support. Using your right wrist, thump hard five times with the base of your wrist in the centre of the baby's back. The aim is to create a blast of air from the air remaining in the lungs, which should then dislodge the object in the child's airway. If the object doesn't come up, turn the baby onto its back and press hard five times in the middle of its breastbone. Again, you should press hard enough to create an explosive blast of air that has a chance of dislodging the object.

We highly recommend that you take a course in first aid for babies and children, which will give you the chance to practise this technique. It's a good general rule that children shouldn't run around and play with food or toys in their mouths.

Certain diseases and abnormalities, such as muscular or nervous-system diseases that result in a weak cough and swallowing reflexes, increase the risk of choking. If your child experiences such difficulties, you should ensure that you get help from a speech therapist to find out which sorts of food should be provided and how your child can eat safely.

Violence by another person

Each year, a small number of children die each year due to violence. Tragically, in nine out of 10 such cases, it is a parent who causes the child's death. The younger the child is, the more common it is for a mother to kill her child, and to take her own life.

Mothers and fathers are equally common as perpetrators of deadly violence to their child. Mothers who kill their own children are often suffering from a psychotic disorder, as a result of which they completely lose their grip on reality. Most new mothers experience the 'baby blues' after delivery. About one out of every 10 of these women will develop a more severe and longer-lasting depression after delivery. About one in 1,000 women develops a more serious condition called postpartum psychosis.

Effective treatment is available for psychosis. The most important thing you can do if you recognise that a parent is showing signs of serious mental illness is to ensure that they get the care they need. The symptoms can include extreme anxiety, very serious sleeping problems, and a feeling that life is completely unmanageable. If you recognise these symptoms in someone close to you, seek help for them from the nearest emergency psychiatric clinic. If the person refuses to accompany you to see a psychiatrist, call a helpline or emergency psychiatric clinic for advice. Some clinics have mobile teams who can come to visit someone who is suffering from serious mental illness and will not attend hospital voluntarily. In such cases, compulsory care may be required until the person feels better. Society has both the right and a duty to provide compulsory care for someone who presents a danger to themselves or to others due to serious mental illness.

Fathers who kill their children have often tended to have been previously violent, jealous, and controlling towards their partner, and may have also abused family pets. If you live with a partner who has violent, controlling, or jealous tendencies, contact social services or a women's shelter, tell your GP or midwife, or call a national helpline. If you yourself have violent tendencies and a need to control your partner, contact your health centre, your local social services, or a helpline. If you have already hit your partner, take responsibility for your actions and leave your partner alone until you have resolved your aggression problems. Move away from each other if you are unable to respect your partner when living together.

Unpleasant and disturbing thoughts about intentionally harming a child — for example, *Just imagine if I were to stick this knife into my child's chest*, or *Just imagine if I were to throw my child off the balcony* — are common among new parents. Many people have such thoughts on the odd occasion, while for others these thoughts come more frequently and are associated with anxiety. At least one in 10 women experience serious compulsive thoughts or compulsive actions during the period after giving birth, compared with 2–3 per cent of women at other times.[1] In addition, almost half of all new mothers have milder forms of compulsive thoughts while their children are babies.[2] We have been unable to find any studies to correlate the statistics for fathers.

It may be reassuring to know that the presence of disturbing thoughts doesn't lead to parents harming their children. These unpleasant thoughts are common and don't lead to any harm to the children, even if they can be frightening for the person who experiences them. They should be regarded as part of the generally elevated levels of anxiety and emergency preparedness that are so often associated with becoming a parent, and they probably serve some evolutionary purpose that we do not yet fully understand. However, if you have so many compulsive thoughts that daily life is difficult, talk to your GP or child and maternal health nurse for advice. If you start avoiding everyday activities, such as cutting bread or going out on the balcony, or if you start doing something compulsively, such as washing your hands or repeatedly checking that the stove is off, you need help. A common strategy in the event of anxiety is to avoid the thing that makes you anxious, but this is also a poor strategy, since the anxiety is allowed to grow and limit your life. A psychologist or a doctor can help you to manage anxiety or compulsions.

Burns

Even though on average only one child a year dies from burns in Sweden, including in house fires, burns are a frequent and painful reason for children needing emergency healthcare. In particular, children aged one or two are most at risk of a burns accident when they have just learnt to walk.

One common type of burn (albeit one that is very rarely fatal) is scalding, where a child who can just reach up to a table pulls down a cup of hot coffee, or a pot of tea, and suffers burns on the neck, or the stomach, or maybe the legs. Kettles or coffee machines with cords are a particular risk if the cord hangs out so the child can pull it. It is sensible to ensure that kettles, teapots, and coffee pots are pushed back against the wall on the benchtop, and to get a hob guard so that children can't reach hotplates and pans that are close to the edge. Barbecues need constant adult supervision if there are children nearby, and this is necessary as long as they remain hot, even after the flames have gone out.

If you have an open fireplace, a wood-burner, or a gas heater in your home, it's almost impossible to be sufficiently vigilant when your child is near it. Install a guard of some kind. If you have other heating in

268

your house, take a break from using the fireplace until your child is old enough to keep away from it.

If your child suffers a burn, remove wet clothing and nappies in the case of scalding, cool the burnt skin under cool running water for 15 minutes, and then examine the injury. If their skin is only reddened or there are small blisters, it's safe to stay at home and allow the skin to heal. If you see larger blisters or injuries, go straight to a hospital. In the event of severe burns, call the emergency services and request an ambulance. If you are unsure what to do, call a medical information service for advice.

Poisoning

Children rarely die from swallowing a poisonous substance, but many require medical treatment. There are a few types of household chemicals that are potentially deadly or that can cause incurable severe injuries. These items should be stored out of reach so that children cannot get to them under any circumstances. For information about such chemicals, there are excellent helplines that you can access online at any time.

Corrosive substances

Substances that are strongly alkaline (such as lye and ammonia) and strongly acidic are corrosive, and if children eat or drink them they can suffer from very serious corrosion injuries of both the mouth and the oesophagus. Think about whether you need to have such substances at home if you have children; if you decide that they are absolutely necessary, store them at a height that is out of reach to them. Some dishwasher detergents and air fresheners are corrosive, and caustic soda is extremely corrosive — as are bleach, ammonia, oven cleaners, drain cleaners, and some toilet cleaners. These are heavy-duty chemicals. When they are used in a laboratory, rigorous safety precautions are followed. If you mix these substances at home, chemical reactions will occur. Depending on the substances and their concentrations, the mixed solution may or may not still be corrosive, and, during the process, severely toxic substances may be released in a gaseous form.

Agnes has a university degree in chemistry, and when her children were small she found the thought of having lye and chlorine bleach in her household so scary that she never bought them. Cecilia, brought up in a green-wave alternative family, knew only about cleaning with soft soap. Between us, we have never used heavy cleaning chemicals in our own homes.

Volatile liquids

Lamp oil, white spirit, petrol, and lighting fluid are all low in viscosity and are volatile liquids. (In other words, they vaporise readily.) Due to these properties, they tend not to run down into the stomach when ingested; they mostly end up in the lungs instead, causing chemical lung inflammation, which can be extremely serious.

Keep a close eye on white spirit when redecorating, and consider alternatives to lighting fluid when lighting the barbecue, or at least ensure it is closely guarded. Never rely on 'child safe' caps!

Medicines

Medicines vary widely in toxicity, and certain over-the-counter medicines are among those that can cause the most serious poisonings. Both iron tablets and pain-relief tablets containing paracetamol can result in life-threatening poisoning symptoms in doses that a child can easily ingest. You should ensure that you always store medicines in a locked cabinet or at a height that children can't reach.

Batteries

Batteries contain acid that can cause corrosion injuries in the digestive tract if swallowed. In 2013, an Australian child died from gastrointestinal bleeding caused by a button battery she had swallowed when nobody was watching and therefore no one knew the cause of her bleeding. In

Australia, swallowed button batteries result in 20 toddlers being admitted to hospital each week in New South Wales and Queensland alone.

Try to ensure that children don't have the opportunity to handle batteries, and seek medical attention immediately if you suspect that they have swallowed a battery, even if you are unsure. Batteries can easily be seen on an X-ray of the abdomen. If a child has ingested a battery, it will need to be removed from the stomach quickly, which is done in hospital with a gastroscope.

We believe that it is also important that parents use their power to argue for consumer-product legislation that reduces the risk of small batteries ending up in the mouths of toddlers.

Magnets

Small, strong magnets are dangerous. If a child swallows two magnets, there is a risk that they will end up in different parts of the intestine or the stomach, and will then be attracted to each other. If the magnets are strong enough, they can exert so much pressure on the tissue that it can break and form a gastric ulcer. If you are worried that a child has swallowed magnets, seek urgent medical attention. Magnets can be seen under X-ray, and if there is more than one in the stomach they will need to be removed using a gastroscope.

WHAT'S THE STORY WITH PLASTIC TOYS AND DUST?

Many parents today, particularly the well educated, spend a great deal of time and money trying to protect their children from plastics, 'chemicals', and dust. There is a constant stream of hazards that parents are told they have to protect their children from, and we would not be surprised if new claims have cropped up since the publication of this book.

Dust

Dust has long been accused of causing illnesses, although the specific illnesses have varied over time. In the early 20th century, dust was believed to cause tuberculosis and other infections. Cleaning and keeping the house tidy became the duty of the housewife and wasted an awful lot of women's time, without helping at all against tuberculosis, diphtheria, or any other infectious diseases that were significant causes of death at the time. As the infectious diseases became less of a threat, it was decided instead that dust caused allergies. Once again, cleaning was launched as an important preventive measure, even though it proved just as ineffective as it was for infections. Now some people are claiming that dust contains chemicals that can disrupt a child's hormones, and that's why you need to be vacuuming and scrubbing away at all domestic surfaces.

Dust is a glorious mix of different substances. In a house near a desert, it will mostly be sand that has blown in on the wind and fallen to ground. At a kennel, the dust will largely be dog hair and dander, maybe accompanied by a few flakes of dry feed. In a regular family home, dust is made up of skin flakes, textile fibres, hair, and all sorts of other things. Dust is dry and sterile. Bacteria can't grow in it. It never caused tuberculosis (which was caused by tuberculosis bacteria) and, equally, it doesn't cause allergies (a disease caused by our own immune systems going astray — see chapter 11). The theory linking dust to allergies is absurd: why would someone who is allergic to pollen or cow's milk fall ill from household dust? The only damage dust can do is to your sense of aesthetics and the cleanliness of your socks. When it comes to children's health and development, it really doesn't matter whether you vacuum your home or not.

The plastics scare

A parent of a newborn baby is expert at finding imaginary dangers. As if this wasn't enough, there are many people who exploit this inclination for parents to worry as a means to spread all sorts of messages. While the mothers of yesteryear were encouraged to clean and scrub to combat tuberculosis or allergies (in both cases to no avail), today's parents are concerned that dust contains 'chemicals'. The word 'chemical' simply means substance or compound, but when hearing the word most people think of molecules that are human-made rather than created in nature. There is a general misapprehension that such molecules are harmful, while 'natural' substances are healthy or harmless. In fact, some of the most poisonous known substances are entirely natural, and most of the molecules manufactured by humans are not particularly harmful, unless you consume them in extremely high doses — and most things are harmful at very high dosage.

There are some chemicals such as lye and white spirit that are really harmful in a household, as we mentioned earlier. In the agricultural and mining industries, many workers are exposed to harmful levels of industrial chemicals such as pesticides and agents used to extract minerals from ores. These industries also risk contaminating their neighbourhood, even to the extent of causing environmental and health disasters. This might be why people are so scared of chemicals. But leaping from this to being worried about minuscule amounts found in plastic products is not factually based.

In the 1990s, a Danish doctor put forward a hypothesis that abnormalities and cancers in children were due to them absorbing chemicals in the womb. According to this theory, many different types of everyday chemicals are structurally similar to our hormones, and so disrupt our hormonal functions. Particular suspicion was directed at substances in various forms of plastic. The theory has been researched for around 20 years without any conclusive evidence being found that people are damaged by the chemicals we are exposed to in daily life. A 2016 meta-analysis (a summary of a large number of studies) shows no correlation between the levels of a host of everyday chemicals in the blood and the risk of the diseases and abnormalities that are suggested to be due to 'hormone-disrupting chemicals'.[3] The hypothesis turned out to be wrong, which is absolutely normal in research: you put forward a theory and test it, and it may turn out to be right, or — more often — wrong. Unfortunately, in the meantime, books have been written about the dangers of rubber ducks, and many anti-plastic activists have scared new parents and instructed them to discard all plastic cups and spoons for no good reason.

We're surrounded by masses of human-made chemicals. They are the basis of our very prosperity: without plastics we wouldn't have smartphones, computers, or televisions. Without plastic wrapping, meat and many other food products couldn't be found on supermarket shelves. Then there is all the plastic in fridges and dishwashers. According to our laws on chemicals, the chemicals present in food and consumer products must be tested to establish limits, so we can know what levels we can expose ourselves to without any risk, and which levels pose a risk. When it comes to regular chemicals such as those in household plastics, the doses children might ingest at home or at preschool are a long way below the limit of the tolerable daily intake (TDI) value. You can safely assume that the researchers who recommend the TDI limits have also included a good safety margin.

For some reason, plastic is the substance of choice for terrifying people today; tomorrow, the hazard is just as likely to come from something else. Conspiracy theories assert that we are surrounded by a mass of hazards that no one is telling us about or that we don't understand. But there is no evidence to show this to be true — on the contrary, every decade, fewer and fewer children are dying or being seriously hurt.

According to the Mayo Clinic in the US, some research has shown that bisphenol A (BPA), an industrial chemical that has been used to make plastics and resins since the 1960s, can seep into food or beverages from containers made with the chemical. Exposure to BPA is a concern because of possible health effects on the brain and prostate gland of foetuses, infants, and children. It can also affect children's behaviour. Additional research suggests a possible link between BPA and increased blood pressure. However, the Food and Drug Administration has said that BPA is safe at the very low levels that occur in some foods. This assessment is based on a review of hundreds of studies.

Some people contend that life was more pleasant and more 'natural' one hundred years ago, but life expectancy has risen hugely since then, and infant mortality is down a hundredfold. Prior to 1805, 20 per cent of Swedish children died before the age of one. By 2015, the percentage had fallen to 0.25 per cent. Remember that this statistic includes all the infants who died because they were born extremely prematurely and with severe congenital disorders. Never before in the history of the world has a child had a better chance of reaching adulthood than today.

RESIST!

It's only natural to be worried when you hear prophets of doom trying to sell their messages about the dangers in everyday life. The big problem is that it's theoretically impossible to prove something can never, ever be harmful. If plastic is a theoretical risk, why not vinyl or coloured cotton fabrics, too? Why not claim that wood, air, rose scent, or cinnamon buns are dangerous? In terms of the philosophy of science, we can never be entirely sure about any of these things. It's just not possible to create a life with zero risk. And it's also not healthy to keep striving for a risk-free life.

If you tend to worry a lot, we suggest you try to put up some resistance. You don't need to get rid of the plastic; a better idea is to switch off the inflow of advice. Stop following people on social media who focus on frightening new parents. Say, 'Thanks, but no thanks' to unsolicited advice. Some people seem to take pleasure in frightening others, which is all very well if they want to tell ghost stories or produce horror films, but they have no right to frighten you just because you've had a baby. These people are like Krösa-Maja, the old crofter woman in Astrid Lindgren's books about Emil of Lönneberga. She was miserable, and had the lowest status in the farming community, and the only thing that cheered her up was scaring other people with her terrifying stories. Avoid all the Krösa-Majas when you're expecting or have had a baby!

As we've just said, never before in human history has a child had a greater chance of reaching adulthood, and that's a fact worth bearing in mind. Unfortunately, this has not reduced our worrying. In fact, it sometimes seems the opposite is true. You don't get rid of worries by trying to minimise risks. Instead, this strategy tends to feed your anxieties, as you think about all the terrible things that could happen while you're working on your risk minimisation. The best way to quell your anxiety if it's of a moderate nature (if it's really strong, you'll need the help of health professionals) is to focus on something else entirely, so you don't have time to dwell on potential hazards. If you're on parental leave, it may be time to go back to work rather than staying at home, worrying. Or take a course, go out jogging, have a night out with your adult friends, or do something else to keep your mind otherwise engaged. Anxiety and worry don't just affect you; they can be a huge burden on family life.

Severe anxiety is much more common among mothers than fathers. This may be because women are generally more inclined toward anxiety and depression than men are, but it may also be related to women all too often bearing primary responsibility for their child, and also for the worry. As you already know, we believe that parents should share their parental responsibility equally. Sharing the worry — or what has come to be referred to as the mental load — is another aspect of co-parenting. If you share the parental responsibility equally with your partner, you can also discuss concerns with each other, which often has a calming effect. If one parent has taken on all the parental responsibility, they'll naturally find it hard to accept that the other parent does not share their concern. In this situation, an absence of anxiety will be interpreted as a lack of parental competence, which could be true, but in many cases may simply be a misunderstanding.

IN BRIEF

It is important to separate facts from beliefs and opinions. When infants die in high-income countries today, it is almost always because of congenital disorders or extremely premature birth, and there is nothing you can do about either situation. What you do need to do to protect your baby is to place them on their back to sleep; keep a close eye on them whenever you are around traffic and water; lock away caustic soda, lighter fluid, batteries, and medicines; be sure to check that the child is nowhere around the car or the swimming pool; and stick to your national immunisation program. Only clean your home as much as you feel like doing. Don't listen to the scaremongers, and apply your critical thinking every time you hear about a new threat that is supposed to be harmful for your baby — particularly if the 'solution' involves more housework and less freedom for you ...

CHAPTER THIRTEEN

Nature, nurture, and the importance of the child flock

There is a widespread belief that perfect parenting during the early years 'vaccinates' children against future unhappiness and is essential in order for them to grow into contented and successful adults. Faced with the enormous responsibility for creating a harmonious person, it is all too easy for parents to falter. In this final chapter, we take issue with the idea of a newborn baby being a 'blank slate'. We also discuss the genetics of personality, and the role that a child's surroundings play in their development. Finally, we provide some advice about key factors for the building of a well-functioning family life.

In our culture, there is a long-established belief that a child's personality is primarily formed by the way they have been cared for and raised. Do it right, and your child will turn out well; do it wrong, and everything might fall apart. All manner of ills — from anorexia, autism, and drug addiction, to an inability to form solid relationships as an adult — have been blamed on parents. Newspaper letters pages and online comments overflow with angry complaints about parents who have not brought their children up well enough.

The debate about what determines an individual's personality and life path has probably been running for as long as humans have had language — it's a fascinating subject. What role is played by heredity, environment, or fate in making us who we are? Fate, or the mystical and religious dimension of life, is not a theme for this book; theology is not our strongest point. We will, however, use this chapter to discuss the role of heredity and environment on a child's future personality and destiny. By 'heredity', we mean the biological, genetic inheritance from the people who provided the genetic material for their baby's creation (usually the parents, but in the case of egg or sperm donation, the donor or, for adoption, the biological parents). We look at the significance of the 'environment' later in the chapter.

HEREDITY AND ENVIRONMENT

We don't need to speculate on how great an impact heredity has on different personality traits, as we have sound research results to inform us. These results have primarily been achieved by using two types of studies: on twins and on adoption. In twin studies, researchers measure likenesses among identical twins compared to likenesses among non-identical twins of the same gender. Identical twins share the same genes, whereas non-identical twins, like other siblings, share half their genes with one another. If a trait is 100 per cent genetically determined, two identical twins would always possess the trait, while siblings (or non-identical twins) on average would possess the trait only half of the time. On the other hand, if parenting style and the family environment are the single most important factor, and genes do not play a role at all, identical twins and siblings would be equally likely to share the trait in question.

Another type of study into the importance of genes versus environment compares likenesses between adopted children and their adoptive parents with likenesses between children and their biological parents. By studying the differences between identical and non-identical twins, full siblings, half siblings, and children who grow up with or without their biological parents, it's possible to determine how much of a character trait depends on genes and how much on environment.

For example, it has been found that around 50 per cent of intelligence in childhood (measured as an intelligence quotient, or IQ) is genetically determined. This means that half the variation in IQ within a group of children can be explained by the genes they inherit from their parents. When their IQs are measured in adulthood, the inherited component rises to 70–80 per cent.[1] So, the older you get, the greater the role your genes play in the type of intelligence measured as IQ. The IQ of identical twins gets closer and closer as they grow older.

The effect of the family environment on IQ accounts for around 15–20 per cent of the variation in IQ between children. But when we measure IQ in adulthood, we tend not to see any effect from the family environment in which the child grew up. Parenting thus appears to play a certain role in a child's IQ while they live at home, but the effect disappears in adulthood.

The attentive reader will have noticed that the totality of what can be explained by the factors of genes and family environment doesn't add up to 100 per cent. To reach 100 per cent you need to add another factor — one that researchers call the individual environment, which is unique to each child.

THE FAMILY ENVIRONMENT AND THE INDIVIDUAL ENVIRONMENT

The family environment relates to the factors shared by all the children who grow up in the same family. Some examples include living in in rural or urban areas, having rich or poor parents, having access to books or numerous screens at home, and so on. The individual environment is much more difficult to pin down: it is made up of factors in the environment that differ between members of a single household, such as birth position in the family, friends and classmates, leisure activities, illnesses, and accidents.

What about eating habits? Are they part of the family environment, or the individual environment? This is where the distinction gets a little trickier. The food that is served at home is part of the family environment as long as the children always eat exactly what is put in front of them. But if one twin eats the meat on the plate and the other just eats the gravy and the potatoes, that becomes part of the individual environment — as do the sweets that are bought with their own pocket money, and the food they are offered at a friend's house.

It's the family environment that determines whether there's a ball to play with, but whether a child actually plays with the ball, and how often, is part of the individual environment. The fact that parents read bedtime stories is perhaps part of the family environment, but what a child reads by themselves forms the individual environment of that child. The income level of the parents, and where they live, is part of the family environment, but how the parents behave with each of their children is more individualised than we might like to believe. Although many of us work hard to treat siblings fairly, we can't treat two siblings with different personalities exactly equally. We talk more about this distinction later in this chapter.

Genes and individual environment have the greatest impact

Almost all personality traits are determined more by the individual environment than by the family environment, but most of all by our genes. According to a meta-analysis of the field, heredity (genes) accounts for 48 per cent of the variation between individuals' language skills, for example, while the family environment only accounts for 19 per cent.[2] Heredity accounts for 60 per cent of the variation in spatial awareness and 48 per cent of the variation in memory, while the family environment accounts for none of the variation in these traits. Personality tests show similar results. For the character trait of neuroticism, which is characterised by a tendency to worry and experience negative emotions, heredity accounts for 42 per cent in men and 50 per cent in women. The family environment accounts for 5 per cent of the variation in neuroticism among men and 0 per cent among women.

But if the key factors are genes and the individual environment, how come, time after time, we see well-balanced and calm parents having pleasant and well-behaved children, while the children of argumentative parents are often angry and find it hard to concentrate? Of course, genetics comes into play here, too, to some extent. Personality traits are partly hereditary – around 50 per cent on average. In families where both the children and the parents are genetically inclined to be hot-tempered, there will be arguments, and arguments breed arguments. Conversely, good behaviour by one person will often be warmly received by another. A cheerful child with a sunny disposition will get smiles and kisses from their parents, which will make the child happy, and so a virtuous circle is created. This pattern is particularly common in families where both the child and the parents have genes that enable them to always look on the bright side of life.

Given that anxiety (neuroticism) is 42–50 per cent inherited, it's by no means fair to blame parents for 'spoiling' clingy and whining children; they may just have been born that way. In some of these cases, at least one parent will also be a worrier. In other cases, two entirely non-neurotic parents may happen to have an anxious child. If, as a parent, you end up with a problem-free child who brings you only joy, you're unusually lucky — not only with your child, but also lucky because you have been born with the ability to see everything and everyone in a positive light. Enjoy that optimistic outlook. If, on the other hand, you have a somewhat unhappy child with fewer immediate charms, it's not your fault.

THE SOCIAL ENVIRONMENT

The social environment is the environment common to everyone in a society. In a society where food is scarce, obesity genes cannot be expressed. No one, whatever their genetic make-up, can become overweight if there is only enough food to sustain life. However, in a society where calorific food is readily available to all, people with a tendency to be overweight will often show this predisposition. Studies of nature versus nurture are almost always carried out within a single country or cultural sphere. Such studies will examine, for example, differences between fat and thin people in the US, and between fat and thin people in Japan, but not between fat and thin people the world over, because global studies would only reveal that access to food is the most important factor.

The same principle applies to societal patterns of violence and criminality. The fact that there is four times as much deadly violence in the US as in Sweden has cultural and historical explanations. Regardless of genetic make-up, the risk is very high that a child will become a drug addict or a criminal if they grow up in a slum ruled by drug dealers. Even if parents do everything they can to imprint good values on their child, there is a real risk that in such an environment the child will end up losing their way in life.

Likewise, no one learns to read in a society that has no written language. But in a society with universal access to schooling, where reading and writing skills are valued highly, most children will learn to read

— although some will master the skill easily and extremely well, while others with a genetic tendency towards dyslexia will find reading more difficult. Yet acceptance of the fact that children's prospects are largely controlled by genetic factors certainly doesn't mean that we should become cynical and asocial. While we maintain that it is meaningless to hold individual parents responsible for their children going astray, we also believe that working to achieve social change benefits all children, and that action at a policy and legislative level is effective.

When Sweden became the first country in the world to ban the corporal punishment of children, in 1979, many people thought that to make this behaviour illegal was an idiotic move. After all, at that time mild smacking was generally seen as acceptable, provided you didn't injure the child (which would be considered abuse). We now know that the legislation led to a change in views about violence towards children, and that fewer children are being physically punished today than before the law was in force. Naturally, not all children were physically punished prior to 1979; those who had kind parents weren't. And, inevitably, there are children who do get hit today, even though it's forbidden. But the children of both kind and more aggressive parents are physically punished much less often now than was previously the case, thanks to a change in legislation.

Today, 57 countries have completely forbidden parents from physically punishing their children. Only six out of the 28 countries in the European Union still permit parents to physically punish their children, and the French parliament recently voted to forbid it. In Canada and the UK, corporal punishment is legal, but in Scotland it is unlawful to hit children under the age of three. Interestingly, in the US, in 49 of the 50 states it is explicitly legal to punish your children physically, according to the state laws. In Australia, children may be physically punished by parents provided it is 'reasonable', but Tasmania is considering reviewing the legislation that allows such punishment. Corporal punishment is largely banned in government and non-government schools in Australia.

As of 2016, an estimated 128 countries have prohibited corporal punishment in schools, including all of Europe, and most of South America and East Asia.

Neurodiversity

People are partly like each other, and partly different. Even if everyone's heart is the same shape, we all have different personalities and talents. Historically, human societies with a wide range of abilities and behaviours have probably had a greater chance of success than societies where everyone has been similar.

Today, some behavioural patterns are creating such great problems in schools and workplaces that they have been given their own names and diagnoses. These include attention-deficit hyperactive disorder (ADHD) and autism spectrum disorder (ASD). The fact that these types of behaviour do create problems in schools and workplaces doesn't mean that there are only disadvantages associated with people whose brains work in these ways. On the contrary, people with these behaviour types are important for the development of our society. We look at some of these behaviours in this book about pregnancy and babies because the patterns can emerge as early as during the first year of a child's life, even if diagnoses are not made until later in childhood.

ATTENTION-DEFICIT HYPERACTIVE DISORDER (ADHD)

People with ADHD have a poorly functioning attention filter, and have difficulty focusing their attention in a controlled manner on a single task. They tend to find it particularly hard to concentrate on boring, unexciting tasks. They are impulsive, find it hard to regulate their activity level, and tend to be either extremely active or very inactive. As a general rule, their working memory is poor. Children with ADHD are often intense, ingenious, and fun to be with, but many of them — particularly boys — get into arguments easily, and undiagnosed ADHD in girls often causes problems with anxiety. When school starts to set demands in terms of self-organisation and planning, it is often hard for children with ADHD to perform in line with their talents.

ADHD is one of the most heritable behavioural conditions we know of: it is at least 75 per cent genetic. Strangely enough, the newspapers are full of assertions that everything from particular foods to plastic products causes ADHD, but this simply isn't the case. Since ADHD is so genetic, at least one parent almost always has an ADHD personality, even if it was undiagnosed when the parent was a child. Extremely premature birth is an environmental factor that increases the risk of one type of ADHD, and certain infections in children's brains can also cause similar conditions. Bad parenting, on the other hand, is definitely not something that can cause ADHD in children.

Just as you can't be overweight in a society where there's hardly enough food, the behavioural pattern that we now diagnose as ADHD wouldn't have caused any noticeable disadvantage for an individual in a society where physical performance and activity was important for survival, and where almost no one sat in their room reading books. A housewife who found it hard to sit still and was constantly on the go with various activities, and whose attention was so scattered that no animal in the yard, no plant, and no child escaped her notice, would certainly have been popular on a 19th-century farm. This type of behaviour and personality may be mostly the result of genetics, but the extent to which it is seen as a problem or expressed in a diagnosis is a product of how society is organised. Many believe that the incidence of ADHD is increasing, but what has actually risen is the propensity to make a diagnosis.

Someone with ADHD often finds being at school the hardest time. If they make it through school, they have increasingly better chances of finding a job where an ADHD brain is an asset. If you're looking for adults with ADHD, the most likely professions include artists, entrepreneurs, estate agents, emergency physicians, and consultants. Unfortunately, you will also find them in prison, as ADHD in men is a risk factor for ending up in a life of crime, possibly due to poor impulse control.

It's not possible to change a child's personality, but the parents of children with ADHD can try to adapt the environment so that their child can function as well as possible. There are also medications that are effective in many cases, and that can make it much easier to live with ADHD in society. These medications are generally not suitable before a child reaches school age, and in many cases an adapted environment and ADHD-friendly strategies and routines suffice for a child to function well.

Autism spectrum disorder (ASD)

Another functional variant that has been given its own diagnosis is autism spectrum disorder (ASD). Originally, a diagnosis of autism required severe developmental delay, and poor language and communication in general. With time, less severe developmental variants have been included in the autism spectrum, so that ASD with normal (or high) intellectual skills, which was until recently named Asperger syndrome, is now incorporated into the autism spectrum. Someone with autism has difficulties understanding other people's views, and often prefers set routines. Many people with high functioning ASD end up getting into arguments from time to time because of their tendency to always put facts first. Their ability to be entirely absorbed by their own strong interests and convictions can bore others. ASD is also strongly genetic.

Even though the number of people with an autism diagnosis has increased over time, the reason is not that this functional variant is more common now than before. It might be that certain sections of our society (not least schools) find it harder to make provisions for people who are not socially agile and who do not adapt quickly to change, and that autism traits have a more negative impact on people's lives today than before. Another possible reason is increased awareness of ASD among medical providers.

As we mentioned before, societies thrive when their citizens have diverging capabilities. This positive contribution is definitely true also for autism traits. The Swedish teenager Greta Thunberg, who has ASD, started school strikes and a global movement for climate change. She has said herself that her ability to see things in black and white, and her being entirely unconcerned with social norms, was essential when she took action, and that she would probably not have been able to do this without her autism traits. People with ASD may make significant contributions as writers, and there are several living examples of famous, successful researchers with this diagnosis. There are no medications for ASD, but learning how these conditions work and adapting life accordingly is usually an effective approach.

If you, your child, or someone else in your family has ADHD or ASD, and your situation doesn't feel satisfactory, it is a good idea to seek professional help. In the case of less complex behavioural problems, suitable places to consult include maternal and health clinics, school health workers, psychology clinics, and paediatric clinics. In more serious cases, where everyday life is barely manageable at all, seek a referral from your GP to a child and adolescent psychiatry clinic, or an adult psychiatry clinic.

Early signs of ADHD and ASD

When a child of school age is diagnosed with ADHD, or ASD of a milder type, parents more often than not report that they had seen signs early in their children's lives. Some of these signs are nonspecific, and common even among babies who later on develop normally; others are less often seen among children with later typical development.

Nonspecific signs in a young child include difficulties in being put to sleep; difficulties in eating; an inability to clearly express what they want; and a reflexive outburst or tantrum when their will is not met. Obviously, these traits are also common in typically developing children; but, in retrospect, parents of children who later on are diagnosed with

ADHD or ASD tend to emphasise these difficulties seen early on in life.

More concerning is a child who at the age of one year does not seem to understand a word of what their parents say, or who does not respond to their name. A two-year-old who produces no recognisable words is also late in their language development, but it is important to see this in an individual context. If that child understands well what is being said to them, makes themself understood by specific signs, and shows joy in interacting with other people, there is not much to worry about. On the other hand, if a two-year-old communicates only through nonspecific sounds (either cheerful or discontented ones), or by making nonspecific gestures, then it is time to talk to a paediatrician or child psychologist for a comprehensive development evaluation.

Distinguishing normal development from early signs of autism, ADHD, or general developmental delay requires a thorough knowledge of developmental psychology and thorough experience in this kind of evaluation. Even for the most experienced psychologist, it is often not clear exactly which diagnosis at this early age will most accurately describe a child later in life. It is nevertheless very valuable for children with developmental variations to be diagnosed early. For children with ASD, early intervention with intensive behavioural training programs is very effective in helping them to function better; the earlier these interventions are started, the better.

EASY AND DIFFICULT CHILDREN

Diagnosed or not, parents tend to be blamed for unruly children, and the people around them can sometimes go so far as to offer unsolicited advice on how to cure a particular trait. Luckily, nature has equipped us with an abundance of parental love, so even slightly less loveable children are usually considered amazing by their parents. But evolution has also equipped children, to a greater or lesser degree, with the ability to charm others. This skill can vary greatly, and it's not something that parents are either responsible for or should take the credit or blame for.

If you have a child who demands extra effort, it's often a good idea to try to share some of their care with other adults. If there are two of you doing the parenting, it's naturally important to share the responsibilities even after parental leave has ended; however, it often takes more than two adults to look after a demanding child if the parents also need to work and have some respite. Look at your circle of family and friends, and ask for help where you can. Let your child spend as much time at daycare as the family needs.

The fact that research has not managed to show that the family environment has a particularly great effect on personality traits is no reason not to offer a child a good environment in which to grow up. The parent–child relationship is unequal. Children don't choose their parents, and a parent has considerable power over them for their entire childhood. We believe that all parents, therefore, have a moral duty to try to behave well and to create a pleasant home environment.

Difficult children will fare better in families where the parents make an effort to treat them well than in families full of violence, threats, and shouting. If you have an easy child, it's important to be supportive, non-judgemental, and understanding when you encounter other parents with more difficult children, as this will make life much more enjoyable for everyone. There's no guarantee that you would have been a better parent to the difficult child you see on the bus, or that you would have been more upbeat if you'd been the parent of the anxious, whining child you meet at your parent and toddler group.

PARENTING IN PRACTICE

In many Swedish families today, perhaps in well-educated families in particular, there is a tendency to let a child's wishes take centre stage — in some cases, at the expense of the rest of the family's and other people's needs. The intentions of this approach are good, but in the desire to not repress the child, the balance can tip in favour of the young. The loss of parental authority is not always a good thing. Children have immature brains, and are not particularly good at foreseeing or understanding the consequences of their actions, or at putting them in a broader context. Parents also need to understand that other adults are irritated by children who interrupt and constantly demand attention.

Upbringing and rules

Parents are well within their rights to determine the rules and standards that apply in their own home. Parents have the responsibility for, and the right to make decisions about, their child until they reach the age of eighteen. Discuss how you want things to work in your family. Parenting is often easier when there are clear rules and parameters for how everyone gets on at home.

There is likely to be less conflict if children know that when a parent looks them in the eye and tells them off in a serious voice, there is no point in continuing to argue — whether the matter is bedtime, ice-cream, or any other point of difference. A rule that changes every day is, of course, not a rule; routines need to be consistent if your children are going to respect them.

On the other hand, rigid routines that just create more stress in your family do not make life easier for anyone. Parenting is a continuous balance between consistency and flexibility, and if you have a co-parent you can discuss these matters with, you are lucky. Otherwise, discuss them with your friends and close people. New questions arise constantly in parenthood as your child grows, and new decisions need to be made, and old ones revisited.

Don't try to be perfect

Many people who want to be perfect parents feel unnecessarily guilty about normal human reactions, such as being irritated, feeling a lack of interest at times (for example, when a child wants to play in the middle of the night), or having the desire to escape the home and seek refuge with a nice group of grown-ups. It's not possible to be a perfect parent, for the simple fact that there are no perfect people. It's also worth asking whether perfection is, in fact, a desirable goal: a child who grew up with two perfect parents would probably be in for a bit of a shock as soon as they encountered life outside the family bubble. In the real world, not everyone is nice, and you constantly have to deal with injustices, unreasonable behaviour, and people who, for whatever reason, don't like you. It's a very strange modern notion that parents should strive to create a perfect environment for their child.

Children need to learn that not all adults think and work the same way. Mum might not be nearly as patient as Dad; one parent might be grumpy in the morning, while the other falls asleep on the sofa while reading a bedtime story. By all means, draw up a few joint rules for the

matters you both think important. But then respect each other's indi-
viduality and the unique relationship you are separately developing with
your child. Try to refrain from criticising each other's parenting style, as
such criticism is really distressing for everyone.

Don't use violence

To avoid harm, there are some things that are important to understand:
you mustn't use violence. It's easy to get angry at children, and with the
combined effects of sleep deprivation, hunger, arguing with your partner, and a screaming child, you can easily end up in a state of completely
powerless, hopeless rage. Not only is violence terrifying for a child and
potentially physically dangerous, but if you behave violently you will
also find yourself in a foul mood and feeling like a bad person.

So what counts as violence? Kicking, hitting, shoving, pinching,
burning, violently shaking, or biting a child are all examples of physical
violence. As a parent, you may at certain times need to restrain a child
who is violent, out of control, or generally unruly. Some children need
to be held down in order to have their nails clipped or their hair cut.
This is not unacceptable violence, and, as a rule, children don't need to
be held down many times before learning that there's no point trying
to squirm free. You may need to use an angry voice in order to show
firmly that a child has done something entirely unacceptable, and, as
we've said, you may sometimes have to hold the child down with force
to protect them from hurting themselves or others.

Children differ in terms of how often they behave violently, and they
are cautious and compliant to different degrees. How often they need to
be held down and told off will vary. Having a very angry child will test
your patience. It is good to remember that, as a general rule, children
get angry or obstinate when they are unable to cope with the demands
placed on them. If you have a child who often reacts with anger, it may be
worth thinking about ways to reduce the demands placed on them. It's
not easy to determine what is and isn't acceptable anger when bringing

up a child. If you're not sure whether your own way of showing anger and setting boundaries is appropriate, you can ask someone you trust to discuss their observations of you and your child's interactions. If you, or your child, often react angrily, seek professional advice. Help is out there.

Don't abuse alcohol or drugs

Enjoying a glass of wine or two is generally acceptable in many societies, and it is unlikely that children will be harmed by this. It's okay to have a drink with your friends at the pub from time to time when your child isn't there, so long as you aren't blind drunk, violent, or unpleasant when you come home. But having parents with a substance-abuse problem is very hard on children and can also be dangerous, because being under the influence of alcohol or drugs clouds your judgement.

If you feel that alcohol or drugs play too significant a role in your life, or if your child, your partner, or a close friend asks you to drink less, or says that you turn nasty when you're drunk, take your situation seriously. Don't try to tell yourself that everyone else is being over-sensitive — it's common for those who abuse alcohol or drugs to deny or play down the problems that it causes for their family and others. Tell your GP, or another health service, that you're worried about your drug use. Talk about your situation honestly, and ask for advice about how best to deal with your concerns.

It is never your child's job to take care of your needs

The relationship between parents and children is not one of equality. As a parent, you are responsible for taking care of your child's basic needs, providing emotional support where you can, and giving your child the opportunity to learn and develop. Your child doesn't have any corresponding responsibilities towards you. Children tend to have a strong emotional link to their parents, but they have no emotional responsibility for their parents, and absolutely no obligation to like them or to show that they like them.

You have the right to decide where a young child should spend their time, but if you think your child should be with you because you feel lonely or otherwise unhappy, or if you think your child should ensure that you're fine, then yours is no longer a healthy parent–child relationship. These types of dependent thoughts and emotions tend to appear when you are over-burdened or aren't feeling mentally well. Professional counselling is often needed in order to feel well again, and mental well-being is essential in order to function properly as a parent. If you are experiencing difficulties, your GP, maternal and child-health centre, or a psychiatrist can help.

If you refrain from the use of violence and the active abuse of alcohol or drugs, and if you ensure that you don't try to force your child to meet your needs, you are well on the way towards good parenting. But no parent can raise a child alone; children also need other children.

THE CHILD FLOCK

The concept of parents taking at least a year off work to stay at home and look after a young child is relatively new. In the old Swedish farming communities, women worked at least as hard as men, but with additional duties, too, and there was no such thing as parental leave. Babies were swaddled or had to lie alone in their cradle while their mother worked, and later had to be looked after by their siblings, who were sometimes only five or six years old themselves. Children spent much of the day in a 'child flock' that played together and raised each other. Infant mortality was high, particularly due to infections, but also because young children obviously couldn't always protect their baby siblings from tumbling to their deaths or drowning in the well.

The child-flock model still exists in many parts of the world, and this is probably how children have lived for much of human history. Children are remarkably happy with other children, and this ease in company can be seen from a very young age. Younger children look admiringly at their older siblings or playmates, and often put up with fairly harsh treatment just to be included. Younger children imitate older ones, and learn how the child society works. Child-to-child modelling behaviour can be seen clearly with language learning. Children who mix with other children quickly learn to talk like them and not like their parents. This phenomenon is particularly apparent when families move to a new country with a different language, where the parents often continue to speak a broken version of the new language while the children soon speak exactly like their friends.

Preschool — the supervised child flock

Preschool, early-childcare centres, and playgroups are some of the places in society where child flocks still exist. We see this as a contemporary — and considerably safer — version of the traditional child flock. They are much more reminiscent of how children have grown up during human history than everyday contemporary life at home with an adult, but without any older siblings or other children. In Sweden, as we've seen, municipalities are obliged to offer a preschool place to all children who have reached the age of one, and the vast majority of children are enrolled at a preschool. In many other countries, childcare is not universally available, and is often so expensive that only high earners can afford it. This is a pity, because preschool not only serves the needs of the working parent, but also of the child, who needs to adjust to other children and learn from them.

The extent to which children show an interest in other children varies greatly. Some have natural social skills and quickly take their place in the child flock, where they fit in easily and become popular. Other children find it harder to interpret social signals and to understand how to relate to others in a group. They may prefer to be at home, playing by themselves. But these children may have more of a need to practise being in the child flock than their more outgoing contemporaries. Early-childhood teachers tend to be very good at helping children with social difficulties to gradually become accustomed to being in a group, and to learn how to interact with others.

One fascinating thing about children is their ability to learn quickly that different rules apply in different settings. At preschool, most children try the food, hang up their coats, and put away toys when playtime is over. Back at home, they may only eat sausages and pasta, they want help taking off their coats, and tidying up seems to be an alien concept! It is testament to their inborn social talents that they know exactly who it pays to cry for (their parents) and who it doesn't (other children and preschool teachers). The idea that children need to have the same rules everywhere is absurd. Being skilled social beings, children learn very early on the behaviours that work best in different contexts. This isn't a harmful lesson at all — on the contrary, it's a way of practising social skills.

Finding other children during parental leave

Children should meet other children regularly, even during parental leave. If children don't have any playmates by the age of 8–10 months, they will often be clingy and try to play with their parents, who on the whole won't have the patience to pick up thrown building blocks 250 times every half-hour for days, weeks, and months on end. However, at a playground or a parent and toddler group, the same children can play peacefully for hours. Sometimes they may not play with the other children, but alongside them. Something about being in a child flock seems to make children of this age happy and calm.

If you have lots of friends yourself and are social, you will probably have friends with children who you can easily spend time with in an energising way during your parental leave. If, however, you find group social settings less easy, you may need to plan more for your children to meet other people. Your child-health centre's parent group is a good way to meet other parents with children of the same age, and a parent and toddler playgroup is another. In large towns, there are courses and book clubs for parents on leave, and many churches and other community organisations run baby music sessions and parents' groups that are open to everyone. We recently read about some mothers' groups in Australia that combine surfing with taking care of each other's children!

ATTACHMENT THEORY

One theory that is highly popular among psychologists, and has featured prominently in the media and social debate, is that children need to calmly 'attach' to one person at a time. According to this theory, a child will become confused if it is cared for by several different adults or older children. Attachment theory was developed by the psychoanalyst John Bowlby in the 1950s; Bowlby also proposed that housewives should devote themselves to their children full-time.

The idea that children might be born with an ability to attach to more than one adult was seen as unreasonable. However, since maternal mortality has been high throughout human history, a child can obviously attach to others in their immediate surroundings who offer care and food. Attachment theory has subsequently been revised, and it is now accepted that children can also attach to their fathers, and are able to attach to more than one adult.

But not all advances or nuances in theory trickle down to the self-appointed experts. We appear to be stuck on a particular meaning of the word 'attachment'. We often hear that 'the mother should take (almost) full parental leave because the child must attach to one parent', or that it is important to breastfeed for as long as possible, 'for the sake of attachment'. These claims tend not to be made by attachment researchers or child psychologists, but rather by people who haven't read in-depth analyses of the theory.

There is no scientific support for many of the assertions about attachment. You will recall that in chapter 1 we reported that even male rats (not, perhaps, the world's most empathetic creatures) behave entirely adequately if they have to care for helpless young rats. Like all mammals, our brains have simply been pre-programmed to automatically start caring for helpless babies if we are left alone with them for long enough. And newborn babies' brains are pre-programmed to trigger caring behaviour in older children and adults. The reason why we click on videos of cute kittens and puppies on social media is that it feels so good when these emotions are activated, whether or not we have children.

One central concept of attachment theory is the idea that the way in which children and parents form an early attachment is of significance for the adult individual. This is, of course, a claim that creates a great deal of concern, and paves the way for feelings of guilt in those who have a child with psychological or social problems. As we discussed previously, the causal link can be the opposite: children are born with different personalities, and a child that is anxious, insecure, and whiny will probably have a similar personality as an adult. Such a child will also seem 'insecure in the attachment' for the simple reason that this is part of their personality. It cannot be surmised that the child would have turned out completely differently if only the parent had known to attach to the child a little better.

The theory that it is the parent (usually, the mother) who is crucial to the child's emotional development has hurt many parents deeply. In the 1960s, it was thought that autism — a highly genetically determined personality trait — was due to a mother who was lacking in warmth, a so-called refrigerator mother. In the same way, rational mothers who have sought care for their children's mental problems have been blamed for causing their children's problems because they are coldly analytical instead of being warm and emotional like a real woman should be, according to psychoanalysts. Anorexia and schizophrenia are also diagnoses for which mothers were once blamed. Modern child and adolescent psychiatry has done away with these theories, and hopefully this type of harm will no longer occur. However, many mothers' lives have been blighted in the past by feelings of guilt.

Throughout evolutionary history, the female human — just like all other female primates and mammals — has had to gather food for herself and her children in order for them both to survive and for their genes to be passed on. Unless they were looked after by older children in the flock or by other adults, children would have been dragged around while their mothers searched for food. Except during this short period – the past fifty years in the world's wealthy nations – human children have probably never had parents who have devoted much of their waking time to meeting their needs. In our view, it is unreasonable to base an entire theory of a person's psychological development on a microscopically small side-bar in human history.

HAVE REALISTIC EXPECTATIONS OF YOUR CHILD

Infancy and childhood is a period of enormous development – intellectually, emotionally, and physically. It is important not to burden children with demands that are too great and that they are unable to meet. Child-health nurses and preschool teachers usually know what you can expect of your child at different ages, and it is well worth talking to them if you have any questions about your child's progress. Individual children develop at different rates.

If a child is much later in passing most milestones than children of the same age, or if they have real difficulties in coping with the rules or daily routines of preschool, a psychological assessment may help to ascertain the child's abilities and whether there's a need for extra resources. Contact your maternal and child-health clinic, or seek a referral to a pediatrician from your GP if you are concerned about this. As we have previously mentioned, the developmental and neurological evaluation of children is a dire task, and it is important that you as a parent feel confident with your healthcare provider's assessment. If you don't, ask for a follow-up or a referral to another specialist. While the absolute majority of worries that parents have about their children's development end up being about nothing abnormal, the first sign of neurological disease is almost invariably something noticed by a parent.

Here is a simplified guide to what most infants can do up to the age of 18 months.

Newborn

A healthy newborn baby shows that it wants to eat, suck, and swallow without choking too much. A newborn sleeps and wakes, but tends not to have a predictable daily rhythm. We don't expect more skills from a newborn than this. But during their first year of life, babies make enormous progress, and you don't need to train them. The program is there, in their brains, and if you give them food and protection, and help them with their hygiene, you will be able to watch your child develop skill after skill.

One month

At one month, a baby can normally return a smile and make eye contact. Many babies can hold their heads up unaided. It's good to let babies lie on their tummies for short periods every day to improve their neck strength. Many will have begun to develop signs of a daily rhythm, but they will feed 24 hours a day; if you're lucky, they might feed slightly less at night than during the day. Many babies start to enjoy people talking and singing to them during their waking hours.

Two months

At two months, babies begin to open their hands if they've previously had them clenched. Their necks should be stable, and babies that have been allowed to play on their tummies will usually be able to hold their heads and shoulders up while lying on their front. Your baby will respond to you with cute babbling sounds when you talk to it.

Four months

At four months, babies typically have begun to use their hands to grip things and bring them into view to investigate them. Many discover their feet, and like to lie and play with them. Many babies of this age show an interest in tasting the food you eat.

Six months

At six months, babies are usually able to sit up, but might be a bit inse-cure if they lose balance. Whatever they get in their hands they put in their mouths to taste. Six-month-old babies will normally have learned to roll from their tummies onto their backs, and will have a range of different sounds that they practise frequently.

Ten months

At ten months, babies will usually have a good pincer grip (thumb against forefinger) that they can use to pick up small things like peas and beads. Most will have learned to pull themselves up on furniture from a sitting position, and they will often be able to walk while holding onto the furniture for balance. The baby will understand individual words, and will usually enjoy playing peek-a-boo.

Eighteen months

Most babies reach the toddler stage of being able to walk without support between the ages of 12 and 18 months, but walking can happen earlier or later without signifying anything out of the ordinary. Most babies say their first words at around 12 months, and by 18 months the vast majority will have learned at least 10 words. Some may begin to string words together into short sentences, but this is unusual. An 18-month-old can usually follow simple instructions and point to parts of the body if they've been taught to name them.

Although children learn a tremendous amount in one-and-a-half years, there are still many things they can't do. As a parent, you need to keep track of when your child needs to eat, wee, and sleep, and the level of warm clothing they need to be wearing. You also need to organise your child's activities, whatever they may be. If you adopt more or less the same daily routine, your child will usually pick this up quite well, which can save you a lot of work when getting your child to stop playing so they can get dressed and go out.

Young children often have some sort of idea about night and day, but it is worth bearing in mind that their perception of time will otherwise not be particularly well developed. At this age, children are unable to understand the meaning of 'We'll go and play on the swings in two hours' time'; instead, they will only hear 'swings', and then get angry when they don't get to play on them immediately.

Young children only have a very basic understanding of cause and effect — to find that a light comes on when you press the button on the lamp can be a very exciting discovery. This means that any type of consequential reasoning with your child along the lines of 'If you eat your carrots, you'll get some ice cream after' or 'If you don't brush your teeth, you'll need fillings, and you don't want that' is far too difficult for them to grasp.

Children believe that you know everything they know. Consequently, they will quickly become extremely frustrated if you don't help them with what they want, despite them not having clearly expressed what it is they want. The ability to understand that their parent is not a mind-reader will not appear in normally developing children until the age of four, while children with autism will develop this ability later, if at all. Children with strong wills and emotions often find daily life quite difficult until they work out that other people don't understand everything they need or feel. It is worth remembering that this mismatch is just a stage — a stage that is often quite difficult for parents, too.

SOME FINAL WORDS

If taking care of your baby in the first year feels mucky, sleepless, noisy, and thankless, remember that this stage passes. You won't always be a parent to a helpless little bundle with no language. In a few years' time, you'll have a highly individual new person sharing your home.

Of course, you can't know from the start how your child will turn out, but it is incredibly rewarding to follow children on their journey through life, and to understand and support their life choices. In early childhood, most children learn the same things, but the older they get, the more you see their individual preferences and personality coming through. Some love balls, and develop their own football skills at lightning speed; others find stones fascinating, and absorb all the knowledge they can about minerals and rocks. Some children love to get other children to play well together, and are impressively social at an early age.

We want to make it clear that most of the choices you make as a parent of a newborn will not play a major role in determining what kind of adult your child will become. Naturally, you — or you and your partner, if you are co-parenting — will decide whether you want to focus on a particular form of parenting, and what guidelines will apply in your family.

But don't lose heart if certain methods don't work out. The sort of adult your child grows into will be influenced more by their genes than by your active efforts to shape them according to your own aspirations.

As well, children can have their own ideas about how they want their parents to be, and are also well equipped to transform them — sometimes into their willing servants! The best you can do is to try to arrange your daily life so that it's as fulfilling as possible for you and your child, or children, for as long as you live together.

Acknowledgements

Even though Agnes's daughter gave us the idea for this book, a book will never appear out of ideas, however much you talk about them. There have been many people involved in the sometimes hard work of writing *Parenthood the Swedish Way*, and we want to mention some of them by name. Sara Nyström, our Swedish editor at Albert Bonniers förlag, worked very closely with us to form our ideas into a book. Literary agent Christine Edhäll, together with her colleagues at Ahlander Agency, surprised us by saying she believed the book would be of interest even outside Sweden, and convinced us by selling the rights to 15 countries in the first round.

For this English-language edition, we've had the most professional and devoted editorial team at Scribe Publications, who have turned the initial text and translation into a book we are very proud to present to the English-speaking world. Tamsin Wagner, Margot Rosenbloom, and Henry Rosenbloom, your contributions to this book cannot be overstated. Your hand with the English language is magical, but, even more, we appreciate your remarks when we've been unclear or inconsistent in our arguments, and everything you've taught us about parenting in Australia, New Zealand, and the UK.

We would also like to thank the following two people, both of whom have been very generous with their time and knowledge: Dr Alexis Shub, maternal fetal medicine subspecialist at Mercy Hospital for Women, Melbourne, and senior lecturer in the Department of Obstetrics and Gynecology at the University of Melbourne, for helping us with fact-checking this English-language edition; and Dr Mireille Vanpee, senior attending in paediatrics and neonatology, who has also read the whole manuscript and given us valuable comments.

Notes

Chapter One: Looking ahead

1   Mansdotter, A., L. Lindholm, and A. Winkvist, *Paternity leave in Sweden: costs, savings and health gains. Health Policy.* 2007. 82(1): 102–15.

2   Rosenblatt, J.S., *Nonhormonal basis of maternal behavior in the rat. Science.* 1967. 156(3781): 1512–4.

3   Harris, J.R., *The nurture assumption: why children turn out the way they do.* Rev. and updated ed. New York: Free Press, 2009, p. 448.

4   Moberg, Y., *Är lesbiska föräldrar mer jämställda? Rapport.* 2016:9. IFAU. Available from: www.ifau.se/globalassets/pdf/se/2016/r-2016-09-ar-lesbiska-foraldrar-mer-jamstallda.pdf.

5   Malmquist, A., *Lesbiska småbarnsföräldrar: utmaningar i en tid av möjligheter.* Göteborg: Makadam, 2016, p. 143.

6   Sandmark, H., *Work and family: associations with long-term sick-listing in Swedish women — a case-control study. BMC Public Health.* 2007(7): 287.

7   Oláh, L.S., *Gender and family stability: dissolution of the first parental union in Sweden and Hungary. Demographic Research.* 2001. 4(2): 29–96.

8   Oláh, L.S., *Gendering fertility: second births in Sweden and Hungary. Population Research and Policy Review.* 2003, 22(2): 171–200.

9   Faludi, S., *Backlash: the undeclared war against American women.* New York: Crown, 1991, pp. xxiii, 552.

Chapter Two: Pregnancy facts

1   Niebyl, J.R. *Clinical practice. Nausea and vomiting in pregnancy. N. Engl. J. Med.* 2010. 363(16): 1544–50.

2   Erick, M., *Hyperolfaction and hyperemesis gravidarum: what is the relationship? Nutr. Rev.* 1995. 53(10): 289–95.

3   McParlin, C., A. O'Donnell, S.C. Robson, F. Beyer, E.Moloney, A. Bryant, et al., *Treatments for hyperemesis gravidarum and nausea and vomiting in pregnancy: a systematic review. JAMA.* 2016. 316(13): 1392–401; Boelig, R.C., S.J. Barton, G. Saccone, A.J. Kelly, S.J. Edwards, and V. Berghella, *Interventions for treating hyperemesis gravidarum. Cochrane Database of Systematic Reviews.* 2016(5); A. Matthews, D.M. Haas, D.P. O'Mathúna, and T. Dowswell, *Interventions for nausea and vomiting in early pregnancy. Cochrane Database of Systematic Reviews.* 2015(9).

4   Jednak, M.A., E.M. Shadigian, M.S. Kim, M.L. Woods, F.G. Hooper, C. Owyang, et al., *Protein meals reduce nausea and gastric slow wave dysrhythmic activity in first trimester pregnancy. Am. J. Physiol.* 1999. 277(4 Pt 1):G855–61.

5   National Collaborating Centre for Ws, Children's H., *National Institute for Health and Clinical Excellence: Guidance. Ectopic Pregnancy and Miscarriage: Diagnosis and Initial Management in Early Pregnancy of Ectopic Pregnancy and Miscarriage.* London: Rcog National Collaborating Centre for Women's and Children's Health. 2012.

6   Simpson, J.L., *Causes of fetal wastage. Clin. Obstet. Gynecol.* 2007. 50(1): 10–30.

7   Nybo Andersen, A.M., J. Wohlfahrt, P. Christens, J. Olsen, and M. Melbye, *Maternal age and fetal loss: population based register linkage study. BMJ* (Clinical research ed). 2000. 320(7251): 1708–12.

8   Feodor Nilsson, S., P.K. Andersen, K. Strandberg-Larsen, and A.M. Nybo Andersen, *Risk factors for miscarriage from a prevention perspective: a nationwide follow-up study. BJOG: An International Journal of Obstetrics & Gynaecology.* 2014. 121(11): 1375–85.

9   Jahanfar, S., and S.H. Jaafar, *Effects of restricted caffeine intake by mother on fetal, neonatal and pregnancy outcomes. Cochrane Database of Systematic Reviews.* 2015(6).

10 Balogun, O.O., K. da Silva Lopes, E. Ota, Y. Takemoto, A. Rumbold, M. Takegata, et al., *Vitamin supplementation for preventing miscarriage. Cochrane Database of Systematic Reviews.* 2016(5).

11 Haas, D.M., and P.S. Ramsey, *Progestogen for preventing miscarriage. Cochrane Database of Systematic Reviews.* 2013(10).

12 Fellman, V., L. Hellstrom-Westas, M. Norman, M. Westgren, K. Kallen, H Lagercrantz, et al., *One-year survival of extremely preterm infants after active perinatal care in Sweden. Jama.* 2009. 301(21): 2225–33.

13 Radestad, I., *Correct information about fetal movements saves life. Lakartidningen.* 2011. 108(42): 2102.

14 Mertz, D., J. Geraci, J. Winkup, B.D. Gessner, J.R. Ortiz, and M. Loeb, *Pregnancy as a risk factor for severe outcomes from influenza virus infection: a systematic review and meta-analysis of observational studies. Vaccine.* 2016.

15 McMillan, M., K. Porritt, D. Kralik, L. Costi, and H. Marshall, *Influenza vaccination during pregnancy: a systematic review of fetal death, spontaneous*

abortion, and congenital malformation safety outcomes. Vaccine. 2015. 33(18): 2108–17.

16 Castillo-Solórzano, C., S.E. Reef, A. Morice, N. Vascones, A.E. Chevez, R. Castalia-Soares, et al., *Rubella vaccination of unknowingly pregnant women during mass campaigns for rubella and congenital Rubella syndrome elimination, the Americas 2001-2008. J. Infect. Dis.* 2011. 204(SUPPL. 2): S713–S7.

Chapter Three: Do's and don'ts during pregnancy

1 Smith, G.C., and J.P. Pell, *Parachute use to prevent death and major trauma related to gravitational challenge: systematic review of randomised controlled trials.* BMJ (Clinical research ed). 2003. 327(7429): 1459–61.

2 Beral, V., E. Banks, and G. Reeves, *Evidence from randomised trials on the long-term effects of hormone replacement therapy. Lancet.* 2002. 360(9337): 942–4.

3 Cnattingius, S., *The epidemiology of smoking during pregnancy: smoking prevalence, maternal characteristics, and pregnancy outcomes. Nicotine & tobacco research : official journal of the Society for Research on Nicotine and Tobacco.* 2004. 6 Suppl 2: S125–40.

4 Dahlin, S., A. Gunnerbeck, A.K. Wikstrom, S. Cnattingius, and A.K. Bonamy, *Maternal tobacco use and extremely premature birth: a population-based cohort study. Bjog.* 2016. 123(12): 1938–46.

5 Gunnerbeck, A., A.K. Wikstrom, A.K. Bonamy, R. Wickstrom, and S. Cnattingius, *Relationship of maternal snuff use and cigarette smoking with neonatal apnea. Pediatrics.* 2011. 128(3): 503–9.

6 Jones, K.L., and D.W. Smith, *Recognition of the fetal alcohol syndrome in early infancy. Lancet.* 1973. 302(7836): 999–1001.

7 Olegard, R., K.G. Sabel, M. Aronsson, B. Sandin, P.R. Johansson, C. Carlsson, et al., *Effects on the child of alcohol abuse during pregnancy. Retrospective and prospective studies. Acta Paediatr. Scand. Suppl.* 1979. 275: 112–21; Kyllerman, M., M. Aronson, K.G. Sabel, E. Karlberg, B. Sandin, and R. Olegard, *Children of alcoholic mothers. Growth and motor performance compared to matched controls. Acta Paediatr. Scand.* 1985. 74(1): 20–6.

8 Hollstedt, C., L. Dahlgren, and U. Rydberg, *Outcome of pregnancy in women treated at an alcohol clinic. Acta Psychiatr. Scand.* 1983. 67(4): 236–48.

9 Updated alcohol consumption guidelines give new advice on limits for men and pregnant women [press release]. 2016-01-08.

10 Janerich, D.T., and S.T. Mayne, *Alcohol and pregnancy: an epidemiologic perspective. Annals of epidemiology.* 1990. 1(2): 179–85.

11 Patra, J., R. Bakker, H. Irving, V.W. Jaddoe, S. Malini, and J. Rehm, *Dose-response relationship between alcohol consumption before and during pregnancy and the risks of low birthweight, preterm birth and small for gestational age (SGA)-a systematic review and meta-analyses. Bjog.* 2011. 118(12): 1411–21.

12 Henderson, J., R. Gray, and P. Brocklehurst, *Systematic review of effects of*

low-moderate prenatal alcohol exposure on pregnancy outcome. Bjog. 2007. 114(3): 243–52.

13 Polygenis, D., S. Wharton, C. Malmberg, N. Sherman, D. Kennedy, G. Koren, et al., *Moderate alcohol consumption during pregnancy and the incidence of fetal malformations: a meta-analysis.* Neurotoxicol Teratol. 1998. 20(1): 61–7.

14 Flak, A.L., S. Su, J. Bertrand, C.H. Denny, U.S. Kesmodel, and M.E. Cogswell, *The association of mild, moderate, and binge prenatal alcohol exposure and child neuropsychological outcomes: a meta-analysis. Alcoholism: Clinical and Experimental Research.* 2014. 38(1): 214–26.

15 Bay, B., U.S. Kesmodel, *Prenatal alcohol exposure: a systematic review of the effects on child motor function. Acta Obstetricia et Gynecologica Scand.* 2011. 90(3): 210–26.

16 Patra, J., et al., *Doseresponse relationship between alcohol consumption before and during pregnancy and the risks of low birthweight, preterm birth and small for gestational age (SGA) – a systematic review and metaanalyses.* Bjog. 2011. 118(12): 1411–21.

17 Flak, A.L., S. Su, J. Bertrand, C.H. Denny, U.S. Kesmodel, and M.E. Cogswell, *The association of mild, moderate, and binge prenatal alcohol exposure and child neuropsychological outcomes: a meta-analysis. Alcoholism: Clinical and Experimental Research.* 2014. 38(1): 214–26.

18 Bay, B., and U.S. Kesmodel, *Prenatal alcohol exposure: a systematic review of the effects on child motor function. Acta Obstetricia et Gynecologica Scand.* 2011. 90(3): 210–26.

19 Andersen, A.M., P.K. Andersen, J. Olsen, M. Gronbaek, and K. Strandberg-Larsen, *Moderate alcohol intake during pregnancy and risk of fetal death. Int. J. Epidemiol.* 2012. 41(2): 405–13.

20 van Wijngaarden, E., S.W. Thurston, G.J. Myers, D. Harrington, D.A. Cory-Slechta, J.J. Strain, et al., *Methyl mercury exposure and neurodevelopmental outcomes in the Seychelles Child Development Study Main cohort at age 22 and 24 years. Neurotoxicol Teratol.* 2016.

21 Bergdahl, I.A., M. Ahlqwist, L. Barregard, C. Bjorkelund, A. Blomstrand, S. Skerfving, et al., *Mercury in serum predicts low risk of death and myocardial infarction in Gothenburg women. Int. Arch. Occup. Environ. Health.* 2013. 86(1): 71–7.

22 Haider, B.A., and Z.A. Bhutta, *Multiple-micronutrient supplementation for women during pregnancy. Cochrane Database of Systematic Reviews.* 2015(11). Cd004905.

23 Amegah, A.K., M.K. Klevor, and C.L. Wagner, *Maternal vitamin D insufficiency and risk of adverse pregnancy and birth outcomes: a systematic review and meta-analysis of longitudinal studies. PLoS One.* 2017. 12(3): e0173605; De-Regil, L.M., C. Palacios, L.K. Lombardo, and J.P. Peña-Rosas, *Vitamin D supplementation for women during pregnancy. Cochrane Database of Systematic Reviews.* 2016(1).

24 Weiss, J.L., F.D. Malone, D. Emig, R.H. Ball, D.A. Nyberg, C.H.

Comstock, et al., *Obesity, obstetric complications and cesarean delivery rate: a population-based screening study. Am. J. Obstet. Gynecol.* 2004. 190(4): 1091–7; Cnattingius, S., E. Villamor, S. Johansson, A.K. Edstedt Bonamy, M. Persson, A.K. Wikstrom, et al., *Maternal obesity and risk of preterm delivery. JAMA.* 2013. 309(22): 2362–70.

25 Aune, D., O.D. Saugstad, T. Henriksen, and S. Tonstad, *Maternal body mass index and the risk of fetal death, stillbirth, and infant death: a systematic review and meta-analysis. JAMA.* 2014. 311(15): 1536–46; Bodnar, L.M., W.T. Parks, K. Perkins, S.J. Pugh, R.W. Platt, M. Feghali, et al., *Maternal prepregnancy obesity and cause-specific stillbirth. Am. J. Clin. Nutr.* 2015. 102(4): 858–64.

26 Villamor, E., K. Tedroff, M. Peterson, S. Johansson, M. Neovius, G. Petersson, et al., *Association between maternal body mass index in early pregnancy and incidence of cerebral palsy. Jama.* 2017. 317(9): 925–36.

27 Tieu, J., E. Shepherd, P. Middleton, and C.A. Crowther, *Dietary advice interventions in pregnancy for preventing gestational diabetes mellitus. Cochrane Database of Systematic Reviews.* 2017. 1:CD006674.

28 Brown, J., N.A. Alwan, J. West, S. Brown, C.J. McKinlay, D. Farrar, et al., *Lifestyle interventions for the treatment of women with gestational diabetes. Cochrane Database of Systematic Reviews.* 2017. 5:CD011970.

29 Jarde, A., M. Morais, D. Kingston, R. Giallo, G.M. MacQueen, L. Giglia, et al., *Neonatal outcomes in women with untreated antenatal depression compared with women without depression: a systematic review and meta-analysis. Jama psychiatry.* 2016. 73(8): 826–37.

Chapter Four: Birth

1 Gyhagen, M., S. Akervall, and I. Milsom, *Clustering of pelvic floor disorders 20 years after one vaginal or one cesarean birth. Int. Urogynecol. J.* 2015. 26(8): 1115–21.

2 Elvander, C., et al., *Birth position and obstetric anal sphincter injury: a population-based study of 113 000 spontaneous births. BMC Pregnancy Childbirth.* 2015. 15: 252.

3 Laine, K., et al., *Incidence of obstetric anal sphincter injuries after training to protect the perineum: cohort study. BMJ Open.* 2012. 2(5).

4 Kuhle, S., O.S. Tong, and C.G. Woolcott, *Association between caesarean section and childhood obesity: a systematic review and meta-analysis. Obes. Rev.* 2015. 16(4): 295–303.

5 Cardwell, C.R., et al., *Caesarean section is associated with an increased risk of childhood-onset type 1 diabetes mellitus: a meta-analysis of observational studies. Diabetologia.* 2008. 51(5): 726–35.

6 Hyde, M.J., and N. Modi, *The long-term effects of birth by caesarean section: the case for a randomised controlled trial. Early Hum. Dev.* 2012. 88(12): 943–9.

7 Olsen, O., and J.A. Clausen, *Planned hospital birth versus planned home birth. Cochrane Database of Systematic Reviews.* 2012(9). Cd000352.

Chapter Five: Feeding a newborn baby

1   Adlerberth, I., F. Jalil, B. Carlsson, L. Mellander, L.A. Hanson, P. Larsson, et al., *High turnover rate of Escherichia coli strains in the intestinal flora of infants in Pakistan. Epidemiol Infect.* 1998. 121(3): 587–98.

2   Heise, A.M., and D. Wiessinger, *Dysphoric milk ejection reflex: a case report. Int. Breastfeed J.* 2011. 6(1): 6; Cox, S., *A case of dysphoric milk ejection reflex (D-MER). Breastfeed Rev.* 2010. 18(1): 16–8.

3   Smith, H.A., and G.E. Becker, *Early additional food and fluids for healthy breastfed full-term infants. Cochrane Database of Systematic Reviews.* 2016(8).

4   Crepinsek, M.A., L. Crowe, K. Michener, and N.A. Smart, *Interventions for preventing mastitis after childbirth. Cochrane Database of Systematic Reviews.* 2012. 10: Cd007239.

5   Svensson, K., S. Lange, I. Lonnroth, A.M. Widstrom, and L.A. Hanson, *Induction of anti-secretory factor in human milk may prevent mastitis. Acta Paediatr. Scand.* 2004. 93(9): 1228–31.

6   Flint A., K. New, M.W. Davies, *Cup feeding versus other forms of supplemental enteral feeding for newborn infants unable to fully breastfeed. Cochrane Database of Systematic Reviews.* 2016(8).

7   Jaafar, S.H., J.J. Ho, S. Jahanfar, and M. Angolkar, *Effect of restricted pacifier use in breastfeeding term infants for increasing duration of breastfeeding. Cochrane Database of Systematic Reviews.* 2016(8).

8   Hesselmar, B., F. Sjoberg, R. Saalman, N. Aberg, I. Adlerberth, and A.E. Wold, *Pacifier cleaning practices and risk of allergy development. Pediatrics.* 2013. 131(6): e1829–37.

Chapter Six: Moving on to solids

1   Kramer, M.S., and R. Kakuma, *Optimal duration of exclusive breastfeeding. Cochrane Database of Systematic Reviews.* 2002(1). CD003517.

2   Qasem, W., T. Fenton, and J. Friel, *Age of introduction of first complementary feeding for infants: a systematic review. BMC Pediatr.* 2015. 15: 107.

3   Du Toit, G., et al., *Randomized trial of peanut consumption in infants at risk for peanut allergy. N. Engl. J. Med.* 2015. 372(9): 803–13.

4   Perkin, M.R., et al., *Randomized trial of introduction of allergenic foods in breast-fed infants. N. Engl. J. Med.,* 2016. 374(18): 1733–43.

5   Adlerberth, I., et al., *High turnover rate of Escherichia coli strains in the intestinal flora of infants in Pakistan. Epidemiol. Infect.* 1998. 121(3): 587–98.

6   Segar, J.L., *Renal adaptive changes and sodium handling in the fetal-to-newborn transition. Seminars in Fetal and Neonatal Medicine.*

7   Aperia, A., et al., *Renal response to an oral sodium load in newborn full term infants. Acta Paediatr. Scand.* 1972. 61(6): 670–6.

8   Aperia, A., et al., *Development of renal control of salt and fluid homeostasis during the first year of life. Acta Paediatr. Scand.* 1975. 64(3): 393–8.

9   Aperia, A., et al., *Renal sodium excretory capacity in infants under different dietary conditions. Acta Paediatr. Scand.* 1979. 68(3): 351–5.

10 Colle, E., E. Ayoub, and R. Raile, *Hypertonic dehydration (hypernatremia): the role of feedings high in solutes. Pediatrics.* 1958. 22(1, Part 1): 5–12.

11 Greer, F.R., et al., *Infant methemoglobinemia: the role of dietary nitrate in food and water. Pediatrics.* 2005. 116(3): 784–6.

12 Martinez, A., et al., *Methemoglobinemia induced by vegetable intake in infants in northern Spain. J. Pediatr. Gastroenterol. Nutr.* 2013. 56(5): 573–7.

Chapter Seven: Getting some sleep

1   Carpenter, R., et al., *Bed sharing when parents do not smoke: is there a risk of SIDS? An individual level analysis of five major case-control studies. BMJ Open.* 2013. 3(5).

2   Dwyer, T., and A.L. Ponsonby, *Sudden infant death syndrome and prone sleeping position. Ann. Epidemiol.* 2009. 19(4): 245–9.

3   Beal, S., *Sleeping position and SIDS. Lancet.* 1988. 2(8609): 512.

4   Li, D.K., et al., *Use of a dummy (pacifier) during sleep and risk of sudden infant death syndrome (SIDS): population based case-control study. BMJ.* 2006. 332(7532): 18–22; Mitchell, E.A., et al., *Dummies and the sudden infant death syndrome. Arch. Dis. Child.,* 1993. 68(4): 501–4; Fleming, P.J., et al., *Pacifier use and sudden infant death syndrome: results from the CESDI/SUDI case control study. CESDI SUDI Research Team. Arch. Dis. Child.,* 1999. 81(2): 112–6; McGarvey, C., et al., *Factors relating to the infant's last sleep environment in sudden infant death syndrome in the Republic of Ireland. Arch. Dis. Child.* 2003. 88(12): 1058–64.

5   Carpenter, R., et al., *Bed sharing when parents do not smoke: is there a risk of SIDS? An individual level analysis of five major case-control studies. BMJ Open.* 2013. 3(5).

6   Symon, B.G., et al., *Effect of a consultation teaching behaviour modification on sleep performance in infants: a randomised controlled trial. Med. J. Aust.* 2005. 182(5): 215–8; Wolfson, A., P. Lacks, and A. Futterman, *Effects of parent training on infant sleeping patterns, parents' stress, and perceived parental competence. J. Consult. Clin. Psychol.* 1992. 60(1): 41–8; St James-Roberts, I., et al., *Use of a behavioural programme in the first 3 months to prevent infant crying and sleeping problems. J. Paediatr. Child Health,* 2001. 37(3): 289–97.

7   Stremler, R., et al., *Effect of behavioural-educational intervention on sleep for primiparous women and their infants in early postpartum: multisite randomised controlled trial. BMJ.* 2013. 346: f1164.

8   St James-Roberts, I., et al., *Infant crying and sleeping in London, Copenhagen and when parents adopt a 'proximal' form of care. Pediatrics.* 2006. 117(6): e1146–55.

Chapter Eight: Poo, vomit, crying, and colic

1   Douglas, P., and P. Hill, *Managing infants who cry excessively in the first few months of life. BMJ.* 2011. 343: d7772.
2   Wake, M., et al., *Prevalence, stability, and outcomes of cry-fuss and sleep problems in the first 2 years of life: prospective community-based study. Pediatrics.* 2006. 117(3): 836–42.
3   Qubty, W., and A.A. Gelfand, *The link between infantile colic and migraine. Curr. Pain Headache Rep.,* 2016. 20(5): 31.
4   Hall, B., J. Chesters, and A. Robinson, *Infantile colic: a systematic review of medical and conventional therapies. J. Paediatr. Child Health,* 2012. 48(2): 128–37.
5   Schreck Bird, A., et al., *Probiotics for the treatment of infantile colic: a systematic review. J. Pharm. Pract.* 2017. 30(3): 366–374.
6   Sung, V., et al., *Treating infant colic with the probiotic Lactobacillus reuteri: double blind, placebo controlled randomised trial. BMJ.* 2014. 348: g2107.
7   Dobson, D., et al., *Manipulative therapies for infantile colic. Cochrane Database of Systematic Reviews,* 2012. 12: Cd004796.
8   Kramer, M.S., and R. Kakuma, *Maternal dietary antigen avoidance during pregnancy or lactation, or both, for preventing or treating atopic disease in the child. Cochrane Database of Systematic Reviews.* 2012(9): CD000133.

Chapter Nine: Infections

1   Hall, C.B., *Respiratory syncytial virus: its transmission in the hospital environment. Yale J. Biol. Med.* 1982. 55(3–4): 219–23.

Chapter Ten: Vaccination

1   Anderson, E.J., et al., *Protecting the community through child vaccination. Clinical Infectious Diseases.* 2018. 67(3): 464–471.
2   Centers for Disease Control and Prevention (US) and National Immunization Program (Centers for Disease Control and Prevention), *Epidemiology and prevention of vaccine-preventable diseases.* Dept of Health & Human Services, Public Health Service: Atlanta, Ga., p. v.
3   Folkhälsomyndigheten, *Folkhälsomyndighetens statistik om Haemophilus influenzae typ B.* 2017; available from: www.folkhalsomyndigheten.se/folkhalsorapportering-statistik/statistikdatabaser-och-visualisering/sjukdomsstatistik/haemophilus-influenzae-invasiv/?t=com.
4   Shiri, T., N.D. McCarthy, and S. Petrou, *The impact of childhood pneumococcal vaccination on hospital admissions in England: a whole population observational study. BMC Infectious Diseases.* 2019. 19(1): 510.
5   Galanis, I., et al., *Effects of PCV7 and PCV13 on invasive pneumococcal disease and carriage in Stockholm, Sweden. Eur. Respir. J.* 2016. 47(4): 1208–18.
6   Folkhälsomyndigheten, *Folkhälsomyndighetens sida om polio.* 2017;

available from: www.folkhalsomyndigheten.se/smittskydd-beredskap/
vaccinationer/vacciner-a-o/polio/.

7   Toole, M.J., *So close: remaining challenges to eradicating polio. BMC Med.* 2016.
     14.

8   Ginsberg-Fellner, F., et al., *Diabetes mellitus and autoimmunity in patients with
     the congenital rubella syndrome. Rev. Infect. Dis.*, 1985. 7 Suppl 1: S170-6.

9   O'Donnell, N., *A report on a survey of late emerging manifestations of congenital
     rubella syndrome.* New York: Helen Keller National Center, 1991.

10   Lambert, N., et al., *Rubella. Lancet.* 2015. 385(9984): 2297-307.

11   Riedel, S., *Edward Jenner and the history of smallpox and vaccination. Proc. (Bayl.
     Univ. Med. Cent.).* 2005. 18(1): 21-5.

12   Tiwari, T.S., A.L. Baughman, and T.A. Clark, *First pertussis vaccine dose and
     prevention of infant mortality. Pediatrics.* 2015. 135(6): 990-9.

13   Lang, S., et al., *Two centuries of immunisation in the UK (part 1). Archives of
     Disease in Childhood.* 2019. archdischild-2019-317314; Lang, S., et al., *Two
     centuries of immunisation in the UK (part II). Archives of Disease in Childhood.*
     2019. archdischild-2019-317707.

14   Folkhälsomyndigheten, *Beslutsunderlag om rotavirusvaccination i det
     nationella vaccinationsprogrammet.* 2016.

15   Dye, T.J., N. Gurbani, and N. Simakajornboon, *Epidemiology and
     pathophysiology of childhood narcolepsy. Paediatr. Respir. Rev.*, 2016.

16   Godlee, F., J. Smith, and H. Marcovitch, *Wakefield's article linking MMR
     vaccine and autism was fraudulent. BMJ.* 2011. 342.

17   Hviid, A., et al., *Measles, mumps, rubella vaccination and autism: a nationwide
     cohort study. Ann. Intern. Med.*, 2019.

Chapter Eleven: Allergies — the immune system's phobias

1   Henderson, J., et al., *Associations of wheezing phenotypes in the first 6 years of
     life with atopy, lung function and airway responsiveness in mid-childhood. Thorax.*
     2008. 63(11): 974-80.

2   Gronlund, H., et al., *The major cat allergen, Fel d 1, in diagnosis and therapy. Int.
     Arch. Allergy Immunol.*, 2010. 151(4): 265-74.

3   Strachan, D.P., *Hay fever, hygiene, and household size. BMJ.* 1989. 299(6710):
     1259-60.

4   Strachan, D.P., *Epidemiology of hay fever: towards a community diagnosis. Clin.
     Exp. Allergy*, 1995. 25(4): 296-303.

5   Butland, B.K., et al., *Investigation into the increase in hay fever and eczema
     at age 16 observed between the 1958 and 1970 British birth cohorts. BMJ.* 1997.
     315(7110): 717-21.

6   Matricardi, P.M., et al., *Exposure to foodborne and orofecal microbes versus
     airborne viruses in relation to atopy and allergic asthma: epidemiological study.
     BMJ.* 2000. 320(7232): 412-7.

7   Illi, S., et al., *Early childhood infectious diseases and the development of asthma up to school age: a birth cohort study. BMJ.* 2001. 322(7283): 390–5.

8   Ismail, I.H., et al., *Reduced gut microbial diversity in early life is associated with later development of eczema but not atopy in high-risk infants. Pediatr. Allergy Immunol.* 2012. 23(7): 674–81.

9   Hesselmar, B., et al., *Pacifier cleaning practices and risk of allergy development. Pediatrics.* 2013. 131(6): e1829–37.

10   Braun-Fahrlander, C., et al., *Prevalence of hay fever and allergic sensitization in farmer's children and their peers living in the same rural community.* SCARPOL team. Swiss Study on Childhood Allergy and Respiratory Symptoms with Respect to Air Pollution. *Clin. Exp. Allergy.* 1999. 29(1): 28–34; Riedler, J., et al., *Austrian children living on a farm have less hay fever, asthma and allergic sensitization. Clin. Exp. Allergy.* 2000. 30(2): 194–200.

11   Genuneit, J., et al., *The combined effects of family size and farm exposure on childhood hay fever and atopy. Pediatr. Allergy Immunol.,* 2013. 24(3): 293–8.

12   Hesselmar, B., et al., *Does early exposure to cat or dog protect against later allergy development? Clin. Exp. Allergy.* 1999. 29(5): 611–7.

13   Perzanowski, M.S., et al., *Effect of cat and dog ownership on sensitization and development of asthma among preteenage children. Am. J. Respir. Crit. Care Med.,* 2002. 166(5): 696–702.

Chapter Twelve: Harmful or harmless?

1   Miller, E.S., et al., *Obsessive-compulsive symptoms during the postpartum period. A prospective cohort. J. Reprod. Med.* 2013. 58(3–4): 115–22.

2   Miller, E.S., et al., *Obsessions and compulsions in postpartum women without obsessive compulsive disorder. J. Women's Health (Larchmt),* 2015. 24(10): 825–30.

3   Bonde, J.P., et al., *The epidemiologic evidence linking prenatal and postnatal exposure to endocrine disrupting chemicals with male reproductive disorders: a systematic review and meta-analysis. Hum. Reprod. Update.* 2016. 23(1): 104–125.

Chapter Thirteen: Nature, nurture, and the importance of the child flock

1   Bouchard, T.J., and M. McGue, *Genetic and environmental influences on human psychological differences. Journal of Neurobiology.* 2003. 54(1): 4–45; Finkel, D., et al., *Heritability of cognitive abilities in adult twins: comparison of Minnesota and Swedish data. Behav Genet.* 1995. 25(5): 421–31.

2   Bouchard, T.J., and M. McGue, *Genetic and environmental influences on human psychological differences. Journal of Neurobiology.* 2003. 54(1): 4–45.

Index